COLERIDGE FILLE

OXFORD UNIVERSITY PRESS
AMEN HOUSE, E.C. 4
London Edinburgh Glasgow New York
Toronto Melbourne Capetown Bombay
Calcutta Madras
HUMPHREY MILFORD
PUBLISHER TO THE UNIVERSITY

Sara Coleridge at the time of her marriage
From the portrait by Miss Jones

COLERIDGE FILLE

❀

A BIOGRAPHY OF
SARA COLERIDGE

❀

Earl Leslie Griggs

OXFORD UNIVERSITY PRESS
LONDON NEW YORK TORONTO
1940

PRINTED IN GREAT BRITAIN

PREFACE

EDITH COLERIDGE'S *Memoir and Letters of Sara Coleridge* (1873) and Mrs. E. A. Towle's *A Poet's Children* (1912) contain the only biographical accounts previously written about Sara Coleridge, unless we are to include such obituary notices as Professor Henry Reed's essay. This lack of attention is not easy to explain. Although Sara Coleridge was distinctly a minor figure, she left behind a volume of poems and a prose tale, both intended for children, and she very capably edited her father's *Biographia Literaria*, *Notes and Lectures upon Shakespeare*, and *Essays on His Own Times*. Devoting so much of her time and energy to these tasks, she enhanced her father's reputation rather than her own, and thus Samuel Taylor Coleridge's magnificent contributions to English literature and her brother Hartley's fragile but significant achievements have completely obscured and overshadowed her.

The following study deals not only with the facts of Sara Coleridge's life but with her intellectual activities as well. Her wide reading, her ratiocinative gifts, and her theological interests equipped her to become the best of her father's early editors. She possessed a remarkably keen and penetrating understanding of Coleridge's mind and character, and the story of her life is necessarily interwoven with his. New light is, therefore, thrown upon Coleridge; his domestic life, his passionate devotion to his children, and his anguish over their problems are brought into clearer focus than in biographies of the poet; and this study may in some measure serve to explain and to extenuate his apparent lack of responsibility towards his family. Sara's various defences of her father in works which she edited also add to our understanding of him.

An examination of the large collection of Sara Coleridge's letters, diaries, and miscellaneous writings (many of which are unpublished) reveals not only the picture of a talented and intellectual woman but also the portrait of an attractive and thoroughly feminine personality. The sweet charm and the innate goodness of the woman, 'nobly planned', are, in the long run, fully as impressive as the penetrating intelligence. Although she was forgiving by nature, occasionally she turned with righteous indignation upon those who assailed her father's reputation. She loved only once, but with an intensity and devotion which made her marriage to Henry Nelson Coleridge idyllic and his death a major catastrophe. She was universally beloved and admired. As a child she was the darling of Wordsworth and until his death held a warm place in his affections. Southey willingly served *vice patris* to her until her marriage, and loved her almost as much as he did his own children. As a young woman and matron she was everywhere esteemed, and James Gillman is reported to have once said that he could deny her nothing. In her widowhood Aubrey de Vere, who seems to have preferred her society to that of the social life of London, spent many quiet hours in her presence. Carlyle sought her out in public gatherings. And no one spoke of her save with praise or affection.

During the long interval when Coleridge was separated from his wife and children, and when Sara was growing to womanhood, he heard much of her beauty and charm; but he preferred to imagine to himself his wistful, large-eyed child as a woman. Then in 1822 he saw her again. The creator of 'the lovely lady, Christabel', was prepared for an exquisite vision; but the flesh and blood daughter, who was as modest as she was beautiful and intelligent, far surpassed even the creation of his imagination. And in his declining years, the storms and trials of his mortal journey almost over, his beloved daughter brightened his ageing heart.

In preparing my manuscript I have carefully acknowledged all quotations from published sources; but since this study has been drawn mainly from unpublished manuscripts, many of the quotations are without annotation. In quoting from manuscripts I have reproduced all eccentricities in spelling and punctuation, unless I seemed to be copying not what the author intended but mere slips in hasty composition.

I wish again to acknowledge the kind assistance of the Rev. G. H. B. Coleridge, who continues to foster and encourage my Coleridgean efforts. Without his willing co-operation, extending far beyond permission to use and publish manuscripts in his possession, this study could never have been brought to completion.

To the Administrators of the Faculty Research Fund of the University of Michigan I am indebted for grants made to assist me in the gathering of material. To Dr. Clarence S. Yoakum I am especially grateful for encouragement and personal advice.

To my friend and colleague, Professor Albert C. Baugh, I am indebted for a careful reading of the proof. I wish also to acknowledge again the kind assistance of Mr. C. J. Connolly of the British Museum in reading manuscripts.

Most of all I am indebted to my wife, whose devotion to research has made this work a collaborative enterprise.

EARL LESLIE GRIGGS

UNIVERSITY OF PENNSYLVANIA

CONTENTS

ILLUSTRATIONS

I

MILD AS MOONLIGHT

'SHE smiles,' so Coleridge wrote of his ten-months-old baby, 'as if she were basking in a sunshine, as mild as moonlight, of her own quiet Happiness.'[1] And as Sara Coleridge grew up, her father reiterated his first opinion. 'Every one is delighted with her,' he wrote to his wife five years later, 'indeed it is absolutely impossible that there can be a sweeter or a sweetlier behaved child.'[2] For Coleridge loved his daughter excessively, even though he spent only a few brief periods with her. His was a deeply affectionate nature, and perhaps the estrangement from his wife and the frustration of his hopes for domestic tranquillity drew him closer to his children. They were, indeed, deserving of his solicitude and tenderness—Hartley, the eldest, a strange, unworldly child, whose mind grasped metaphysical obscurities before he learned to distinguish fact from fancy; Derwent, Coleridge's 'fat child', whose hardy, practical nature stood him apart from his imaginative brother; and Sara, a wisp of starlight, flashing fairy-like about the fields, or saying in the depths of childish despair, 'I'se miseral'. To Coleridge his children were a constant source of wonder, and as their personalities unfolded he delighted his friends with unsurpassed descriptions, for he, better than any one else, understood them. '*Hartley*', he wrote to a friend,

is considered a genius by Wordsworth and Southey; indeed by every one who has seen much of him. But what is of much more consequence and much less doubtful, he has the sweetest temper and most awakened moral feelings of any child I ever saw. . . . *Derwent* is a large, fat, beautiful child, quite the *pride* of the village, as Hartley is the *darling*. . . . Verily the constitutional differences in the children are great indeed. From earliest infancy Hartley was absent, a mere dreamer at his meals, put the food into his mouth by one effort, and made a second effort to remember it was there and swallow it. With little Derwent it is a time of

[1] E. L. Griggs, *Unpublished Letters of Samuel Taylor Coleridge*, London, 1932, i. 293.　　　　　　　　　　　　　　[2] Ibid. 425.

rapture and jubilee, and any story that has not *pie* or *cake* in it comes very flat to him. . . . Our girl is a darling little thing, with large blue eyes. . . . Next to the Bible, Shakespeare and Milton, *they* are the three books from which I have learned the most, and the most important and with the greatest delight.[1]

Coleridge and his wife were an ill-assorted pair, and undoubtedly the fact that little Sara grew up in a broken home left an indelible mark upon her. Seven years before her birth her parents had married in Bristol in 1795, but even the most sanguine person could have foreseen only disaster. In the full flush of pantisocratic enthusiasm, when he and Robert Southey hoped to establish a Utopia on the banks of the Susquehanna River, Coleridge had become engaged to Sara Fricker, a sister of Southey's fiancée, not because he loved her but because his idealistic scheme called for young married emigrants. Not long after he gave his word to Sara Fricker, the 'emigration scheme' came to naught; but Coleridge, pressed no less by his own sense of duty than by Southey's insistence, consented to marriage. Yet the first few years of married life were happy ones, the advent of two sons, Hartley and Berkeley, obscuring any lack of congeniality that may have existed. Even then, however, Coleridge was hardly an ideal husband. He was too erratic, too self-absorbed for that. Mrs. Coleridge, natively intelligent, but simple hearted, asked no more than a peaceful home and the security of a regular income, and during his early married life Coleridge struggled desperately to provide these things. Frequently, and often for long periods, he absented himself from home, pursuing the quixotic fancy of the moment, now the author and circulator of the *Watchman*, now a Unitarian minister at Shrewsbury, and now the potential tutor of Mrs. Evans's children, but his treatment of Mrs. Coleridge was considerate and his letters were tender. His unbounded admiration for his new-found friends, Dorothy and William Wordsworth, and his growing tendency to seek inspiration from them rather than from her undoubtedly served as a source of irritation. Tied down as she was by two small babies, she could not join him on rambles across the country, nor engage

[1] E. H. Coleridge, *Letters of Samuel Taylor Coleridge*, 1895, i. 443-4.

in the spirited discussions going on about her. Her interest lay in her home and she was half-jealous of the poetic muse which Coleridge and Wordsworth were pursuing. Indeed, later when the *Lyrical Ballads* appeared, she took an almost malicious delight in noting the volume's lack of popularity. 'The Lyrical Ballads', she wrote to a friend, 'are laughed at and disliked by all with very few excepted.'[1] As a result of her failure to enter into the spirit of Coleridge's enthusiasm, disagreements arose, mild enough at first, but leading eventually to outbursts of temper and mutual recrimination.

In the autumn of 1798 Coleridge and the Wordsworths went to Germany. Here Coleridge remained about a year, gaining a knowledge of the language, mastering the philosophy, and delving deeply into the literature of Germany, doing exactly what he set out to accomplish. He wrote frequently and affectionately to his wife in England, and when little Berkeley died, he suffered all the pangs of tender fatherhood. As soon as he could he returned to Nether Stowey.

Then occurred the turning-point in Coleridge's domestic life. In October 1799, while on a visit to Wordsworth, Coleridge met Sarah Hutchinson, Wordsworth's future sister-in-law, and what began as a mere flirtation ended in deadly seriousness. His love for Sarah Hutchinson was really the tragedy of his life. For the next ten years it dominated his whole being. It disrupted for ever his domestic life, which if it had not been passionately happy had at least been reasonably calm. Slight misunderstandings and uncongeniality now assumed menacing proportions. Even the unfortunate circumstances of his marriage loomed into his consciousness and took on a new significance. Frustrated at the very onset of the affair, for his own conscience rendered any immoral relationship unthinkable, he was driven to despair, and his home became intolerable to him. Whereas his wanderings had previously been due to a restlessness in his nature or to attempts to earn his 'bread and cheese', now he turned away in sheer desperation. In the summer of 1800, after a few months spent in London, he had moved with his wife and

[1] Stephen Potter, *Minnow among Tritons*, 1934, 4.

3

Hartley to Greta Hall, Keswick, in order to be near Dorothy and William Wordsworth, who had settled in Grasmere, thirteen miles away. At Greta Hall his son Derwent was born in the early autumn. Coleridge should have been happy in his mountain home, but his love for Sarah Hutchinson lay like a canker at his breast. At intervals he made fitful attempts to restore domestic tranquillity, but his heart was elsewhere. Further factors in his family tragedy were his failing health and his indulgence in opium. The drug soon blunted his finer sensibilities and made him ignore his obvious obligations to his wife and children. That Coleridge blamed his wife almost exclusively for his marital difficulties (and the Wordsworths and others have seen fit to do likewise) merely hid but did not erase his own responsibility. If Mrs. Coleridge was irritable, high-strung, and exasperating, he was equally culpable. Had he been freed from his slavery to opium, his better nature might have rescued him; as it was, he lacked the moral courage to set his house in order.

In April 1802, after a visit to Sarah Hutchinson, Coleridge wrote his *Dejection, an Ode*.[1] Sarah Hutchinson was the inspiration for this tragic poem, in which he deplored the loss of his 'shaping spirit of imagination', and blamed that loss upon his personal afflictions, meaning particularly his thwarted love for Sarah. Recognizing clearly that the beauty and inspiration of the external world could affect only those who remain actively receptive, that we 'receive but what we give', he sought refuge in intellectual pursuits, escape from his tortured emotional nature in 'abstruse research'. Like the hero and heroine of Browning's *Statue and the Bust*, he would neither claim his love, nor accept without regret his present situation.

Coleridge and his wife did, however, make a last sincere

[1] It is worth noting that the first version of *Dejection, an Ode* recently appeared in an article by E. de Selincourt (vide 'Coleridge's Dejection: an Ode', in *Essays and Studies by Members of the English Association*, vol. xxii, Oxford, 1937, 7–25). The poem as there published is twice the length of the accepted version and contains a good many specific references to Sarah Hutchinson. In publishing his poem, first in the *Morning Post* and later in *Sibylline Leaves*, Coleridge of course omitted such personal references.

effort to achieve domestic harmony during the months immediately prior to Sara's birth, and in so doing endeavoured to discover the sources of infelicity and to remove them. Even here Coleridge was blundering, if not tactless. On one occasion they determined to search out each other's faults, but Coleridge, trying to confess his own, filled an astonishing letter to his wife with a long summary of her own deficiencies. Not long before Sara Coleridge was born on December 23, 1802, he was away from home, travelling with his friend and benefactor, Thomas Wedgwood, and among several really tender letters to Mrs. Coleridge we find one in which he advises her to make Sarah Hutchinson her companion during her confinement, for the 'opportunity of having her by yourself and to yourself, and of learning to know her, such as she is, really is'.[1]

The autumn preceding Sara Coleridge's birth was extraordinarily mild, foreshadowing, perhaps, her lovely temperament. A few days before Christmas, Dorothy Wordsworth discovered 'flowers of various kinds' in bloom—'the topmost bell of a foxglove, geraniums, daisies, a buttercup in the water . . . small yellow flowers . . . in the turf. A large bunch of strawberry blossoms'.[2] A week later, when she went over to Keswick to see the new baby, she found a tuft of primroses in bloom. Dorothy thought of picking them, but did not do so and found them on her return to Grasmere. She was so impressed that years afterward she recounted the incident to Sara. Coleridge was away from home at the time his daughter was born, and the news was communicated to him by the Wordsworths. He said he was unexpectant of a daughter, child and man-child being for him synonymous terms, but he must have forgotten what he had written to his wife:

If a Girl, . . . You must take your choice of Sara, Gretha, or rather Algretta, Rotha, Laura, Emily, or Lovenna.[3]

Mrs. Coleridge, apparently preferring the least poetical name, determined on Sara. When the little girl's birth was

[1] E. L. Griggs, op. cit. i. 226–7.
[2] W. Knight, *Journals of Dorothy Wordsworth*, 1897, i. 157.
[3] E. L. Griggs, op. cit. i. 225.

recorded in the family Bible—the same Bible, let us recall, which Cottle had provided, along with such domestic articles as a tin dust pan and a pair of slippers, at the onset of the Coleridge's honeymoon—it was in Mrs. Coleridge's handwriting, and not, as were the records of the earlier births, in Coleridge's own. This was, indeed, portentous of what was to follow, for Sara was always her mother's rather than her father's child. And how different the Coleridge of 1802 was from the young poet who hung over the crib of little Hartley! In 1796, the year of Hartley's birth, Coleridge was at the height of his poetic powers. Life lay before him like a vale of sunshine. He was the idol of his friends—indeed, every one who met him marvelled at his genius. Cottle, Poole, the Wordsworths, Hazlitt, each fell under the spell of his magnetic personality. Little Hartley delighted, astonished, and puzzled his father. The song of the nightingale led Coleridge to plan for his son's future; the frost busily tracing patterns suggested a natural education for his sleeping baby. No father could have worshipped his son more; certainly none has ever succeeded in more poetical rhapsodizing over his child. But by 1802 the picture has changed. Coleridge's poetic imagination is dead. His dreams lie scattered about him. His love for Sarah Hutchinson eats at his heart. His health seems irreparably bad. He blunts his sensibilities with opium. His vision of a happy home has faded away. Small wonder, then, that his wife, not himself, recorded Sara's birth.

Yet Sara did inspire love in Coleridge's heart. During the year following her birth there is less turmoil in his life. Proudly he records Wordsworth's praises of the baby:

[Sara] is quietness itself, very lively and joyous, but all in a quiet way of her own—she feeds on her quietness—and "has the most truly celestial expression of countenance I ever beheld in a human face". . . . The words "quoted" are Wordsworth's not mine, and Wordsworth's words always mean the whole of their *possible meaning*. She has blue eyes.[1]

The coming of a daughter awakened, too, Coleridge's sense of responsibility to his family; during her first year he

[1] E. L. Griggs, op. cit. i. 271-2.

6

joined an Equitable Assurance Society. He also made a will providing that the interest on £1,000 should go to Mrs. Coleridge after his death, an event which ill health and the ravages of opium led him to consider imminent, and that on his wife's demise the sum itself should be payable to Sara.[1] This insurance policy, it is worth noting, was not permitted to lapse; on Coleridge's death it provided for his wife and children, and even to-day, more than a hundred years later, it having been advantageously invested, pays dividends to the Coleridge heirs. During Sara's first year, Coleridge took his three children to Crosthwaite Church, where they were publicly baptized, as J. Dykes Campbell says, 'to please the good people'.

After the futile attempt to restore domestic harmony in 1802, Coleridge and his wife gradually drifted farther and farther apart. Two years later his marital difficulties and his constant recourse to opium had so undermined his health that he determined to seek the beneficent effects of a southern climate, finally deciding on Malta, but he never ceased to regret his separation from his children. 'You told me nothing about sweet Sara——' he wrote to his wife in 1804, tell me everything—send me the very *Feel* of her sweet Flesh, the very look and motion of that mouth—O I could drive myself mad about her.[2]

A few months later he wrote in an agony of homesickness from Malta,

I do not know what it is to have one *happy* moment, or *one* genial feeling. . . . No visitation of mind in fancy, but only the same dull gnawing pain at the heart—sometimes, indeed, tho' seldom relieved by a flow of tears when I can cry aloud to myself— My children my children.[3]

That he loved his children his letters afford ample proof, but he saw little of them. For them this could mean only tragedy, and one ventures to see in the sad, wistful, and introspective natures of Hartley and Sara the result of a household divided against itself. Sara, particularly, who was born when Coleridge had become almost a stranger to his home, grew up without his guiding care.

[1] Ibid. 262.   [2] Ibid. 304.   [3] Ibid. 333.

Whence came, then, her training, her amazing mastery of languages, her intellectual acquirements? During her childhood she astonished every one by her knowledge and intelligence. Coleridge, Southey, and Wordsworth each reported in glowing terms the gradual unfolding of her mental powers. As a mere child she read Italian with ease and had mastered the rudiments of French and Latin. Coleridge found her well versed in English literature. Her whole life, indeed, was distinguished by profound intellectual interests and achievements. She enjoyed, however, no formal training, but was educated by Robert Southey and her mother. The desire for knowledge lay deep within Sara Coleridge, and where other children would have welcomed the lack of formal schooling she took advantage of every opportunity to develop herself. To her father she owed her intellectual curiosity and her bent for metaphysical and theological speculation no less than her lively though fragile poetic imagination, but to Robert Southey, who stood *vice patris* for so many years, and to her mother, whose intellectual powers are often unjustly disparaged by those anxious to spare Coleridge in his marital tragedy, Sara was indebted for guidance, discipline, and training, for her knowledge of languages, and for her critical acumen.

Greta Hall, where Sara was born and where she spent the first twenty-seven years of her life, is a large, rambling structure lying on the outskirts of the village of Keswick. Behind it rise Skiddaw and the majestic peaks of Cumberland—'broad-breasted brethren', Charles Lamb called them; in the fields before the house the River Greta winds its way, almost tracing a horseshoe in its circuitous meanderings; while far in the distance stretches a chain of lakes. It is a beautiful spot, with ever-varying views. The mountains, now clothed in mists, now proudly rearing their heads in the sunshine, the lakes before, now peacefully laughing in the breeze, now angrily reflecting the tempestuous skies, the River Greta gliding like a snake across the broad fields, the green gardens almost surrounding the house, all suggest a fairyland of lights and shadows. The house itself is not so attractive, but at least it was large enough to accommodate the numerous inmates who called it home. The house and grounds were a constant source of pleasure to the children. They roamed at will in the woods behind the house or along the banks of the Greta. There was a path running alongside the river down to a forge, with hidden nooks and shady banks to explore. Inside the house, too, there was much to amuse them. The many rooms were filled with books from Southey's ever-expanding library, which grew to fourteen thousand volumes. Some of the rooms were named, Peter and Paul being two of the most used. At the top of the house there was a dark lumber room, supposed to be the abode of a bogle, which the imaginative Coleridge children feared exceedingly. The Coleridges occupied the larger portion of the house, the owner, William Jackson, and his housekeeper, Mrs. Wilson, living in the other side. Southey came on a visit in 1803, bereft of his infant daughter, and hoping that the baby, Sara, might fill the void in Mrs. Southey's heart. Here the Southeys remained permanently. As Coleridge was almost continuously away from home, Southey came to look upon Greta Hall as his own. Mrs. Coleridge and her children stayed on, however, and gradually Southey became the head of the family.

The occupants of Greta Hall swelled it to capacity, even though the two portions were eventually made into one. There were Mrs. Coleridge and three children. To the Southeys were born seven more children, four surviving childhood. Mrs. Lovell, a widowed sister of Mrs. Southey and Mrs. Coleridge, and her son became a part of the family. Two maiden sisters, Eliza and Martha Fricker, and their brother George, were also occasional residents of the house. Visitors, often such distinguished men of letters as Scott, Francis Jeffrey, Shelley and his young wife Harriet, or such well-known figures as Thomas Clarkson, Humphry Davy, William Wilberforce, and Dr. Bell, were hospitably received. The Wordsworths, too, were frequent guests at Greta Hall, living as they did not far away in Grasmere. 'Indeed we are a house *quite* full when we are altogether', Mrs. Coleridge once wrote to Poole:

At Christmas we seemed like bees in a Hive—for now Eliza is

here we are 4 women—Southey—8 children 3 servants—and
Hartley thought we were not quite thick enough—so he sends
for a youth of his own age to come and Scait upon *Derwentwater*—he staid a fortnight—and at the same time Miss Barker
had little Dorothy Wordsworth and another young lady at her
house, who were half the time here.[1]

At such times as this Greta Hall must have been more like
a hotel than a private home, but Sara was undoubtedly
stimulated and her personality developed by such a large
family circle. From her earliest years she was privileged to
enjoy the company of a lively, intelligent household, enriched by the presence of visitors from London, Edinburgh,
and even America.

Nor can we omit some reference to the cats of Greta Hall.
When Southey arrived there little Hartley had two cats,
Lord Nelson and Bona Marietta. There followed a long
progeny—Bona Fidelia, Madame Bianchi, Pulcheria, Ovid,
Virgil, Othello, Pope Joan, Rumpelstilzchen, and Hurly-
burlybuss. Such an imposing array of names suggests the
varied interests of the household, from contemporary affairs
to German fairy stories. To the children, of course, the
strange appellations must have brought both hilarity and
imaginative stimulation.

It seems certain that no formal arrangements were ever
made between Southey and Coleridge. Mrs. Coleridge and
Mrs. Southey being sisters, what began as an extended
family visit turned into permanent residence. That petty
jealousies and misunderstandings arose in this overcrowded
household, that Mrs. Coleridge and her children felt keenly
their dependent position, and that Sara particularly developed an almost morbid sensibility as a poor relation are
not to be wondered at; yet life in this strange *ménage* was far
from unhappy, and Southey watched over his brood with
serene kindness and treated every one impartially. It would
require the mystical powers of an Indian seer to discover
what financial assistance Coleridge rendered his family. He
made over to Mrs. Coleridge his only regular source of
income, the Wedgwood annuity—an allowance of £150

[1] Stephen Potter, op. cit. 27.

given to Coleridge in 1798 by the munificence of the Wedgwood brothers, the annual sum being remitted directly to
Mrs. Coleridge after 1817[1]—but, being himself so tortured
by poverty and harassed by financial embarrassments, he was
unable adequately to support his family. Thus a double
burden fell upon Robert Southey. He was called upon not
only to guide and direct the young Coleridges but to bear in
part the expenses of their subsistence.

In her later life Sara Coleridge often spoke and wrote of
her girlhood at Greta Hall. Sometimes, indeed, she deplored
the conflicts that inevitably arose, but more often she remembered the gay occasions when visitors arrived, her
conversations with Southey, who never closed his study to
the children, whatever labour he was undertaking, and her
intimacy with her cousin, Edith Southey. Robert Southey
she loved and admired. She recognized his steadiness of
purpose, his indefatigable energy, his untiring good nature.
Coleridge, she knew, even in girlhood, was the greater man;
but she probably had more affection for Uncle Southey, 'the
nurse, the guide, the guardian of [her] heart, and soul of all
[her] moral being'.

The brothers-in-law, Robert Southey and Samuel Taylor
Coleridge, form indeed a great contrast. Coleridge, one of
fortune's ne'er-do-wells, lived a somewhat irresponsible and
unproductive existence; nevertheless, he left behind him
three of the most remarkable poems ever written, a body of
critical work unequalled in his century, and a vast mass of
philosophical and theological material. The grandeur of his
conceptions stamps him as the foremost thinker of his day.
Yet his indulgence in opium, his wretched health, his domestic
troubles, his frustrated love, and an innate weakness of will
thwarted the full expression of his genius, and much that he
began he could not complete. When he was only thirty years
of age—in the very year of his daughter's birth—he sang in
Dejection, an Ode a sad farewell to his poetic genius; a few
years later he courageously undertook a weekly publication,
The Friend, which, after appearing at irregular intervals for

[1] In 1812 Josiah Wedgwood withdrew his half of the annuity, thus leaving
only the £75 guaranteed by Tom Wedgwood's will.

twenty-seven numbers, expired with the words 'to be continued in the next Number'; his contribution to literary
criticism, the *Biographia Literaria*, breaks off its philosophical
argument at its most crucial point. This impotence of will
is the misfortune of Coleridge's life; the amazing thing is that
his work, fragmentary as it is, should rank so high in English
literature. Southey, on the other hand, undertook his literary career with an orderliness from which he never devi-
ated. What he began he carried to completion. Less gifted
than his brother-in-law, nevertheless he was more popular
among his contemporaries. At thirty-nine he was made Poet
Laureate. The bibliography of his works reaches staggering
proportions. Whereas Coleridge wandered, physically and
mentally, and lacked purpose in satisfying his insatiable
curiosity, Southey, scarcely less enthralled by the strange,
the unusual, and the far afield, made good use of his scholarly
excursions. Thus Southey lived a quiet and contented
family life, while Coleridge's domestic affairs, like his literary
concerns, lay in ruins about him.

Despite, however, Coleridge's failure to live a methodical
life, he never ceased to deplore his inability to provide for
his family. There was, it is true, one period when opium took
full possession of him, but, with this exception, he planned
for the well-being of his children, spasmodic though his
efforts were. Hartley enjoyed more of his father's company
than either Derwent or Sara, and on him Coleridge lavished
an unlimited affection. Coleridge was, perhaps, desultory
in his educational methods, but such a precocious boy as
Hartley scarcely needed conventional training. Coleridge
sought, too, to instil moral principles in his children. To
Derwent, not yet seven years old, he once wrote:

It will be many times the number of years, you have already
lived, before you can know and feel thoroughly, how very much
your dear Father wishes and longs to have you on his knees, and
in his arms. . . . For you are a big Thought, and take up a great
deal of room in your Father's Heart: and his eyes are often full
of tears thro' Love of you, and his Forehead wrinkled from the
labor of his Brain, planning to make you good, and wise and
happy. And your *Mother* has fed and cloathed and taught you,

day after day, all your life; and has passed many sleepless nights, watching and lulling you, when you were sick and helpless; and she gave *you* nourishment out of her own Breasts for so long a time, that the moon was at its least and its greatest sixteen times before you lived entirely on any other food, than what came out of her body, and she brought you into the world with shocking pains, and yet loved you the better for the Pains, which she suffered for you, and before you were born for eight months together every drop of blood in your body, first beat in *her* Pulses and throbbed in *her* Heart. So it must needs be a horribly wicked thing ever to forget, or wilfully to vex a Father or a Mother, especially a Mother. God is above all: and only good and dutiful children can say their Lord's Prayer, and say to God, 'our Father', without being wicked even in their Prayers. But after God's name, the name of Mother is the sweetest and most holy. . . .[1]

In the same genuine desire for the spiritual welfare of his children, and, we may add, with a rather remarkable understanding of the child's level of comprehension, Coleridge wrote for his little four-year-old daughter a beautiful poem, *A Child's Evening Prayer*.

> Ere on my bed my limbs I lay,
> God grant me grace my prayers to say:
> O God! preserve my mother dear
> In strength and health for many a year;
> And, O! preserve my father too,
> And may I pay him reverence due;
> And may I my best thoughts employ
> To be my parents' hope and joy;
> And O! preserve my brothers both
> From evil doings and from sloth,
> And may we always love each other
> Our friends, our father, and our mother:
> And still, O Lord, to me impart
> An innocent and grateful heart,
> That after my great sleep I may
> Awake to thy eternal day! *Amen.*[2]

In justice, however, while we must deplore the Coleridge children's lack of the presence and guidance of a father—of

---

[1] E. L. Griggs, op. cit. i. 366–7.

[2] These pleasant lines, it is important to remark, are an anticipation of Sara Coleridge's own poems for children a generation later.

such a father, one of them says—Southey was undoubtedly the better teacher. Had Coleridge been able to overcome his aversion to his wife and live with his children, their lives would have been immeasurably enriched by his love and guidance; fortunately Robert Southey was equally a worshipper of childhood. With a boyish heart he was able to enter into the games and amusements of the children. He invented stories, sometimes of goblins and witches, sometimes such immortal tales as *The Three Bears*. He could easily be persuaded to leave his books to go down to Derwentwater or to the mountains for picnics. He dreaded leaving his family for even a short time, once giving up a journey to Lisbon unless his wife and child could accompany him. 'It certainly is not worth while to sacrifice a year's happiness', he wrote to Mrs. Southey:

for your sake as well as my own, and for little Edith's sake, I will not consent to any separation; the growth of a year's love between her and me, . . . is a thing too delightful in itself, and too valuable in its consequences, both to her and me, to be given up. . . .[1]

On another occasion Southey rejected an opportunity to sit in Parliament because he could not bear to be away. No home is complete, he once said, unless there be a child rising three years and a kitten rising six weeks. When he returned from a visit to Waterloo, he deliberately stayed overnight at the Wordsworths' that the children might be awake to enjoy his home-coming in broad daylight. Always was he solicitous for the happiness of the children at Greta Hall, and indeed everything was calculated to spare them any unnecessary pain. Nor was their enjoyment his only concern. By example, no less than by instruction, he brought them up in a religious manner. When his daughter Isabel died he called every one into his study and read aloud the fifteenth chapter of the First Epistle to the Corinthians. Little Sara, certainly, basked in the warmth of Southey's love; indeed, her later success in training her own children owes much to the example of Robert Southey.

Although Coleridge and Southey were ostensibly friends,

[1] C. C. Southey, *The Life and Correspondence of the late Robert Southey*, 1850, ii. 348–9.

they were hardly suited to one another, and there were misunderstandings between them almost from the beginning of their association. Southey's meddling interference in bringing about Coleridge's marriage embittered Coleridge; and the fact that Southey later had to assume a share of the financial and moral responsibility for the Coleridge children tended to make him openly hostile to their father. Southey's own income was none too secure. He met his expenses only by dint of constant and unceasing literary efforts, and he must have resented the additional burden falling upon him. He was, of course, too matter-of-fact in the management of his literary and domestic affairs to tolerate or even understand Coleridge. Gradually he began to lose faith, and as he did so, what had once been buried in his heart now came out in conversations and correspondence with friends. When Coleridge's *Christabel*, *Lay Sermons*, *Biographia Literaria*, *Sibylline Leaves*, and *Friend* were published in rapid succession and the reviews were almost unanimous in their animosity, Southey never lifted a finger, although he had become the 'chief support' of the *Quarterly Review*. Had he wished to come to Coleridge's defence, certainly he could have done so; especially when the reviews unjustly attacked Coleridge's personal life, Southey might at least have defended Coleridge against calumny and falsehood. Southey's silence declared, as effectively as his open criticism in his letters, his complete renunciation of Coleridge's friendship.[1] Nor could Sara and her brothers fail to notice their uncle's attitude, and they wept where they could not protest. Mrs. Coleridge was keenly aware of the children's feelings about their father. '[They] are miserable', she wrote to Poole,

if their father is mentioned for fear they should hear anything like blame attached to it, but I believe I mentioned to you before their great sensibility on this unhappy subject.[2]

[1] Not long after Southey had bitterly condemned his brother-in-law in letters to Cottle and to the Ottery Coleridges in 1814, Coleridge, generous as always, vigorously defended him in two letters in the *Courier*, answering the malevolent attacks upon Southey's piratically published *Wat Tyler*. Southey showed no gratitude for Coleridge's magnanimous action. Of Southey's obvious feelings about Coleridge there can be no question.

[2] Stephen Potter, op. cit. 32.

15

Is it any wonder, then, that Sara literally sat at the feet of visitors from London for news of her father? Usually she was gratified with glowing reports, for Coleridge continued to cast his magic spell, even until his death. The pity is, indeed, that she should have been deprived of the love and inspiration which only Coleridge could have given her.

Throughout her life Sara Coleridge suffered from delicate health, the source of which she traced to an accident during her early childhood. When she was two years old she slipped from a bridge across the Greta into the river below, but luckily a young workman rescued her before the current carried her away. In Sara's own words:

I was put between blankets on my return to the house; but my constitution had received a shock, and I became tender and delicate, having before been a thriving child.[1]

This accident, one is tempted to interpolate, was probably of less permanent significance than Sara considered it; even she herself admits that before it she 'had been nervous and in-somnolent'. 'A poor little, delicate, low-spirited child I doubtless was',[2] Sara said of herself later. Once she exclaimed to her Aunt Lovell, 'I'se miseral'. Mrs. Lovell, a little too sympathetically, perhaps, suggested a cap to alleviate her self-pity; and from then on until she was eight years old her head was kept covered by a lacy cap, thereby adding to her quaintness.

As a baby, Sara seemed to Dorothy Wordsworth 'the very soul of meekness',[3] though she soon became 'a little quick creature here and there and everywhere'.[4] Indeed Dorothy was enthralled. 'For at least five minutes', she wrote to Lady Beaumont,

I could not get over a shock which I felt at the first glance of my eye upon Sara, she seemed so very little, such a slender delicate creature, fair as a snow-drop and was then almost as pale. But when she twirled about upon the carpet the exquisite grace of her motions, her half-Lady, half-Spirit Form and her interesting countenance made her an object of pure delight. She is as quick

[1] Edith Coleridge, *Memoir and Letters of Sara Coleridge*, 1873, i. 6.   [2] Ibid.
[3] E. de Selincourt, *Early Letters of William and Dorothy Wordsworth*, 1935, 349.
[4] Ibid. 391.

as a Fairy—everything about her diminutive except her eyes which may be called majestic—indeed I never saw finer eyes.[1]

When Sara was a mere baby, Dorothy thought her growing 'exceedingly like her Father'.[2]

Sara was admired by every one. She and Edith Southey, her cousin, both about the same age, were inseparable companions, and Dora Wordsworth was often their playmate. Edith was the most dignified—Hartley considered her stately and insisted that she should marry a title; Dora was the most active and, like an untamed fawn, she bounded over the hillsides; Sara was the frailest and most quaint. There was something wistful and yet ethereal in her large blue eyes and pale complexion. What she lacked in physical strength she made up in energy and liveliness.

When Sara Coleridge, late in life, attempted to set down details of her early years for her daughter's sake, from the blurred remembrance of the past only a few memories remained in the sea of forgetfulness. A journey to Bristol in 1807, with her mother and Derwent, left an indelible impression upon her. For Sara this experience was filled with excitement, but for her parents it was another sad chapter in marital disaster. When Coleridge returned from Malta in 1806 he was broken and dejected. Two years of absence had vivified his dread of further domestication, and he delayed his return to Keswick for several weeks after landing in England. He remained at Greta Hall only a short time, and then departed with Hartley for Coleorton, where the Wordsworths were staying. He was convinced that he must separate from his wife. Mrs. Coleridge felt, however, that a formal separation would disgrace her in the eyes of the world and she wrote pleading with him to postpone his decision. She finally persuaded him to go with her to his brother, George Coleridge, at Ottery St. Mary, the family seat, in order that the separation might 'appear free from all shadow of suspicion of any other cause than that of unfitness and unconquerable difference of temper'.[3] Accordingly, in the spring of 1807 Coleridge and Hartley joined Mrs. Coleridge and the two younger children in Bristol, but when George

---

[1] Ibid. 395.   [2] Ibid. 510.   [3] E. L. Griggs, op. cit. i. 371.

Coleridge learned of the plan he denounced it as immoral and bluntly told Coleridge not to come to Ottery.

Coleridge thereupon tarried with his family for several months, visiting friends in Bristol and Nether Stowey. Thus little Sara was afforded an opportunity to be with her father, from whom she had been almost continuously separated. There seems to have been a lull in Coleridge's domestic turmoil; far from managing a separation, he actually resumed amicable relations with Mrs. Coleridge. On several occasions she even served as his amanuensis. In November 1807, however, he left for London, where, under the auspices of the Royal Institution, he was to give his first course of lectures on Shakespeare. Mrs. Coleridge and the children had in the meantime left for Greta Hall, accompanied by De Quincey, who had recently come under the spell of Coleridge's personality. De Quincey, not yet launched upon a literary career, was charmed with the children, and because he was anxious to meet the Wordsworths, he offered to escort Mrs. Coleridge to Keswick. Little Sara he loved especially; in her childish affection she promised to marry him, and great was her disappointment when he did not claim her hand. The journey was uneventful, but the children were beside themselves with joy as the carriage approached Greta Hall. Hartley screamed with delight at the sight of his beloved nurse, Wilsy, and shouted, 'Oh Wilsy, Wilsy, let me sleep with you!' Sara was calmer. Timidly she approached her cousin Edith, a beautiful, fair-skinned, little girl, with thick yellow hair. Soon they shared a stool near the fire, and, discovering how easily it moved about the room, 'ere long we were sociably travelling around the room together on one stool, our joint vessel, and our childish noise soon required to be moderated'.[1]

After completing his lectures in 1808, Coleridge returned to the north, his separation from Mrs. Coleridge still not carried out, despite the adjurations of the Wordsworths. They insisted that he could enjoy no peace of mind until he had definitely separated from his wife. Otherwise, they

[1] Edith Coleridge, op. cit. i. 12.

argued, both he and Mrs. Coleridge would continue in a
state of vexatious uncertainty, but Coleridge apparently had
not the heart to act decisively.[1] He domesticated himself
with the Wordsworths at Allan Bank, where, during the years
1808 to 1810, he was engaged in the composition of his
weekly periodical, *The Friend*. Sarah Hutchinson, who was
also an inmate of the Wordsworth household at this time,
acted as his amanuensis, and he spent much of his time with
her. Coleridge and his wife, however, seem to have gone on
in an amicable manner, for he occasionally returned for brief
periods to Greta Hall, and she sometimes came over to the
Wordsworths.

Throughout her father's domestic uncertainties, little Sara
had remained a constant source of joy to him, and when he
saw her again on his return to Greta Hall in the autumn of
1808, he was so enraptured with his six-year-old fairy-child
that he could not bear to depart for Allan Bank without her
and begged Mrs. Coleridge to let him take Sara with him.
Proudly he bundled her into a gig, and soon they arrived in
Grasmere. As they drove up, little John Wordsworth, six
months her junior, screamed with pleasure, but as Sara
entered the house excessive modesty forced him to hide. Not
for long, however. Soon he emerged, and, with his face
covered with his pinafore, he kissed her. Every one loved
Sara, but Coleridge had insisted on the visit for his own
delight and he added, 'Sara sleeps with me.'[2]

Coleridge was so grateful to his wife for her kindness in
letting him have Sara to himself that he wrote a tender letter
to her, describing Sara, telling how she had made the
Wordsworth children 'as happy as happy can be'.[3] He found
the child much cleverer than he had supposed. 'She is
indeed', he continued,

a very sweet unblameable Darling—and what elegance of Form
and Motion—her dear eyes too! as I was telling a most wild
story to her and John her large eyes grew almost as large again
with wonderment——'[4]

[1] E. de Selincourt, *The Letters of William and Dorothy Wordsworth. The Middle Years*, 1937, i. 69, 156–7.
[2] E. L. Griggs, op. cit. i. 424.   [3] Ibid. 425.   [4] Ibid. 426.

The opportunity of enjoying his daughter softened Coleridge's feelings towards his wife; but, blundering as ever, he asked her to send him 'a good lot of books by each carrier—no odds, with what you begin'—and when all were dispatched, 'lastly the shelves'[1] were to follow. It is as if Coleridge were surreptitiously moving out!

Sara was overjoyed to find among the visitors at Allan Bank her 'future husband', as she then solemnly regarded Thomas De Quincey. She used to watch her father and De Quincey pacing up and down the room in conversation. Too young to understand what they were saying, nevertheless she was fascinated by their animation. She noted particularly Coleridge's handkerchief hanging forgotten out of his pocket and longed to clutch it.

She was at this time almost morbidly sensitive. Often at night she would make her way downstairs from her own dark and terrifying room to the comforting light of the family parlour. No one save Coleridge seems to have understood the child's fears and to have sympathized with them. He insisted upon a lighted candle in her bedroom at Greta Hall, for he knew what unbidden horrors could force themselves before the trembling consciousness. Yet at Allan Bank, when his daughter was his bedfellow, he awakened her to relate stories of unearthly beings, telling her of things she could not choose but hear. In these days of theoretical education, when we take the wolf out of the tale of *Red Riding Hood* and shield the child from *Grimm's Fairy Tales*, Coleridge would hardly qualify as a schoolmaster; but who would deprive little Sara of those tales which only a mind such as his could concoct, as she lay nestled in his arms? Much, however, as she enjoyed these nocturnal visits with her father, for, as he says, she talked to him by the hour in bed, she preferred to sleep with Sarah Hutchinson, who retired at a reasonable hour and did not keep the poor child waiting alone half the night.

The visit to Allan Bank, however, was not entirely happy. Sara was more introspective and less demonstrative than the Wordsworth children. She needed to become accustomed to her father before she could show her affection for him.

[1] Ibid. 426.

Whereas the young Wordsworths climbed on his lap, romped with him, and warmed in the glow of his affection, Sara hid herself away. Coleridge sought to break down the barriers and contrasted her coldness with the childish caresses of the little Wordsworths, but he merely drove her from him. Soon Mrs. Coleridge came to take her home. The sight of her mother released the tempest of feeling within her; she rushed to Mrs. Coleridge's arms, begging never to be separated again. To Coleridge the scene meant only one thing: his daughter preferred her mother to him; and he turned away to the Wordsworth children. He failed to understand his daughter's heart, failed to distinguish between shyness and lack of affection; and Sara as a result was driven back into herself in a misery of misunderstanding.

In the *Memoir* of Sara Coleridge we find her own description of herself as a child:

What *was* I? In person very slender and delicate, not habitually colourless, but often enough pallid and feeble looking. Strangers used to exclaim about my eyes, and I remember remarks made upon their large size, both by my Uncle Southey and Mr. Wordsworth. I suppose the thinness of my face, and the smallness of the other features, with the muffling close cap, increased the apparent size of the eye, for only artists, since I have grown up, speak of my eyes as large and full. They were bluer, too, in my early years than now.

I had great muscular activity, which I cultivated into agility—great were my feats in the way of jumping, climbing and race-running.

My health alternated, as it has done all my life, till the last ten or twelve years, when it has been unchangeably depressed, between delicacy and a very easy, comfortable condition. I remember well that nervous sensitiveness and morbid imaginativeness had set in with me very early. During my Grasmere visit I used to feel frightened at night on account of the darkness. I then was a stranger to the whole host of night-agitators—ghosts, goblins, demons, devils, bogles, burglars, elves, and witches. Horrid ghastly tales and ballads, of which crowds afterwards came in my way, had not yet cast their shadows over my mind. And yet I was terrified in the dark, and used to think of lions, the only form of terror which my dark-engendered agitation would take.

My next bugbear was the Ghost in Hamlet. Then the picture of
Death at Hell Gate in an old edition of Paradise Lost, the delight
of my girlhood. Last and worst came my Uncle Southey's ballad
horrors, above all the Old Woman of Berkeley. Oh, the agonies
I have endured between nine and twelve at night, before mama
joined me in bed, in presence of that hideous assemblage of
images. . . . What made the matter worse was that, like all other
nervous sufferings, it could not be understood by the inexperi-
enced, and consequently subjected the sufferer to ridicule and
censure. My Uncle Southey laughed heartily at my agonies. I
mean at the cause—he did not enter into the agonies. Even
mama scolded me for creeping out of bed after an hour's torture,
and stealing down to her in the parlour, saying I could bear the
loneliness and the night-fears no longer. . . .

Yet I was a most fearless child by daylight, ever ready to take
the difficult mountain-path and outgo my companions' daring
in tree-climbing.[1]

At this time Coleridge put his two sons under the tutelage
of the Rev. Mr. Dawes, who kept a school at Ambleside.
Here they were adequately prepared for college. They doted
on their younger sister. Derwent endeavoured to instruct her
in Latin, but Hartley, though secretly proud of her learning,
warned her that Latin and celibacy go hand in hand.

To Hartley and Derwent the Wordsworth home was
almost as familiar as Greta Hall; for years they spent
numerous week-ends at Grasmere. Sara's visits were less
frequent, but she was equally welcome. Coleridge, of course,
wanted his children to love the Wordsworth family. He was
especially anxious for them to admire Sarah Hutchinson and
used to talk to Sara 'with much admiration and affection'
about her. The Coleridge children probably sensed that she
was one source of irritation between their father and mother,
and they never overcame an instinctive dislike of her.[2] Sara,
long afterwards, described her unsympathetically:

She had fine, long, light brown hair, I think her only beauty,
except a fair skin, for her features were plain and contracted, her
figure dumpy, and devoid of grace and dignity.[3]

[1] Edith Coleridge, op. cit. i. 24–6, supplemented by a passage from the
unpublished version of the memoir.
[2] G. E. and E. L. Griggs, *Letters of Hartley Coleridge*, 1936, 136, 175.
[3] Edith Coleridge, op. cit. i. 19–20.

It is interesting to note how differently Coleridge, Words-worth, and Southey, now closely associated, reacted to feminine dress. Coleridge liked everything feminine and domestic. He admired white clothing, because he thought it 'expressive of . . . delicacy and purity'. He even approved of Sara's cap, considering it girlish. Once when Mrs. Coleridge had dressed her in a 'new stuff frock', Coleridge took her up, only to put her down without a caress, disliking the unnatural costume. Southey preferred the 'gay, bright, cheerful colours, and even declared he had a taste for the *grand*, in half jest'. Wordsworth was partial to 'all that was rich and picturesque, light and free in clothing. A deep Prussian blue or purple was one of his favourite colours.' He hated white dresses and the sombre, dingy black worn by the peasantry. He once pointed out 'how much better young girls looked of an evening in bare arms, even if the arms themselves were not very lovely, it gave such a lightness to their general air'.[1] It is a curious fact that each of the three daughters, Sara Coleridge, Edith Southey, and Dora Words-worth, expressed even in personality her father's preference in the matter of dress; Sara, the meek and wistful; Edith, the grand and stately; and Dora, the free and impetuous.

Coleridge's residence at Allan Bank was to end in a tragic misunderstanding with the Wordsworths. The details of the Coleridge-Wordsworth quarrel are too well known to need more than passing reference. Coleridge's ill health, his indulgence in opium, and his strange disregard for the neces-sary routine of the household changed him from a stimulating companion to a nuisance and a burden. When, in the autumn of 1810, Basil Montagu, on a visit to the north, invited Coleridge to accompany him to London for an extended stay, Wordsworth warned Montagu of Coleridge's domestic habits. Arriving in London Montagu unfortunately saw fit to repeat this warning to Coleridge—and a friendship of nearly fourteen years' standing was rent asunder. Montagu's gossip was, of course, the fuse which set off the dynamite. The real cause lay deeper. Coleridge's love for Sarah Hutchinson, with which the Wordsworths had long been

[1] Edith Coleridge, op. cit. 20–1.

familiar, was an unwholesome thing. It made Coleridge unreasonable, jealous, and unresponsive. Like a bird of ill omen it hung over his life, giving rise to morose silence or self-condemning agony. Then, too, the presence of both Coleridge and Sarah Hutchinson in the Wordsworth household could only aggravate the situation. Wordsworth slowly began to lose faith in Coleridge, and once the misunderstanding was precipitated, nothing could bring back the old association. Mrs. Coleridge viewed the quarrel with mingled feelings. Much as she deplored the effect of the alienation upon her husband, she was secretly pleased

that even his dearest and most indulgent friends, even those very persons who have been the great means of his self-indulgence, when he comes to live *wholly* with them, are *as* clear-sighted to his failings, and much *less* delicate in speaking of them, than his Wife, who being the Mother of his children, even if she had not the slightest regard for himself, would naturally feel a reluctance to the exposing of his faults.[1]

Grief-stricken and stunned, Coleridge renounced Sarah Hutchinson and the Wordsworth family as well and absented himself from the Lake Country for almost two years. When he at length returned to Greta Hall in 1812, he called for his sons at Mr. Dawes's school in Ambleside and drove in silence past the Wordsworth home. Hartley turned white and was speechless, and Derwent burst into tears, for Allan Bank was still a second Greta Hall to them. Little Sara must have known, too, of the misunderstanding. She and her brothers were innocent victims of an upheaval they could neither comprehend nor remedy, and as with the disagreement between their parents, they could only suffer in silence. Was it any wonder, then, that Sara, like little Hartley, was driven 'to think her own thoughts' even as a child?

While Coleridge lingered in misery and uncertainty at Greta Hall, his beloved daughter bound herself still more closely to him. 'Little Sara', he wrote proudly to the Morgans,

does honour to her mother's anxieties, reads French tolerably, and Italian fluently, and I was astonished at her acquaintance with her native language. The word 'hostile' occurring in what

---

[1] Stephen Potter, op. cit. 16–17.

she read to me, I asked her what 'hostile' meant? and she answered at once, 'Why! inimical; only that "inimical" is more often used for things and measures and not, as "hostile" is, to persons and nations.' If I had dared, I should have urged Mrs. C. to let me take her to London for four or five months, and return with Southey, but I feared it might be inconvenient to you, and I knew it would be presumptuous in me to bring her to you. But she is such a sweet-tempered, meek, blue-eyed fairy and so affectionate, trustworthy, and really serviceable![1]

After a few weeks with his family Coleridge departed for London in what proved to be his last farewell to the Lake Country, no less than to the childhood of his children. Sara was to pass to young womanhood before he saw her again. This farewell brings to an end nearly ten years of indecisiveness in regard to his matrimonial affairs and from now on Mrs. Coleridge is to assume in reality her role of virtual widowhood. Pathetically, however, for years she kept a room in readiness for his return.

In the years that followed the quarrel with Wordsworth, the Coleridge children longed incessantly for their father. When letters from him arrived, and often there were long periods of silence, they were enraptured. When would he return? When might they go to him? 'It would pity anybody's heart to look at Hartley', wrote Dorothy Wordsworth, 'when he enquires as if hopelessly if there has been any news of his father.'[2] Mrs. Coleridge noted 'the flush of hope and joy that spreads over the expressive countenance of poor Derwent at the idea of seeing his father next spring! . . . He was 11 when his father last beheld him.'[3] And so, too, Sara was uneasy about not seeing her father, and Mrs. Coleridge tried to devise some plan to make this possible. It is, indeed, to Mrs. Coleridge's credit that she did not alienate her children from their father, and that each one retained an unceasing respect and passionate affection for him.

The visits of the Coleridge children to the Wordsworths at Grasmere continued as before. Much as she loved the Wordsworths, Sara as a child was not completely happy at

---

[1] E. H. Coleridge, op. cit. ii. 575–6. [2] E. de Selincourt, op. cit. 425.
[3] Stephen Potter, op. cit. 84.

their home. Even in later life she contrasted 'the extreme order, cleanness, and neatness of Rydal Mount' with Allan Bank and the 'Grasmere hut'. She remembered 'the horrible smoke, the dirt, the irregular Scotchy ways, the mischief inflicted on the walls by the children, who were chid and cuffed freely enough, yet far from kept in good order'. Her shy and retiring nature led her to resent somewhat the boisterous, rustic life of the Wordsworths. There was greater care and refinement in the management of children at Greta Hall. At Allan Bank they sometimes arose as early as four o'clock, free to roam barefoot about the kitchen until some one came to dress them. Once, too, Sara was 'washed in a tub in the kitchen, in an exposed sort of way, [with] some men or man coming in or out during the operation'.

Of the adults at Allan Bank, Sara probably felt most drawn to Dorothy Wordsworth. Dorothy's exquisite appreciation of natural beauty, her goodness of heart, and her unaffected and childlike manners made her a great favourite with the children. Wordsworth and his wife, too, were objects of affection, though the poet was often too severe and self-absorbed to be little Sara's playfellow. 'I knew', Sara wrote to Henry Reed many years later,

and honor dear Mr. Wordsworth perhaps as well as I have ever known any one in the world—more intimately than I knew my Father, and as intimately as I knew my Uncle Southey. . . . But in my youth when I enjoyed such ample opportunities of taking in his mind, I listened to 'enjoy' and not to 'understand.' . . . In our spring time of life we are poetical, not literary, and often absorb unconsciously the intellectual airs that blow, or stilly dwell, around us, as our bodies do the fragrant atmosphere of May, . . . and are nourished thereby without reflecting upon the matter. . . . I used to take long walks with Mr. Wordsworth . . . listening to his talk all the way; and for hours have I often listened when he conversed with my Uncle, or . . . when he chatted or harangued to the inmates of his household or the neighbours. But I took no *notes* of his discourse either on the tablet of memory or on material paper: my mind and turns of thought were gradually moulded by his conversation and the influences under which I was brought by his means in matters of intellect.[1]

[1] L. N. Broughton, *Sara Coleridge and Henry Reed*, 1937, 63–4.

Though Coleridge was not to be an inmate of Greta Hall again, it was not an unhappy house. There were gay times when Southey was persuaded to join the family on picnics or excursions to the mountains, or when he proposed a day of boating on the lakes. Little Sara, remarkably agile and sure-footed, bounded on ahead, calling back with girlish laughter as she hurried forward. Then they laid a fire, and after eating, sat around while Southey told strange stories or recited ballads. Finally Sara found her bed, too tired to sleep, to lie awake, haunted by the things Southey had related. She remembered a happy week, begun by a day of roaming over Helvellyn, followed by strenuous boating, horse-back riding for days, and climaxed by an ascent of Scafell. She got 'but half-way up the rock of mountain', and was forced to descend 'in a broken-back state, and from that time to this never had a back like other people's'.

Although Greta Hall was somewhat isolated, Sara was well supplied with youthful companions. Her brothers she adored. The numerous Southey children were a constant source of delight. Together they romped about the open fields. The innumerable pools of water from the river and the lakes afforded many a day of wading. One of their chief pleasures was the garden, 'in which', she later wrote, 'we laboured ... with a zeal and diligence which must have been injurious as disproportionate to our strength. We used to fetch water from the river, in large water cans, dragging the heavy laden vessels up the long steep hill.' Here began her knowledge and appreciation of flowers.

Many years afterwards, when Sara looked back upon these joyous days of her childhood, she wrote a poem describing her youth:

> When Herbert's Mama was a slim little Maid,
> And liv'd among Waterfalls, Mountains and Lakes,
> With Edith her cousin, she rambled and played
> And both of them garden'd with spades and with rakes.
> Sweet Edith was fair as the lilies and pearls,
> And swift as the slender Gazelle's were her feet,
> And over her forehead the small silken curls,
> Wav'd yellow and light as the clusters of wheat

27

A wood full of harebells was close to their home,
It led to a River all broken with rocks:
They lov'd o'er the thyme and the heather to roam
'Mid brackens and brambles they ruin'd their frocks;
They tuck'd up their trowsers to paddle and wade,
And washed their Doll's clothes in the water so cold;
They wove pretty garlands within the cool shade—
Their May Pole was beauteous indeed to behold.

In Winter they put on their great wooden Clogs,
And down to the Lake with young Derwent they ran;
The Sun having chased all the vapours and fogs
Their sport on the Ice in high glee they began.
In Summer they gathered the primroses pale
And filled little Baskets with fruits and with flowers;
To make Primrose Wine and their friends to regale
Was one of their pleasures in Summer's gay hours.

With Dora and Mary they went to the Grove
And picked purple bilberries near the bright Lake;
They oft with each other in gathering strove—
An excellent pie did their bilberries make.
They frequently sate on the bough of a Tree
And climbed to the top of a very high beech;
They sought for the foxgloves and O with what glee
They gathered the globe flowers that grew within reach.

Sara's earliest friend outside of her cousins and Dora
Wordsworth was Mary Calvert. When Sara was nine years
old, her mother took her to visit the Calverts at Allonby, at
the sea-side not far distant. She was delighted with the sands
and sea-shore. Here she found shells, crabs, and flowers, and
many new things to examine and explore. Here too, she
galloped merrily for hours on one of the Calvert's ponies.
Except for Mary, she found the children too boisterous and
rude. The girls annoyed the boys by putting crumbs in their
porridge; they were repaid by mustard in their own the next
day. The boys blamed 'that little vixen, Sara Coleridge',
and mockingly called her 'Cheshire Cat' because she grinned
so much. She must have been a spiteful little girl at times,
matching her wits against the others' strength. Once she
plagued a 'morose, ugly, withered, ill-conditioned, ignorant

creature' by strutting up and down before her door. Her intellect was developed far beyond that of her playmates and gave her a sense of superiority to them. Morbidly sensitive, she nourished too deeply and too long any childish affront and became somewhat introspective.

After the Battle of Waterloo all England, of course, was in a holiday mood over Napoleon's defeat, and Sara, a deeply imaginative little girl, twelve years old, hearing jubilant speeches from every one's lips, was wildly excited. In the summer following Wellington's victory a great celebration was held atop of Skiddaw. Led by Wordsworth and Southey, a large party ascended the mountain. At midnight an enormous bonfire was lighted—'it fairly put out the moon', said Southey—and blazing balls of tow and turpentine were rolled down the mountain side. For miles around, every one gathered at windows and doorways to observe the sight. Poor Sara was not permitted to attempt the journey. She was thought

much too delicate to be permitted such a thing. She saw her cousins . . . set out with tears in her eyes, protesting she could perform the thing with the greatest ease.[1]

Instead she had to watch the distant bonfire from the windows of Greta Hall.

There were sorrows, too, at Greta Hall, sufferings even the kindly Southey was unable to prevent. In April 1816 Herbert Southey, his father's favourite and most promising child, then in his tenth year, died after an illness of six weeks. Sara had become particularly attached to him, Herbert, of all the Southey children being nearest to her in temperament and intellectual interests. Four years older than he, Sara had helped to instruct him, no less than to romp with him in play, and when he died, she, like every one else, was grief-stricken. On the morning of Herbert's death Southey, ever thoughtful of the children, sent Edith and Sara with Dorothy Wordsworth to Rydal Mount 'to save them from all the sorrow that can be avoided, and to mitigate, as far as possible, what is inevitable'.[2] Sara never forgot little Herbert.

[1] Stephen Potter, op. cit. 39.   [2] C. C. Southey, op. cit. iv. 164.

Fourteen years later, in remembrance of him, she named her eldest-born Herbert.

Sara's greatest delight lay in study. From earliest childhood she had been precocious. At the age of four, when she was in Bristol she had amused her mother's friends by repeating the poems of Ann and Jane Taylor. As a very young child she loved to retire by herself to read, at first in English but before long in foreign languages. 'Sara', wrote Dorothy Wordsworth in 1811, 'is an admirable scholar for her age. She is also very fond of reading for amusement—devouring her Book——.'[1] Five years later Dorothy was even more impressed:

[Sara] is a delightful scholar, having so much pleasure in learning. I know no greater pleasure than to instruct a girl who is so eager in the pursuit of knowledge as she is—often do we wish that Dorothy was like her in this respect—*half* like her would do very well.[2]

By the time Sara was twenty years of age she had mastered Spanish, French, German, Italian, and Latin. She soon found herself at home in Southey's immense library. She was a voracious reader. The English classics not less than the ancients she pored over as a young girl, and she spent many hours studying such subjects as botany, theology, and politics. Southey, deeply gratified with her development under his guidance, encouraged her to instruct his younger children, and she gradually became their chief teacher. As a matter of fact, Sara's continual reading took its toll, and she early complained of infected eyes. But she never abandoned her studies.

It was not learning alone, however, which made Sara astonish every one who saw her, for she was strikingly beautiful. Her delicate features, her deep blue eyes, and masses of auburn hair were the delight of all who saw her. Her manner, too, increased the impression of beauty, for she continued to be shy, retiring, and thoroughly feminine. She bore her beauty in an unassuming manner, almost unconscious of it, and retaining always the gentle simplicity of heart which was natural to her.

[1] E. de Selincourt, op. cit. 483.   [2] Ibid. 745.

Although the Southey children showed no particular interest in intellectual pursuits, the atmosphere in which Sara grew up was by no means lacking in mental stimulation. Southey was a scholar, judged even according to modern standards. To him came a long procession of men and women of literary pretensions, as well as those who wished to pay homage to the poet laureate. There was much talk of public affairs, of the Church, and of literature. Sara in childhood and youth was privileged to hear the living voice of Wordsworth, De Quincey, Southey, Coleridge, Scott, and others, and she profited greatly thereby. Being not only the daughter of genius, but remarkably talented as well, she grew wise in the sunshine of her environment.

Although Sara enjoyed no formal training, there was more attention to the education of the children at Greta Hall than might be supposed. Writing to Poole in 1814, Mrs. Coleridge speaks of a regular school, over which the various adults assumed responsibility. Mrs. Lovell taught English and Latin; Mrs. Coleridge and her sister, Eliza Fricker, undertook instruction in French, Italian, writing, and figures; Southey taught Spanish in his spare time; while Miss Barker, a neighbour and friend of the family, gave training in drawing and music. As a result of all this, Sara became so accomplished that Wordsworth, ever solicitous, could say,

Should it be *necessary* she will be well fitted to become a Governess in a nobleman's or gentleman's family, in course of time; she is remarkably clever, and her musical Teacher says that her progress is truly astonishing.[1]

On one of her visits to Rydal Mount, Wordsworth, deeply interested in her intellectual development, heard her daily Latin and Italian lessons and was amazed at her progress as well as her knowledge. As a matter of fact, Sara's love of books and her precocious development led many persons to attribute her fragile constitution to indulgence in study. Mrs. Coleridge said frequently, however, that Sara had a perfectly normal love of exercise, dancing, and the usual pleasures of childhood.

[1] Ibid, 645.

Mild as Moonlight

As a foster-daughter of Southey, Sara was brought up in the Anglican tradition. Southey believed that religious training in youth was imperative and he insisted upon a religious atmosphere in his home. Unsympathetic with Roman Catholicism—indeed he preached his anti-popery on every occasion—Southey brought Sara up as a thoroughgoing Protestant; so much so, indeed, that she was later to turn her controversial powers against the theological arguments of the leaders of the Oxford Movement. Throughout her life Sara retained her faith in the beneficence of the divine will, and she was later to bear her sufferings and misfortunes with a fortitude and piety reminiscent of the early martyrs.

Sara's charm and beauty as a young girl are best exemplified in a portrait painted by William Collins when she was fifteen years old. Her slight, graceful figure reposes on a rock seat, against a background of black clouds. She looks into space, and there is the same far-away look in her eyes as in Wilkie's portrait of her brother Hartley. The seriousness of her expression merges into contemplative sadness. The forehead is high, the nose and mouth delicately chiselled. Surely, Collins caught something of the wistfulness, the haunting imagination, and the tender sweetness of his subject. The romantic manner of the painting is here entirely fitting, for it presents the fragile charm of Sara Coleridge against the black, unrelenting background of her life. In speaking of her, Collins called her 'Coleridge's elegant daughter Sara', but in his painting there is little elegance. We have, indeed, poise and self-possession, but the strongest impression is of demure charm and especially of haunting wistfulness.

The Collins Portrait of Sara Coleridge as a young girl

II

THE FLOWER BLOOMS

AS Sara Coleridge grew to womanhood, she continued to live at Greta Hall. Her brother Hartley left in 1815 to enter Merton College, Oxford, never to return to Greta Hall, except for occasional visits, and Derwent departed for Cambridge five years later. She kept in close touch with her brothers, however, and followed their careers with sisterly solicitude. Although she loved and respected Southey and was devoted to his children, especially her cousin Edith, with whom she shared every girlish confidence, although she enjoyed every favour her aunts, Mrs. Southey and Mrs. Lovell, could bestow, Sara was naturally drawn most closely to her mother and brothers. Mrs. Coleridge entered middle life a little disillusioned as a result of her unhappy marriage; always absorbed with the lesser details of life, she watched her growing children with pride and misgivings. Would her sons follow in their father's footsteps, becoming, like him, waifs of fortune, or would they find themselves places in the world? She fretted, worried, distressed herself and others, now elated, now in despair. Thus it fell to Sara to soothe her mother.

When Hartley left for Oxford he was a shy, unspoiled child of nature. 'Without being an ugly fellow', Southey wrote at this time,

he is a marvellously odd one—he is very short, with remarkably strong features, some of the thickest and blackest eyebrows, . . . and a beard which a Turk might envy. [Though] his manners are almost as peculiar as his appearance, . . . his disposition is excellent, his principles thoroughly good, and he has instinctively a devotional feeling which I hope will keep them so.[1]

He had no vicious habits, and in learning, as Southey remarked, had 'Greek enough for a whole college'. He was, however, fearful of being laughed at by his more sophisticated class-mates. Wordsworth, whose paternal interest began

[1] Lord Coleridge, *The Story of a Devonshire House*, 1905, 215–16.

when Hartley was a babe in arms and lasted until his death in 1849, endeavoured to impress upon him the necessity 'of applying himself zealously and perseveringly to those studies which the University points out to him'.[1] In spite of his own fears and those of Southey and Wordsworth, however, Hartley pursued his way with a steady and sedulous purpose, avoiding any sort of irregularity and practising the strictest economy. So gratifying was his conduct that Southey and Wordsworth began to interest themselves in Derwent's college career, Hartley having so well rewarded their efforts. Hartley took his degree with second class honours in 1819; shortly thereafter he was appointed Fellow of Oriel College, in recognition of his obvious intellectual gifts. Coleridge, with whom Hartley had spent most of his college holidays, was delighted. Mrs. Coleridge could hardly believe the news, Sara and Derwent were overwhelmed with pride and joy, and Hartley himself was so incredulous that he thought the good tidings only a dream.

Then, a year later, everything crashed in ruins about him. He could not adapt himself to the routine of a college don, and after holding his fellowship during the probationary year he was notified that it would not be renewed. The authorities charged him with general indifference to academic routine and habits of drunkenness. Though he was guilty of occasional spells of intemperance and was careless about college duties, he was undoubtedly judged too harshly. Great was the shock of his failure to his family. The news came upon Coleridge as a 'very heavy affliction ... with all the aggravations of surprise, sudden as a peal of thunder from a cloudless sky',[2] and he later spoke of it as one of the four major sorrows of his life. He did everything in his power to have the decision of the Oriel authorities reversed. With great pains he wrote out for Hartley long letters, asking for a reconsideration of the case; although his health was wretched, he made a journey to Oxford to consult the provost and expostulate with him. He suffered bitter agony over

[1] E. de Selincourt, op. cit. 645.
[2] Thomas Allsop, *Letters, Conversations and Recollections of S. T. Coleridge*, 1858, 40-1.

the injustice to Hartley; for Coleridge recognized that his son's failure at Oxford would probably undermine Hartley's whole life.

To no one was this grievous calamity more painful than to Hartley's sensitive young sister, who had had such high faith in him, and who later confessed that her brother's failure cast a shadow over her 'tender mournful girlhood'. Nor was Mrs. Coleridge less distressed. She considered the outcome 'the worst news that ever reached my ears'.[1] 'Poor H.', she wrote to Poole a little later,

is preparing a volume of Poems for the press, but I fear is at a loss for a publisher; he talks of writing for present support, but *what*, and *how* Alas, I know [not]. It's impossible for me to have any peace of mind until he [is] in a regular way of providing for himself.[2]

After more than two years in London, during which Hartley tried in a rather desultory manner to support himself by writing for magazines, Coleridge, anxious to have him among friends in the north, sent him to Ambleside to share teaching duties with Mr. Dawes, Hartley's old schoolmaster. The long letter which Coleridge wrote to Dawes about Hartley is a striking and yet pathetic one. It shows only too well how tenderly he loved his son and how, at the same time, he was tortured by Hartley's strange inability to adapt himself to the world. After Mr. Dawes's retirement the school failed, but certainly Hartley was in no way responsible for the failure. Henceforth he followed no regular occupation, but remained in the Lake Country, the beloved responsibility of every one there. He does not seem to have gone very often to Greta Hall, where Sara and Mrs. Coleridge lived until 1829, fearing perhaps the well-intentioned but unpleasant rebukes of his mother. The fact that Sara saw so little of her brother, although he was living only a few miles away, must have been an affliction to her, and she bitterly regretted his inability to live a regulated existence. At times, when under emotional stress or when an irresistible impulse seized him, he would be intoxicated for days. Yet he never wholly abandoned himself to drink and to the end

---

[1] Stephen Potter, op. cit. 85.   [2] Ibid. 90–1.

of his life deplored a vice he could not conquer. The whole country-side adored him, and, drunk or sober, he was welcome in every house. His family contributed to his support, usually through the medium of the Wordsworths, who loved him as a son. More gifted than any one of the Coleridge children, he failed to make full use of the talents entrusted to him. During his long exile, for all agreed that he must remain in the Lake Country, he wrote a considerable amount, but rarely was he able to prepare anything for publication. A slight volume of poems of exquisite charm, an excellent volume of prose, whimsically entitled *Biographia Borealis*, and a series of delightful essays in the manner of Charles Lamb make up his published work. Beyond these productions, one finds among Hartley's remains a large number of unfinished fragments, sad testimony to his inheritance; for his life retold, in miniature, Coleridge's own story of thwarted ambition, abortive hopes, and unfulfilled promise. To the end of his days Hartley continued, as his father had once written, to 'wander like a breeze'; but he remained innocent and humble, ever conscience-stricken, and filled with regrets for his shortcomings, and he retained 'a young lamb's heart among the full-grown flocks'.

For Sara, then in her most impressionable years, the wreck of Hartley's hopes spread an ever-lengthening shadow over her life. Her greatest joy in girlhood was from his college successes. Like every one else, she worshipped him; during unhappy episodes at Greta Hall, when members of the Southey family, less tactful than Robert Southey, the 'poet-oracle of her childhood', openly resented her dependence upon him, she could look to Hartley with pride. When he was cast adrift, however, she realized that he was henceforth to be a responsibility rather than a consolation.

Derwent, too, for a time caused worry and irritation. During his college years at Cambridge he became something of a dandy, indulging in extravagant amusements and ignoring his responsibilities. Mrs. Coleridge, who had developed a nagging, complaining, scolding attitude in her letters, wrote many rebukes. Coleridge hoped that Derwent was merely in his 'caterpillarage', but he was anxious none the less. Soon, however, Derwent came to his senses, and settled down as clergyman and teacher at Helston in Cornwall. In 1827 he married Mary Pridham, who was to be a great favourite of Sara's in the years following. In 1841 Derwent became the first Principal of St. Mark's, Chelsea, a newly established training-school for teachers. In later life he became a distinguished editor and scholar.

But let us return to the details of Sara Coleridge's life. Until 1822 Sara was rarely away from the Lake Country. In 1819 Mrs. Coleridge had taken her to Liverpool, partly to visit their old friends, the Cromptons, but mostly to have her fitted with supports for her back. Sara had long been developing a slight curvature of the spine, and it was hoped that medical treatment would prove effective. Apparently she improved, for there is but little reference henceforth to this particular malady.

When arrangements were being made for sending Hartley to college, Coleridge, now a wretched victim of opium at Calne, had been strangely silent; but once he saw his son again, his moral responsibility reawakened and henceforth he contributed, as far as he was able, to the college expenses of both his sons. From the time he bade farewell to his children in 1812, thus depriving himself of the pleasure of seeing them develop into maturity, he yearned tenderly for them. After Hartley entered college in 1815 and Derwent in 1820, Coleridge saw his sons frequently during their vacations, but Sara, who was only in her tenth year when he left the north, he did not see again until she had grown to womanhood. 'Would to God!' he wrote passionately to his wife in 1817,

I could but hit upon the possibility of seeing my dear Sara. I would work night and day to bring it about—but unfortunately we have no bed room and she could not sleep out.[1]

He had found for himself, indeed, a haven at last with the Gillmans at Highgate; for in 1816 he had begun a temporary residence with them, in order that he might cure himself of his slavery to opium, a residence which continued until his

[1] E. L. Griggs, op. cit. ii. 207.

death in 1834. The Gillmans ministered to him, made him an intimate member of their household, and to them he owed that Indian summer of his life. Yet their Highgate home was hardly his home, and he had, necessarily, to consult their wishes rather than his own. 'Poor C.', Lamb wrote feelingly, 'I wish he had a home to receive his daughter in. But he is but a stranger or a visitor in this world.'[1] Of Sara, Coleridge had only a memory-picture of a little girl of ten. In November 1818 Charles R. Leslie, the portrait painter, took with him to Highgate Collins's portrait of Sara. 'When Collins was in Cumberland', Leslie later wrote to a friend,

he made a sketch of Coleridge's daughter, a very interesting girl of fifteen, and it is by far the best portrait he ever painted. The sentiment . . . is exquisite. I took it to show Coleridge as one of my own, to see if he would discover the likeness, which he did; a proof that it must be very strong, as he has not seen her for many years and had not the most distant idea that it was intended for her.[2]

Coleridge was haunted by the picture, and he was delighted to learn from Hartley that the 'exquisite sketch' was 'not less faithful as a *portrait*'. He was so happy in the possession of this image of little Sara that he had it hung above the desk in his study, and there it remained until his death.

Late in 1822 Sara and her mother paid a visit to London, arriving during Christmas week. Coleridge welcomed his daughter with open arms, proud no less of her learning than of her feminine charm. Just as Sara had begged for news of her father from every visitor to Greta Hall and had sat enraptured as she heard tales of his overpowering personality and his conversation 'wondrous wise', so, during the long years of separation, Coleridge had sought for tidings of his 'gentle Sara' from those who had been in the north; but even the creator of Christabel was unprepared for the dazzling vision of loveliness which stepped across the threshold one cold December day, and his mind must have been crowded with poignant memories of the past. On one occasion every one stood up at Sara's entrance into a public gathering

[1] E. V. Lucas, *The Letters of Charles Lamb*, 1935, ii. 374.
[2] J. B. Flagg, *The Life and Letters of Washington Allston*, 1893, 142-3.

enraptured at her beauty. Coleridge was so overjoyed with his lovely and talented daughter that he wanted all his friends to admire her, and during her stay at Highgate there was a steady succession of visitors. She was fêted and entertained everywhere. During her childhood her pensive and half-melancholy disposition won her only love and praise and spared her even the unkindness of a rebuke—'every one has a caress ready for her',[1] her mother once said; and now in the bloom of her young womanhood, affection was showered upon her. 'Exquisite Sara', 'flower of the lakes', 'sylph of Ullswater'—these epithets were frequently used to describe her. When Henry Taylor first saw her about this time 'she seemed to him, . . . a form of compacted light, not of flesh and blood, so radiant was her hair, so slender her form, so buoyant her step, and heaven-like her eyes'.[2] Hartley remembered her:

Always so completely unique, so perfectly a Fairy, a being belonging neither to time or space, so like the etherial vehicle of a pure spirit, a visible soul (I remember once when she was sitting at the Piano-forte at Greta Hall she told me I was a *visible fool* for saying so) that I cannot imagine any thing like her, which is not completely the same.[3]

De Quincey thought her 'the most perfect of all pensive, nun-like, intellectual beauties that I have seen in real breathing life'.[4] When Sir Walter Scott came to Keswick, he said of her:

Miss Coleridge *is* really a lovely vision of a creature, with the finest blue eyes, . . . and altogether, face and figure and manner, the very ideal of a novel heroine. They say she is very clever and accomplished. We could see nothing except extreme ignorance of the World.[5]

Sara was less romantic and confided to her cousins:

[Scott] looks like an old, lame, fat, honest, good-natured admiral—I should never have suspected him of being the Ariosto of the North.

---

[1] Stephen Potter, op. cit. 46.
[2] Eleanor A. Towle, *A Poet's Children*, 1912, 119.
[3] G. E. and E. L. Griggs, op. cit. 156.
[4] Stephen Potter, op. cit. xxxv.
[5] *Familiar Letters of Sir Walter Scott*, 1894, ii. 342.

Yet with all her sweetness of manner, charm of personality, and natural beauty, there was an almost 'alarming degree of modesty' about her. She was as little pretentious of her learning as she was affected by her beauty. In early life she wrote an unpublished essay 'On the Disadvantages resulting from the Possession of Beauty'. Therein she noted the temptations to envy, vanity, affectation, frivolity, and extravagance which a beautiful person must resist, and she went on to comment on the morbid fear of growing old and the devotion to the looking-glass which those with personal attractions usually possess in excess. This girlish composition is remarkably sensible for so young a writer, but it is especially indicative of a serious, moral tendency which characterizes Sara's entire life. Small wonder, then, that Coleridge, whose whole being was profoundly devoted to religious and moral inquiry, glowed in paternal pride, as his friends admired his brilliant and gifted, but quiet and unassuming daughter.

One evening Charles Lamb joined Coleridge and his wife and daughter at dinner. He was captivated. 'Yes', he wrote a few days later, 'I have seen Miss Coleridge, and wish I had just such a—daughter.'[1] The evening passed pleasantly enough, though there was one source of irritation. Coleridge, it seems, launched forth in a long theological monologue, but as he touched on various controversial questions, Sara interrupted with, 'Uncle Southey doesn't think so'. Lamb, sensing Coleridge's irritation but ever ready to see the humorous side of things, was greatly amused, and as he rode homeward in a gig later was heard to chuckle to himself, 'Uncle S-Southey d-doesn't think s-so'. If Coleridge was disappointed to find his daughter agreeing with Southey rather than himself, it was not to be very long before her thought became typically Coleridgean. Sara, indeed, found her father to be all she had dreamed, both for his personal tenderness and his inspired conversation.

Charles Lamb later wrote to a friend:

The she Coleridges have taken flight, to my regret. With Sara's own-made acquisitions, her unaffectedness and no-pretensions are beautiful. You might pass an age with her without

---

[1] E. V. Lucas, op. cit. ii. 370.

suspecting that she knew any thing but her mother's tongue. I don't mean any reflection on Mrs. Coleridge here. I had better have said her vernacular idiom.[1]

This visit of Sara and her mother to Highgate marks the reconciliation of Coleridge and his wife. Henceforth Mrs. Coleridge was always to speak and write of her husband with consideration, pride, and even affection. The Gillmans certainly did all in their power to bring Coleridge and his wife and children into harmony, and both Hartley and Derwent spent many of their college vacations with their father. Mrs. Gillman wrote frequently to Mrs. Coleridge, especially when Coleridge was indisposed or too busy to do so. From 1823 on Mrs. Coleridge notes with pleasure her husband's successive publications—a sharp contrast, indeed, to her caustic description of Coleridge in 1816, when, after telling Poole that Southey 'is a most extraordinary being— good and great and deserves to be happy', she went on to say that Coleridge, whose *Zapolya* the managers of Drury Lane had returned for alteration,

instead of instantly setting about [it] . . . got in a fit of despondency and was confined 3 weeks to his bed . . . he will alter his play for next season.

You will also be sorry for another thing respecting him—Oh! when will he ever give his friends anything but pain? he has been so unwise as to publish his fragments of 'Christabel' and 'Koula-Khan' [*sic*] Murray is the publisher, and the price is 4s 6d —we were all sadly vexed when we read the advertizement of these things.[2]

This unpleasant critical attitude is replaced by one of pride in his achievements, sympathy with his ill health, and an understanding of his vexatious problems. She endeavoured, too, to keep from Coleridge any bad news about their children, and regretted any irregularities of Hartley and Derwent more on his account than on her own. When Sir George Beaumont died in 1827 and left legacies of £100 to Mrs. Coleridge, as well as to Wordsworth and Southey, but omitted any reference to Coleridge in his will, she was fearful lest her husband should be wounded, and she was comforted

[1] Ibid. ii. 374.   [2] Stephen Potter, op. cit. 47–8.

to learn from Sara that his only regret was at the passing of a beloved friend. She excused the fact that Coleridge failed to tell her of his appointment to the Royal Society of Literature and of the annuity of 100 guineas accompanying it, on the plea that he needed the money himself. Her resentment towards Coleridge had slowly burned itself out, until she viewed him with compassion rather than condemnation. Whatever bitterness had existed earlier was worn away by time and by their mutual love of their children.

Among the visitors who were welcomed at Highgate to meet Sara, two of her cousins came on December 29, 1822, to pay their respects to their uncle. John Taylor Coleridge, the elder of the two brothers, had long since been an admirer of his uncle. Many years before he had listened spell-bound while Coleridge discussed poetry, religion, language, politics, and metaphysics 'in the most splendid eloquence, without ever pausing for a word'. He wrote to his father that 'so delightful and astonishing a man I have never met with', who made 'altogether . . . the most powerful impression on my mind of any man I ever saw'.[1] John was now a successful young lawyer with a rapidly growing reputation, but he had never lost his interest in literature. His brother, Henry Nelson Coleridge, born in 1798 and named after Lord Nelson, had not seen his uncle since boyhood, but it was with great expectation that he accompanied John to Highgate. He had heard glowing reports from his brother, and several years previously, when Coleridge's *Remorse* had come out, he had read it standing at a bookstall. He was at this time practising as a Chancery barrister, after a brilliant record at King's College, Cambridge. Not wholly unconscious of his physical attractions and his intellectual endowments, he was a rather sophisticated and self-satisfied young man. He and John had looked forward to meeting their young cousin at Coleridge's; John, in fact, 'swore he would kiss Sara, . . . but he quailed in the moment of trial'. As for Henry, he contented himself 'with the most affectionate, prolonged diminuendo and crescendo squeeze with both hands'. Henry was quite pleased by his delightful cousin, but he did not fall in love

[1] Lord Coleridge, op. cit. 191–2.

with her at once. As a matter of fact, he wrote a spirited but somewhat supercilious letter to his sister; the letter deserves quotation here, if only to mark the complete change in Henry's outlook and personality once he became enamoured of Sara.

She is a lovely creature; small, but not in the least diminutive or dwarfish; her figure perfectly proportioned; her hair like Mary's and her eyes like a dove's; fair with a nice carmine; little features. Mrs. C. is not prepossessing; she was wonderfully kind and attentive and watchful; I even read *design* in her eye. She dressed most unbecomingly. Sara neat and elegant. . . . She does not seem at all formidable; you need not alarm yourself. [The whole family, apparently, had been informed of Sara's intellectual attainments.] She uses no hard words and seems very ordinary in her wishes and thoughts. I will engage five to one, she commits waste in the heart of the Special before the week is over; and truly let not the Special despair; he will find this little sylph of Ulleswater sufficiently susceptible, if I do not mistake. And God bless her! she has not a shilling to cross her [palm] with. . . .

You would split to hear the way I *romanced* to Sara! It amused me so myself, that once I slightly tittered, which she took for a nervous and enthusiastic motion.

This is hardly the language we might expect from a young lover, but before many days had elapsed Henry was transformed from a smart, self-conscious fop into a serious-minded man. He and Sara soon became secretly affianced. 'Sara and myself', he wrote in his diary for March 21, 1823,

are solemnly engaged to each other. She has promised never to marry any one but me. She wrote me, while in London, two notes, which I keep under lock and key, and gave me two ringlets of her hair, which I had made into two rings; one of them with my own hair intertwined with hers and set round with pearls I gave to her the last morning, when we parted, and the other, her own hair entirely, I keep myself. She took from her own neck a coral necklace, which I now wear round mine. . . . Fanny [his sister] advises me to keep the matter a secret till I can claim Sara without a chance of refusal.

Now as I value my honour and happiness, I ought to study with all my might to preserve the love I feel in its utmost force and purity. It should ever be before me, and deter me from every base and improper action. I never can meet any woman so exquisitely sweet again, and who loves me more devoutly.

Both Sara and Henry knew that their engagement would be of long duration. Neither possessed any worldly means whatever, and he was not even launched in a profession, but they were so sure of their affection that they minimized the prospect of indefinite waiting. They were cautious enough, however, to plight their troth in secret, for they feared the interference of their families. Sara was as reluctant to tell her father as Henry was to confide in his own relatives, and for a time only her mother and Henry's sister, Fanny, apparently shared the secret. The fact that they were first cousins also added to the probability of parental objection.

The young lovers were remarkably different in character and personality, though greatly resembling one another in hungry intellectual curiosity. Whereas Sara was quiet and introspective, Henry was a brilliant conversationalist and bubbling over with gay spirits. There was about him a sturdy self-reliance. Neither intolerant nor haughty, he was firm in his own convictions and fearless in expressing them. Although he was never very robust, he possessed a zest for living. He made friends easily. When he talked, his face lighted up with colour and animation, giving force to his remarks. Deeply religious, he was, nevertheless, a man of the world. He became a good barrister because of clear and incisive thinking, and he was also to take his place as a man of letters and a scholar. His overwhelming admiration for Coleridge was greatly to influence his thinking, and his political and theological views were to become in large measure Coleridgean. He listened enraptured as Coleridge spoke. 'Uncle Sam', he once confided to his brother, 'talked like a dragon . . . upon a thousand subjects'. At the very first meeting with Coleridge he had been so inspired by the poet's conversation that he felt it must somehow be preserved for posterity; he went home that night and recorded it as best he could in a journal. Thus the *Table Talk* had its beginning. To Sara, Henry's passionate devotion to Coleridge was extremely gratifying. She herself marvelled at her 'myriad-minded' father, and what greater happiness could she ask than a fiancé equally entranced by him? If she loved Henry for his manly beauty, his wit, and his effervescent good spirits, she loved him still more for his worship of her father. Unlike in temperament as she and Henry were, in their regard for Coleridge, in their spiritual aspirations, and in their desire for intellectual pursuits they were in harmony.

After a very pleasant visit in London, Sara and her mother went on to Ottery St. Mary, Devonshire, where they were most hospitably received. Like her brother Hartley, who had spent his spring holiday there in 1817, she made a very favourable impression upon her father's relatives. Henry Nelson Coleridge's father, Colonel James Coleridge, wrote of her:

Sara is indeed a sweet creature, and she has attached herself to me, and indeed to us all. Fanny is delighted with her.[1]

Mrs. Coleridge did not please him quite so well:

We get on with Mrs. Sam and let her run on about all the literary World. And I begged her not to think ill of me because I only read the Bible, search the Encyclopaedia, etc., etc. I shall not quiz her for the love I feel for her Daughter.[2]

He was so captivated with Sara that he proposed contributing £20 annually to Mrs. Coleridge's support.

From Ottery, Sara and her mother proceeded to Stowey and Bristol, where they remained for several weeks renewing old friendships. At this time Sara spent a day with the John Kenyons. She found their society especially interesting, and her friendship for them continued throughout her life.

One of the high-lights of these months of travel was a visit to Derwent at Cambridge. The geologist Adam Sedgwick showed them Roubilliac's statue of Newton, remarking that Newton was a far greater man than Milton. Sara heartily, but silently, disagreed. 'Even then', she wrote later, 'I *felt* Milton as many an able intelligent man can never do.'[3] One is reminded of Dorothy Wordsworth's visit to Cambridge in 1810, when in the company of Thomas Clarkson she stood reverentially before this same statue of Newton.

[1] Lord Coleridge, op. cit. 282.
[2] Ibid. 282.   [3] L. N. Broughton, op. cit. 84.

In June they made their way northward. Some distance from Rydal Mount they met Hartley and John Wordsworth, who had set out to meet them. Hartley's school at Ambleside was over for the summer, and just as in the old days he had again come to the Wordsworths for his vacation. To the great relief of Mrs. Coleridge and Sara he had completed his first half-year in Mr. Dawes's school without any difficulty. The Wordsworths were delighted to talk to Sara and Mrs. Coleridge at great length about Nether Stowey and London, and detained them for several days at Rydal Mount. Dorothy, still rambling over the mountains, as she had done twenty-three years earlier in the company of Coleridge, was especially anxious to hear about her old friend; and it was a sincere gratification for Mrs. Coleridge to be able to say that the visit to Highgate had 'been productive of the greatest satisfaction to all parties'.[1]

This brings to a conclusion the *annus mirabilis* of Sara Coleridge's girlhood. It was marked by a joyous reunion with her father, an acquaintanceship with the Ottery Coleridges, a glimpse of her brother at Cambridge, an introduction to the wonders of London, and, most exciting of all, her engagement to her brilliant and handsome cousin. Life had never seemed so glorious.

[1] Stephen Potter, op. cit. 99.

III

INTERLUDE OF WAITING

IT was probably with some misgivings that Sara returned
to Greta Hall. We can be sure that if she resented her
subordinate position in the Southey household before her
engagement, she must have found it even more difficult afterwards. As a child she had naturally been undisturbed by her
dependent relationship to the family, but now, as she reached
maturity, it weighed heavily upon her. Hartley, reviewing
the whole situation in a letter to his brother years afterwards,
sums up the matter:

A house of bondage Greta-hall was to her, not by any fault,
far less from any intention of its proprietors, our excellent Uncle
and Aunt, but from her own excessive, I might almost say, morbid
delicacy. Tho' she could not but know, that both she and our
Mother were doing daily services, much above the price current
of reciprocal favors, and that their presence was a perpetual
motive of good and kindly feelings, tho' they knew that their
absence would be regretted and the house never look like itself
without them, an uncomfortable sense of obligation, always lay
like an incubus on their gratitude. They were afraid to move,
to speak, every wrinkle of that blood-ill-temper which disorders
not diminishes Aunt S.'s benevolence, even sometimes the young
lady airs of our Lady Cousins, seem'd to their feverish appre-
hensions like a warning to depart.[1]

During the long period of waiting—Sara was not married
until six years later—she and Henry kept up a regular correspondence, full of tenderness and mutual faith, of so personal
a nature that her children consigned it to the flames after her
death.[2] Only a few fragments remain. A host of obstacles
almost overwhelmed her. Marriage would liberate her from

[1] G. E. and E. L. Griggs, op. cit. 108–9.
[2] It was, of course, the cruel and unwarranted publication by Allsop and
Cottle of Coleridge's confidential letters which led the family to destroy every
document the publication of which might cause pain to the living Coleridges.
Thus Mrs. Coleridge burned many of Coleridge's letters to her, as well as to the
Morgans; and other members of the family destroyed documents by Hartley,
Sara, and Henry Nelson Coleridge.

her humiliating and dependent position, but she knew it could not materialize until some indefinite time in the future, when Henry had established himself in the legal profession. But to Sara the engagement was irrevocable. 'She was a maid', Hartley wrote,

> Not easily beguiled by loving words,
> Nor quick to love; but, when she loved, the fate
> Of her affection was a stern religion,
> Admitting nought less holy than itself.[1]

Henry planned a visit to Scotland and the English Lakes in the summer of 1824, in order that he might see Sara; a recurrence of a rheumatic complaint forced him to go to Ottery St. Mary instead. He wrote Sara affectionate letters and sent her 'a beautiful French silk dress—he has made me many handsome presents which I have always discouraged his doing so much as I could'.[2] While at Ottery he sought his father's approval of his engagement to Sara, but the Colonel not only flatly refused to give his sanction but demanded that the young couple break off entirely any understanding with one another. To Sara he could, of course, have no justifiable objection. He had grudgingly contributed to Hartley's college expenses, and as far as he was able, lent assistance to the others. But for his son, who was still far from independent, to consider marriage with the penniless daughter of the ne'er-do-well Sam seemed preposterous.

Undoubtedly this hostile attitude was due in some measure to the fact that Coleridge had long since been regarded as the black sheep of the family. Unlike his brother

---

[1] *Complete Poetical Works of Hartley Coleridge*, Muses Library, 1908, 220.

[2] Sir E. K. Chambers in his recent biography of Coleridge (*Samuel Taylor Coleridge*, 1938, 315) suggests that all was not well between Sara and Henry in 1824 and cites as evidence a passage from a letter of Mrs. Coleridge to Poole: 'The youth *will* persevere, and now affects to think himself ill used: he now wishes to keep up a correspondence as *Brother & Sister*' (Stephen Potter, op. cit. 110). Mrs. Coleridge does not allude to Henry. Before going to London in 1822 Sara had half-heartedly accepted the attentions of a Mr. May, but since his father refused to consent to a formal engagement between them, and since the Southeys disapproved of the affair, she considered the matter closed. On her return to Keswick, however, May renewed his suit. His continued persistence proved so agitating to Sara and her mother that Sara accepted John Taylor Coleridge's offer of assistance and requested him 'to put an end to the affair in whatever way you judge to be the most conciliating and judicious'.

James, who had followed a regular profession, married an heiress, and lived as a country gentleman, Coleridge earned a random livelihood through spasmodic surges of creative activity. Uncle Sam, as the younger generation of Coleridges called him, was looked upon with emphatic disfavour by his more affluent relations. When John plunged into debt at college and sought to justify himself, his Uncle George cautioned, 'By that sin (specious argumentation) fell your Uncle Sam, and I trust that you will have too much sense, and enough religion, to prevent *you* from hoping to win by it'.[1] When both John Taylor Coleridge and his brother Henry Nelson looked longingly at a literary career, their Uncle Sam was set up as a tragic example of such a profession, and they were warned not to emulate him. Nor was Coleridge condemned for his poverty alone. To his family he seemed oblivious to the ordinary conventions of society. Had he not separated himself from his wife? Had he not abandoned his children to the care of others? Did he not close his conscience to the demands of duty? As early as 1809 Coleridge's brother George wrote, 'It is strange, passing strange, but such men there are. My brother Sam will be admirable, in my opinion, but neither respectable, nor venerable';[2] and five years later the Colonel is even more condemnatory. Hartley's '*Mad* Father',[3] he says,

is at Bristol, or God knows where, living on the bounty of his friends. I expect that *that Stream* will dry up and then we must have a heavier blow! unless Opium or something remove him to another World. What a humbling lesson to all men is Samuel Coleridge.[4]

Thus from the quiet of Ottery St. Mary, the scene of Coleridge's birth and early childhood, the Coleridges had passed unfavourable judgement upon the poet; but in spite of the warnings and disapproval of the older generation, Coleridge won the undying love and esteem of his nephews.

John Taylor Coleridge endeavoured to convey to Sara the

---

[1] Lord Coleridge, op. cit. 170.   [2] Ibid. 178.

[3] Southey was, of course, responsible for this notion of Coleridge's mental state; he had written on Oct. 12, 1814, to the Ottery relatives, 'I . . . verily believe that your brother labours under a species of insanity'.

[4] Lord Coleridge, op. cit. 214–15.

wishes of the family about her engagement. The Colonel, he insisted, was opposed to any vague and indefinite understanding; the family's approval might encourage the young lovers to marry in spite of Henry's prospects, and marriage could mean only poverty and disaster. In short, John Taylor Coleridge wrote to her that she ought to consider herself 'entirely disengaged'. This was too much. Had not she and Henry solemnly promised to postpone marriage until he was financially able to support her? Did the family imagine that she would expect to live in luxury after her marriage? 'I am not in the habit', she wrote to John, 'of sitting on cushions and having silk stockings drawn on by the hand of another, but get up early and sit in a room where there never has been a fire on a very hard chair, and walk miles alone, in heavy clogs of wood and iron.' As far as she was concerned, then, she would persevere in her engagement. 'According to current notions of honour', she protested to John on August 17, 1824,

I may be disengaged, but my own feelings will never permit me to think myself so—in the eye of the world I might be justified in bestowing my affections elsewhere, since Henry cannot assure me of his hand as well as his heart; but after what has passed between us, after the vows that we have interchanged, I must ever think that for either of us to make such a transfer while the attachment of the other party remains undiminished, would be a faithless and falsehearted thing and I have the less scruple in making this declaration because I think that Henry's ill health may render him in more ways than one, less likely to make what the world calls a good match than he otherwise might do, though I would not have him know that I should consider him as guilty of any breach of honour or feeling were he to make another and more prudent choice. I even had scruples at one time about declaring to him my resolution of living single for his sake, but judging from my own heart, I thought the comfort of this assurance would be preferable in his mind to a liberty which if all he says be true, he would never avail himself of. For my own part, I knew from the beginning that there was but little chance of our being ever united—I knew also that if I entered into the sort of negative engagement which Henry wished, for an indefinite term till he should think it advisable to ask his father's consent, such a plan would very probably prevent my settling in life, as it is called, altogether, . . . for a man may marry almost when he chooses, but with a woman, especially one in my situation, the season is soon past and after dedicating my affections to him for so long a time how could I calculate upon stifling them all of a sudden and marrying another?—No! when I gave my heart to him I gave it for good and all and never will I take it back till I perceive that he is weary of the gift—then I certainly will never trust any of his sex with it again. . . . Such being my feelings . . . nothing that may be said by any one with regard to this affair can have the slightest power to weaken or strengthen them. . . . I regret also that you think Henry has not managed the affair discreetly—one letter of his I was shewn the contents of—I do not see what more he could have said in token of his submission unless he had given up the point of his fidelity to me—do you think he ought to have done this?

This reads, perhaps, like a passage from an eighteenth-century novel. The interminable sentences are quite in the Coleridgean manner, but the thought is that of a self-controlled woman answering in kind the arguments of her legal-minded cousin.

There were other difficulties, too. Henry's poor health, aggravated by assiduous attention to both law and literature, necessitated a change of climate. Late in 1824 he accompanied his cousin, William Hart Coleridge,[1] to the West Indies. As a result of his travels he published in 1826 a light-hearted account of his experiences in his *Six Months in the West Indies*. In writing his book he failed to reckon with the conservative spirit of his family, who were displeased with its 'gay, laughing Epicureanism . . . and its lively sallies'.[2] Even Hartley was displeased with Henry's volume and questioned whether its author would make a suitable husband for his sister. 'I wish', he wrote,

the dear girl had form'd another attachment. Worldly considerations apart, I do not think . . . [Henry] . . . the likeliest person in the world to accord with the exquisite tenderness and susceptibility of her moral and physical constitution. Ever[y] lover, who

[1] William Hart Coleridge, the first Anglican bishop to be appointed to a foreign diocese, was Bishop of Barbados from 1824 to 1841.
[2] Lord Coleridge, op. cit. 142.

has had the education of a gentleman, must be delicate, but our Sariola will require delicacy in a husband. . . . The *Six Months* is very clever, and tolerably sensible, but there is a flippancy, a vulgarity about it, which I cannot esteem.[1]

In reading the *Six Months* in the summer of 1826 Coleridge, completely ignorant of his daughter's engagement, ran across this objectionable passage:

I love a cousin; she is such an exquisite relation, just standing between me and the stranger to my name, drawing upon so many sources of love and tying them all up with every cord of human affection—almost my sister ere my wife!

On 'complaining [to Mrs. Gillman] of his [nephew's] thoughtlessness in not foreseeing, that . . . [it] might be applied by many persons to Sara',[2] Coleridge first learned of the affair. Two years earlier Henry had sought his uncle's opinion concerning the marriage between first cousins. All unsuspectingly, Coleridge remarked impersonally:

If the matter were quite open, I should incline to disapprove the inter-marriage of first cousins; but the Church has decided otherwise on the authority of Augustine, and that seems enough on such a point.[3]

When his own daughter intended to marry her cousin, however, he could not view the question with the same philosophical equanimity and sought further advice from his friends. Henry Nelson Coleridge he loved and admired, but he was somewhat irked by the fact that Sara had not consulted him and had betrothed herself in secret. To Mrs. Coleridge he wrote:

I have no fortune to leave, no *trust* of this kind in the transfer of which I have any interest or duty: and therefore it has ever been my fixed principle, in respect of marriage, that after my children have reached the years of discretion—as a friend, I was ready to give them my best advice if it were asked while it could be of any service; but as a Father, I had only my Prayers and my Blessing to give.[4]

[1] G. E. and E. L. Griggs, op. cit. 93.
[2] E. L. Griggs, op. cit. ii. 379.
[3] *Specimens of the Table Talk of Samuel Taylor Coleridge*, 1835, i. 55.
[4] E. L. Griggs, op. cit. ii. 379.

Apparently Coleridge determined to accept gracefully, albeit reluctantly, his daughter's decision, especially as it was too late to counsel otherwise:

What I should have thought, had I been her confidant at her first knowledge of Henry's intention, it would now be a great deal worse than idle to say. I do not conceive it to be my duty—I thank God, that I do not—for the man and the father are too strong in my soul, for me not to shrink from the thought of my only Daughter—and *such* a daughter—condemned to a miserable Heart-wasting; or not to regard the alternative [her marriage to Henry] as a *lesser evil*. I have not the heart either to pass such a sentence, or in [any] way to be aidant thereto.[1]

Sara would have confided in her father had the circumstances of her engagement been happier, but with the possibility of marriage so far in the distant future, she wished to prevent the laceration of Coleridge's feelings. Had he known of her suffering, of her sleepless nights alleviated only by doses of laudanum, he would have been equally agitated. For Sara, too, her father's acquiescence was almost a secondary consideration. Having been reared almost exclusively by her mother, naturally she sought her mother's rather than her father's assent.

Mrs. Coleridge heartily approved of Sara's plans. She knew only too well what their common dependency in the Southey household meant. She did not wish Sara to become a governess in some wealthy family—the only means of self-maintenance—and she understood, too, from the example of Eliza and Martha Fricker, that independent spinsterhood was a precarious existence. Sara, too, needed comfort rather than further arguments against her engagement. Mrs. Coleridge saw her placed on the rack, torn between her great love for Henry and the constant temptation to yield to the entreaties and even demands of others, and pursue what was probably a more reasonable course. She was kept in a state of continual uncertainty. 'As for my prospects', Sara wrote to Derwent in 1826,

they are no better than heretofore—my Uncle's nervous state

---

[1] Ibid. ii. 379–80.

prevents any fresh application for his sanction to an engagement between my dear cousin and myself. . . . The idea of having a little of Henry's society would be sufficient to fill me with happiness were it not for the alloy which the disapprobation in this quarter must cause us both; yet for so long a time to be separated from one for whom one feels so much is trying enough and that is nothing compared to the dread of losing his affection from long absence, which it is impossible entirely to remove from one's mind.

A weaker person than Sara Coleridge would have capitulated under the double force of family objections and unpromising prospects. Even pride might have led her to change her decision, for she must have resented her uncle's disapproval. She had made her choice, however, and with the warm assurance of mutual love, she and Henry persevered until all opposition gave way.

During the long period of her engagement she did not entirely give herself over to dejection and despair. Instead she turned to intellectual pursuits. The younger Southey children needed training, and Southey, employed upon literary undertakings, gladly relinquished the task to Sara. To her the labour was most congenial. Blending in her personality both gentleness and firmness and being herself always a student, she became an admirable teacher. Inasmuch as her own training had been private, she had but little sympathy with the disciplinary methods then in vogue. Her understanding of children undoubtedly benefited the Southeys, no less than it was later to profit her own son and daughter.

Even before her first meeting with Henry Nelson Coleridge, Sara had become an author. While engaged upon his *Tale of Paraguay* Southey had come across the curious book of Martin Dobrizhoffer, *An Account of the Abipones, an Equestrian People of Paraguay*. The quaintness of the book's Latinity no less than its strange subject-matter attracted Southey's attention. Surely, he thought, the translation of such a work should be a profitable venture, but he found himself too preoccupied to undertake it. As it happened, Derwent at this time was badly in need of funds for his university expenses, and accordingly Southey suggested that he should attempt to translate the work. Sara, wishing to assist her brother, began translating the third volume in 1819, Derwent under-taking the first. Not long afterwards Coleridge's friend, John Hookham Frere, proffered financial assistance to Der-went. Being also engaged in tutoring at this time, Derwent followed Wordsworth's advice and withdrew from the trans-lation. Sara, however, did not wish to abandon the task, as she liked the employment 'of all things'. To her the work represented an intellectual challenge, and with inde-fatigable effort she carried it forward to completion. The book was published anonymously under the imprint of John Murray in 1822, the young translator being paid £125 for her labours.

No wonder, then, that Henry Nelson Coleridge had been somewhat overawed by the intellectual attainments of the young girl he met under her father's roof at Highgate! Coleridge, too, was extraordinarily pleased. 'My dear daughter's translation of this book is', he said proudly,

in my judgment, unsurpassed for pure mother-English, by any-thing I have read for a long time.[1]

Charles Lamb, humorous as always, was equally impressed by the 'inobtrusive quiet soul who digged her noiseless way so perseveringly through that rugged Paraguay mine', and amazed by the learning of the translator, exclaimed, 'How she Dobrizhoffered it all out, it puzzles my slender Latinity to conjecture'.[2]

Whatever claim to fame the work can make—and Sara Coleridge never sought any—her translation has long since passed into oblivion. The curiosity which drew Coleridge, Southey, and their contemporaries to Bartram's *Travels*, Jacob Bryant's *Mythology*, and Bruce's *Travels to Discover the Source of the Nile* no longer characterizes our reading public. Martin Dobrizhoffer's book, even in the excellent prose style of its English translation, was, alas, not widely read in 1822, and no one cares even to glance at it to-day. In spite, how-

[1] Edith Coleridge, op. cit. i. 34.
[2] E. V. Lucas, op. cit. iii. 22.

ever, of the work's ephemeral quality, the fact that Sara Coleridge not only held herself (and she was not seventeen years of age when she began her labours) to the onerous task of translating a difficult Latin text, but also produced a smooth, graceful, and readable translation, indicates that she possessed the requisites of a true scholar—perseverance, accuracy, and literary expression—and that she was admirably equipped for the leading position which she was later to occupy among her father's editors.

Sara turned almost at once to another task. This time she undertook to translate from the French the sixteenth-century *Memoirs of the Chevalier Bayard, by the Loyal Servant.* While engaged on this work she suffered from severe eye-strain, but Southey, whose own good health rendered him incapable of sympathizing with those less fortunate than himself, humorously traced the affliction to Cupid and thought her eyes 'killing as ever'. Yet Sara persisted, despite the fact that she found the translation of Bayard even more difficult than that of Dobrizhoffer. 'It is all about battles and sieges', she writes,

things which puzzle my little feminine brain. However, I am quite enamoured of my hero, the more so as he reminds me of my first love, Amadis de Gaul, over whose dreadful adventures I used to cry (unreproved then).

'In these Memoirs', she says elsewhere,

the names of places and persons in Italy are so Frenchified and completely disguised, that I am obliged to hunt in Guicciardini and other old authors, for their true spelling.

She was undaunted, nevertheless, and in 1825 Murray published the *Memoirs.* Like its predecessor, *The Account of the Abipones,* the work did not win popularity for the author. Among the members of the Coleridge circle it was well received. Lady Beaumont, who with her husband had been benefactors of Coleridge and Wordsworth a few years earlier, received the volume with great pleasure and wrote a graceful compliment to Sara.

Sara went on to make still another translation from the

French, this time, however, not for publication but because, as she wrote to Derwent, she

> had rather do that than nothing, if it is only for the sake of keeping my hand in. . . . I should have been happier, with my taste, temper, and habits, had I been of your sex instead of the helpless, dependent being I am. The thing that would suit me the best of anything in the world would be the life of a country clergyman. I should delight in the studies necessary to the profession.

She turned to translation not only as a means of keeping out of her consciousness the unhappy circumstances surrounding her engagement but also to earn a small income. Southey was generous enough in providing her with a home, but she found it embarrassing to be so constantly indebted to him. The impossibility of considering her engagement as more than a vague assurance of love and the hopelessness of trying to look forward to any definite date for her marriage, or even the assurance that it would ever take place, made her realize that she might eventually find it necessary to support herself. She fought against her grief and sought to appear cheerful for the sake of those about her, but often her mother found her weeping alone in her room or in the garden outside. In order to keep her mind occupied, to earn a little money, and to be able to feel herself 'a tiny bit of use in this world', she thought seriously of translating a tale by Cervantes, but 'the most amusing of them', she wrote to Derwent, 'are rather too waggish for a damsel's pen to have anything to do with'. The plays of Cervantes were equally obnoxious, and her 'fear of offensive passages such as a female would hardly like to undertake', led her to abandon the idea of translating them.

Throughout youth Sara had drawn deeply from the mind and spirit of Robert Southey. With her mental development she came increasingly to drink at the fountain of Wordsworth's wisdom. In matters of intellect and imagination, she afterwards declared, Wordsworth had enriched and inspired her whole being. In her sorrow as in her joy, she turned to him, gradually finding calm and self-composure. She found great solace in Wordsworth's *White Doe of Rylstone*. She loved his poetry only less than she honoured the poet

himself, and she welcomed every opportunity to be with him.
She was frequently a guest at Rydal Mount, often being
there for weeks at a time. Wordsworth was so devoted to his
daughter Dora that he could not spare her for more than a
few days at Greta Hall, and he was happy in having the girls
together. Sara was keenly alive to the poetical achievements of Wordsworth, and because of her obvious intellectual
superiority to either Dora Wordsworth or Edith Southey,
entered more fully into communion with him. She accompanied him on long walks, listened attentively to his discourse, and gratified him by her appreciative comments.
With almost filial devotion she entered the inner recesses of
his spirit. Wordsworth seems to have been equally devoted
to her. As he once saw her in the company of Edith Southey
and his own daughter, he composed a poem, *The Triad*, in an
effort to describe the three girls. Edith, the poet tells us, is

> . . . worthy of earth's proudest throne!
> Nor less, by excellence of nature, fit
> Beside an unambitious hearth to sit
> Domestic queen, where grandeur is unknown;

His daughter he finds 'Light as the wheeling butterfly'.

> Her happy spirit as a bird is free,
> That rifles blossoms on a tree,
> Turning them inside out with arch audacity.

To Sara, 'Last of the Three, though eldest born', he says:

> Reveal thyself, like pensive Morn
> Touched by the skylark's earliest note,
> Ere humbler gladness be afloat.

Describing her, he continues:

> Her brow hath opened on me—see it there,
> Brightening the umbrage of her hair;
> So gleams the crescent moon, that loves
> To be descried through shady groves.
> Tenderest bloom is on her cheek;
> Wish not for a richer streak;
> Nor dread the depth of meditative eye;
> But let thy love, upon that azure field
> Of thoughtfulness and beauty, yield
> Its homage offered up in purity.

58

What wouldst thou more? In sunny glade,
Or under leaves of thickest shade,
Was such a stillness e'er diffused
Since earth grew calm while angels mused?
Softly she treads, as if her foot were loth
To crush the mountain dew-drops—soon to melt
On the flower's breast.

The Triad certainly shows more of Wordsworth's heart than poetic power, but the poem does catch the individuality of each of the girls.

In 1829, when this poem appeared in *The Keepsake*, all England was aroused over the question of extending the franchise to Roman Catholics. Coleridge, as is shown in his *Constitution of the Church and State*, took a most liberal view of the matter, but Southey and Wordsworth thought otherwise. Sara by this time had come to share her father's political views, and she heartily approved of the Emancipation Act. Southey expressed his views in a manner brooking no contradiction. 'Sara', wrote Mrs. Coleridge,

in general, sits silent when the matter is discussed, but at Rydal-Mount where we were staying for a Month in May, she talked much with W. who is equally strong against the measure, with Southey—but he will listen to another side with more tolerance, and there I heard a little on both sides.[1]

From the time of her visit to Highgate, Sara began to pay greater heed to the thought and philosophy of her father, and set herself not only to read his works but to master their metaphysical and theological implications as well. When the *Aids to Reflections* appeared in 1825, she began reading it at once. 'I must confess', she wrote to John Taylor Coleridge,

that every now and then, in spite of my efforts, I get completely bewildered. Do you not think, that in speaking of Free Will and the other mysteries of Religion, my Father, though he does not attempt to explain what I suppose is inexplicable, puts the subject in a new and comfortable point of view, for sincere Christians?

She says that she cannot help lamenting that her father does not write more popularly, but she quickly 'suppresses the

---

[1] Stephen Potter, op. cit. 148–9.

59

thought as unworthy his daughter'. Southey had often assured her that had her father made proper use of his powers, he 'could have beaten Walter Scott himself', and she naturally regretted Coleridge's miserable, poverty-stricken existence. Southey, Scott, and Wordsworth enjoyed a comfortable sustenance, while her poor father remained dependent and almost penniless. 'I suppose he consults his future fame', she said; and it is gratifying to note that she lived to see the day when edition after edition of his works testified to his posthumous popularity.

Sara was giving a good deal of attention to religious thought, beyond reading the *Aids to Reflection*. In the summer of 1825 she was confirmed, and we find her reading such theologians as Clarke, Hooker, and Cranmer. Her unhappy situation at Greta Hall and the unpromising outlook for the future forced her to seek spiritual consolation. She needed the support of religious contemplation and delved deeply into the writings of the Church.

The visit to Highgate in 1822 had awakened a feeling of mutual pride and deep affection in both Coleridge and Sara, and they longed for more of each other's company. She planned to go to London in 1825, but the domestic arrangements of the Gillmans prevented Coleridge from receiving her. 'It is afflictive enough', he wrote to Derwent, who had neglected writing to his father, 'that we have not one family House, as the natural center for all of you and your Home. . . . I have felt this want very poignantly and not without an after-relish of *mortification*, with regard to your Sister'.[1] In the summer of 1826 Sara started for London, but she was unable to proceed any farther than Kendal. Her beloved cousin Isabel Southey had died only a few days before, and Sara had suffered so much that she was in no physical condition to make the long journey to London. Coleridge grieved over this postponement in her plans and confided to his notebook on July 30, 1826:

The letter was delivered to me which announced that Sara had been taken so ill at Kendal, that it was determined that Mr. Gee [her escort] should set off without her: O it was a bitter

[1] E. L. Griggs, op. cit. ii. 368.

disappointment for her sake even more than for my own. For though I exceedingly regret that the attachment between her and —— ever took place, for four momentous reasons, yet to know her to be unhappy would be worse than regret.

Mrs. Coleridge was determined, however, that her daughter should go, for Sara was undermining her health in brooding over the uncertainty of her engagement. Mrs. Coleridge felt, too, that if Sara did not depart at once, Coleridge's own precarious health might make an indefinite postponement necessary or death itself prevent the journey altogether. Late in 1826, accordingly, Sara set off for London, where she remained for nearly a year, seeing much of her father and spending a great deal of time with Lady Beaumont, whose husband had recently died. More than all this she was reunited with Henry Nelson Coleridge. Together they explored London to their hearts' content. She was ecstatically happy in his company. 'I wish all the dinner parties in the Red Sea that separate me from [him]', she wrote impetuously. She confided to Derwent that she had thought before seeing Henry again that 'it was impossible to love him better than I did in absence but I feel the chain grow tighter and tighter every day'.

From the time of his first meeting with his uncle, Henry Nelson Coleridge had welcomed every opportunity to visit him at Highgate, and had painstakingly and methodically kept a record of the poet's conversation. In January 1827 he presented Sara with a note-book containing fifty-seven different items of what later became Coleridge's *Table Talk*. He was so proud of his uncle's intellectual powers that he delighted in taking his friends to Highgate; more important still, he recognized the value to posterity of any records of Coleridge's conversation. In the front of the note-book given to Sara he wrote:

These are all the Memorabilia, my love, I have. It would be well worth your while to be very attentive to your father's conversation, when you are with him, and endeavour afterwards to preserve some of it, as I have done. Especially as he talks to you on plainer subjects.

With what delight must Sara have discovered that the first

entry in Henry's notes corresponded exactly with his first sight of her at Highgate on December 29, 1822!

To add to Sara's felicity, word apparently came from Ottery of James Coleridge's approbation of her engagement, and though two more years were to elapse before her marriage, the ultimate realization of her hopes seemed assured. 'Sometimes I think', she wrote to Henry of their contemplated union,

it would be greater bliss than I ought to expect in this life; to judge from my present feelings, from the moments of deep delight I have felt in your society and from hearing the sound of your beloved voice, I know and feel sure that if to this were added a sense of security and permanence, if the sad perspective of parting, of possible disasters and various dreaded contingencies were not before me, my condition would be one of real happiness. . . . But however fate may decide, I shall never regret my engagement to you, but still be thankful for the delightful moments I have already enjoyed and which once I despaired of ever enjoying.

So it was that Sara returned to Greta Hall, refreshed after this delightful visit, to wait patiently for her lover to come and claim her hand. The years of weeping and bitter tears, of torturing doubts and fears, of anxiety and uncertainty, were over.

By 1829 Henry Nelson Coleridge had at last established himself in the profession of law, and though his income was woefully small, he and Sara determined upon marriage. But they took the step seriously. There survives a beautiful letter written by Sara, only a few days before her wedding.

My beloved, my head is at this moment full of tender, affecting thoughts of all that is past and of all that is to come. What an interesting, agitating yet consoling interchange of letters are we now about to terminate! I could almost weep to bid farewell to such a correspondence, would that other imperious, though blessed thought, of all we are about to commence, suffer me to dwell long enough upon that. Soon I am about to see you, beloved, never to leave you for any long absence, save that of death; it is a sweet, yet an awful thought. O may our union be still more blest, more unmixed, than our correspondence has been. I am sure it will be so, for all the trying subjects of dissension are now at rest, and hereafter it will be my pride as well as my duty to comply with your wishes, and you, beloved, will, I trust, be happier and more satisfied than you have hitherto had cause to be. You have been most kind in yielding to my desires and suggestions, and I trust I shall never encroach upon your privileges, or abuse your gentle nature, asserting the reign of feminine too pertinaciously. . . . You will not, I know, grudge a few tears to my dearest mother, to dear Keswick, dear Greta Hall, and its dear and interesting inmates; these changes, these farewells, are types of the great change, the long farewell, that awaits us all hereafter, we cannot but be thoughtful upon them. Yet I know and feel that this is to be a change infinitely for the better; and in your blessed and improving society, beloved, I trust I shall learn to look upon the other change as a blessed one too; the sadness of my farewell will be tempered by the prospect of meeting all here frequently upon earth, as I hope all dear friends will be united in heaven. . . . Fear not, my Henry, that such speculations, or rather such a tendency in my nature to speculation and dreaminess, will render me an unfit wife for you. Does not Wordsworth point out to you how the most excursive bird can brood as long and fondly on the nest as any of the feathered race?

Though Hartley Coleridge did not wholly approve of the man his sister intended to marry, no one was more relieved than he by the successful outcome of her engagement. Unlike his mother, who looked 'with an eye of apprehension, if not censure', on any marriage in which absolute financial security was not provided, he saw 'a weary, wasting, perennial evil in engagements indefinitely deferred', and 'an urgent expediency in [Sara] acquiring a home of her own'. For him, fate had decreed bachelorhood. 'My Brother gets a wife— well—' he wrote pathetically,

my Sister is to have a Husband—well—I remain alone, bare and barren and blasted, ill-omen'd and unsightly as Wordsworth's melancholy thorn on the bleak hill-top. So hath it been ordain'd, and it is well.[1]

He promised to be present at the wedding, to walk all night if necessary, but alas, when the day arrived, his fragile, sensitive, introspective, self-condemning nature proved unequal to the trial, and he was not to be found.

[1] G. E. and E. L. Griggs, op. cit. 99.

It was entirely fitting that the Reverend John Wordsworth, the poet's son, who had been Sara's playmate twenty
years earlier, and who as a child had intended to marry her,
should have officiated at the wedding. He was at this time
the clergyman at Crosthwaite Church, where on the morning
of September 3, 1829, the bridal party arrived. The brides-
maids, including Edith Southey and her sister and Dora
Wordsworth, smiled prettily in their pale green dresses, amid
armloads of roses. The weather was glorious. 'Skiddaw
doffed his misty cap and looked out nobly on this lovely
flower of his domain, and the bright sun made the lake
glitter in beauty and throw a radiance round.' The bride in
her rich, brocaded, white silk dress trimmed with tulle and
satin, impressed every one by her 'gentle firmness'. Her
mother and her aunts, Mrs. Southey and Mrs. Lovell, remained at home, fearing perhaps that their tears might dis-
concert her. Her brother Derwent, occupied with his vicarage
in Cornwall, could not attend, and her ageing father, though
he followed with the keenest interest her wedding plans,
dared not hazard the long journey to the north; but Robert
Southey, standing *vice patris* for the last time, gave her away,
and she was among her beloved friends. Henry, 'to whom
this precious Gem of the Lakes is intrusted, shewed deep
feeling, . . . and will prove as worthy of the treasure as he
appears sensible of its value'. After the ceremony the young
couple set off for Patterdale; then, following a brief stay at
Greta Hall, and a final farewell at Rydal Mount, they departed for London, which was henceforth to be Sara's home.

IV

WIFE AND MOTHER

IT was with mingled feelings that Sara prepared to depart
from Greta Hall. She knew she would miss Robert
Southey and his kindly concern for her well-being; she turned
sadly away from the intimate companion of her youth, Edith
Southey, who had been like a twin sister to her; and most of
all, she deplored the necessary separation from her mother,
'the ever near and dear guardian of all my childhood and
youth'. She would gladly have taken her mother with her,
but Henry's modest income required the strictest economy,
and the furnished rooms which they were to occupy in
Gower Street, London, were too small to accommodate a
third person. For Mrs. Coleridge this change meant an
unhappy sacrifice. She felt that she could remain no longer
in the Southey household, especially because Mrs. Southey
had never been completely normal since Isabel's death, and
she determined, apparently without a moment's hesitation,
to depart at once. She decided to settle with Derwent in
Cornwall, although she had scarcely seen him for almost ten
years. To be uprooted in her old age from Greta Hall, where
she had spent the last twenty-nine years, to begin life anew
with a daughter-in-law whom she had never met, and to give
up one who was 'more than a daughter', a beloved treasure
who had rarely been out of her sight, were bitter sequels
to her long years of responsibility and virtual widowhood.
For Sara's sake she rejoiced, but she pathetically tried to
show a degree of stoical resignation, in the face of becoming
a homeless dependant in her advanced years. 'At my age,
perhaps', she confided to her old friend, Thomas Poole,
it ought not to be matter of *very great moment* where the time is
past between the present and the last home—but old age is full
of doubts, fears, and cares, unknown to earlier years.[1]

That Mrs. Coleridge's precarious situation was the utmost
concern to Coleridge is shown by his will, which he made

[1] Stephen Potter, op. cit. 148.

immediately after Sara's marriage. With her departure from Greta Hall, Mrs. Coleridge was left dependent on her children for a home. Derwent was hardly able to care for her, and Hartley, of course, could contribute nothing. Coleridge knew, too, that on his death the Wedgwood annuity, his wife's only source of income, would cease. His will, dated September 17, 1829, was an effort to provide for her welfare after his death. Mrs. Gillman entered most heartily into his plan and sent Mrs. Coleridge a brief summary of the provisions of the will. Nor was Coleridge unmindful of Hartley, for whose use he sent Mrs. Coleridge the £50 legacy left to him by Lady Beaumont.

Sara and her husband were no sooner in their modest London quarters than Coleridge came down from Highgate to welcome them. Eagerly he looked forward to her residence in London. Two years before her marriage he had planned to give her a most sumptuous wedding gift, William Sotheby's polyglot edition of the *Georgics*, which appeared in 1827. In acknowledging the volume which Sotheby had given him, he promised to

deliver [it] to my Daughter on her Wedding Day, as the most splendid way, that I can command, of marking my sense of the Talent and Industry, that have made her Mistress of the Six Languages comprized in the volume.[1]

Wishing to perpetuate Sotheby's work as an heirloom in the family, Coleridge mentioned it in his will:

To my daughter, Sara Coleridge, exemplary in all the relations of life, in which she hath been placed, a blessing to both her Parents—and to her Mother, the rich reward, which the anxious fulfilment of her maternal duties had, humanly speaking, merited, I Bequeath the Presentation Copy of the Georgica-Heptaglotta given me by my highly respected friend, Wm. Sotheby, Esquire, and it is my wish that Sara should never part with this volume but that if she marry and should have a daughter, it may descend to her, . . . as a Memento that her Mother's Accomplishments and her unusual attainments in ancient and modern languages were not so much nor so justly the object of admiration, as their co-existence with piety, simplicity, and a characteristic meekness—

[1] E. L. Griggs, op. cit. ii. 392.

in short—with mind, manners and character so perfectly feminine. And for this purpose I have recorded this my wish, in the
same or equivalent words, on the first Title page of this splendid
Work.[1]

The domestication in Gower Street gave the poet and his
daughter frequent opportunities for the intimate association
which they had both long anticipated, and from 1829 until
his death five years later they were constantly to visit one
another. Henceforth Sara turned to Coleridge for guidance
and inspiration. She was married, too, to Coleridge's
favourite nephew. Henry Nelson Coleridge was a visitor at
Highgate as often as his legal practice would permit. Since
their meeting in 1822, the friendship between him and his
uncle had ripened into intimacy, and the younger man was
welcomed as a son into the group of disciples who gathered
at the poet's feet. The *Table Talk* was the result of this
intimacy and remains the best living record of Coleridge's
conversation during the last eleven and a half years of his
life. How closely the entries in that work approximate to the
actual language of Coleridge, it is difficult to say; they compare favourably with similar accounts by Crabb Robinson
and others privileged to hear the melodious voice of one
whose 'face when he repeats his verses hath its ancient glory,
an Archangel a little damaged'.[2]

There survive a good many letters written by Coleridge to
Henry, both before and after the latter's marriage. Between
uncle and nephew a close and affectionate relationship
existed. On one occasion Coleridge addressed Henry as
'My dear Nephew and by a higher tie Son'; frequently, however, he wrote in a vein of confidential familiarity, treating
Henry more as a friend his own age than as his son-in-law.

[1] The Sotheby volume is now in the possession of the Rev. G. H. B. Coleridge.
In 1852, the very year of her mother's death, Edith Coleridge had the volume
rebound in white vellum. She was apparently moved by Coleridge's inscription,
reading in part:
    'After my decease this splendid Volume presented to me by William
Sotheby, Esqr. . . . is to belong, and I hereby give and appropriate it to,
my beloved and love-worthy Child, *Sara Coleridge*. . . . If she should marry
and should have a Daughter, . . . [she] is to regard it as a Memento provided
by her maternal Grandfather.'
[2] E. V. Lucas, *The Letters of Charles Lamb*, 1935, ii. 190.

On May 8, 1827, Coleridge wrote a bitter and confiding letter to Henry regarding Sir George Beaumont's legacy of £100 to Mrs. Coleridge; and yet could conclude with a playful couplet:

> A bitch and a Mare set Old Troy bells a knelling:
> The Mare was of Wood and the Bitch was call'd Helen!

Another letter ends with love to 'Sara and the bonny Suck Cubus—and to the *original Sara*'. When in 1831 Coleridge's annuity of 100 guineas, as Associate of the Royal Society, was withdrawn and a gift of £200 was proffered through Lord Grey, Coleridge sought Henry's advice, and then remarked half-humorously:

> So that on the supposition that a hundred pound would suffice to prevent me from starving for 12 months, I have a *respite* of a full Year, before [my] deposition to the Work-house.

Coleridge endeavoured, too, to assist Henry in advancing in the legal profession and he frequently used his influence in that direction. He read with great interest his nephew's studies in Greek and offered pertinent criticisms. He was especially pleased when Henry offered to co-operate in the second edition of *Aids to Reflection* and the 1834 edition of the poems, and expressed his confidence in his nephew's discretion and taste by giving him a free hand in editorial procedure.

The most affectionate letters are those asking about Sara. Coleridge made plans to gather Henry, Sara, Mrs. Coleridge, his grandchildren, and himself for a few weeks at the sea. He was always solicitous about his daughter's health. Once when Sara had been ill, Coleridge addressed her:

> My dearest Sara—Night after night has my last and most fervent prayer been that of humble Intercession for you and for my other suffering Friend, Mrs. Gillman!—I thank God who has thus given ear to my Prayers, and trust in his Mercy. Your affectionate Father.

Sara, indeed, was close to his heart. 'I am always thinking and dreaming about Sara', he wrote, as if in his declining years he could never see enough of her.

One blot on the otherwise happy reunion of Coleridge and

his daughter was the lamentable conduct of Hartley in the Lake Country. For several years prior to leaving the north, Mrs. Coleridge had paid out of her slender income the major portion of Hartley's living expenses, and it was not without reason that Coleridge, who had been unable to contribute very much to his son's support, should have made over Lady Beaumont's bequest. Sara's marriage and the departure of his mother and sister from Greta Hall led poor Hartley to dwell introspectively upon his failures. The contrast between his own aimless and fruitless life and the happiness in marriage of Sara and Derwent now became painfully apparent. Self-condemnation overwhelmed him. He abandoned himself to alcohol. For weeks at a time he wandered over the country-side, his whereabouts being unknown to his anxious family. Only the hospitality and kindly care of the dalesmen saved him from starvation. He eluded the Wordsworths and followed an irresistible desire to escape—from himself and his conscience, no less than from any one likely to rebuke him.

Sara in London and Mrs. Coleridge in Helston sought news of him, and the Wordsworths tried desperately to find him. Eventually they were successful in locating him and arranging for his residence with Mrs. Fleming in Grasmere, but only after a long period of anxiety. On March 5, 1830, Dorothy Wordsworth wrote to Mrs. Coleridge that she had somewhat better news to report of Hartley, but she gave a heart-breaking account of his wanderings.

From time to time . . . we heard of him—calling at this house or that—where he was supplied with a meal—and housing at night in Barns etc. . . . We commissioned every one likely to see him with a message requesting him to come to R. Mt, and last Friday evening the message was delivered to him by Mr. Fell; . . . however, he did not arrive. . . . We had during the long time of H.'s wanderings been turning over in our minds all places likely for board and lodging; but till he 'cast up' we could take no steps whatever.[1]

Dorothy went on to describe the arrangements she had effected with Mrs. Fleming and to discuss the bills for which

[1] E. de Selincourt, *The Letters of William and Dorothy Wordsworth. The Later Years*, 1939, i. 451–2.

Mrs. Coleridge had made herself responsible. 'How thankful shall I be', Dorothy continued,

if after the end of the year we find that he has really worked, so as to be able to pay off his debts of honour (of which no doubt he has several at the publick houses) to provide himself with cloaths and to repay you a part at least of what you have made such sacrifices to advance for him. At all events you will have (by being answerable for board and Lodging) the satisfaction of knowing that you at least have done all you can to guard him from perishing of cold and hunger.[1]

One can easily imagine the effect of such distressing news upon the sorely tried mother. She wrote at once to Sara and to the Gillmans, and Mrs. Gillman tactfully brought Hartley's woeful plight to Coleridge's attention. 'I mentioned the subject to your Father as slightly as I well could', she wrote to Sara on March 15, ten days after Dorothy's letter,

because you are aware of his circumstances and it could do no good, but perhaps an injury to his health in the present very precarious state he is in. As it was, three frightful nights were the consequence—although at the moment he seemed to bear up well—A few hours after, I found him on his knees in an agony of Grief—and stole away unperceived——

Wishing to discuss these grievous matters, Mrs. Gillman sent an urgent request for Sara and Henry to stay at Highgate for a week—'I wish so much to see you here to stay a little while'. She offered what comfort she could in speaking of Hartley.

As to the letters it was impossible not to feel heart sick in reading them. With regard to poor Hartley, I never could endure human judgement to be passed on him, having myself always believed, that there was some hidden cause for his conduct, some defect in the powers of his moral Will, which however did not extend to his Intellect—and which leaves him, as it were blameless, an innocent Being, without vice, yet fulfilling none of his duties, giving only pain to those he loves and by whom he knows himself beloved.

During Sara's stay at Highgate Hartley's circumstances were fully talked over with Coleridge, who was now firmly

[1] E. de Selincourt, op. cit. i. 454.

convinced that the provisions for Hartley in his will must be modified. He felt that at no time should Hartley receive a sum of money to be dispensed at his own discretion, and he wished to provide for his son's shelter in the future. On July 2, 1830, he added a codicil to his will, reading as follows:

Most desirous to secure as far as in me lies, for my dear Son, Hartley Coleridge, the tranquillity indispensable to any continued and successful exertion of his literary talents, and which, from the like characters of our minds in this respect, I know to be especially requisite for his happiness, . . . I hereby give and bequeath to Joseph Henry Green, Esquire, to Henry Nelson Coleridge, Esquire, and to James Gillman, Esquire, and the survivor of them, . . . the sum . . . which in the Will aforesaid, I bequeathed to my son, Hartley Coleridge, after the decease of his mother, Sara Coleridge, upon trust, and I hereby request them . . . to hold the sum . . . for the use of my dear Son, Hartley Coleridge, at such time or times, . . . [as] shall . . . [be] conducive to the attainment of my object in adding this Codicil, namely, the anxious wish to ensure for my Son the continued means of a Home, in which I comprise Board, Lodging, and Raiment, providing that nothing in this codicil shall be so interpreted as to interfere with my Son, Hartley Coleridge's freedom of choice respecting his place of residence. . . .

After living a few months in Gower Street, Sara and her husband secured a 'tiny cottage' in Downshire Place, Hampstead. James and Anne Gillman, Coleridge's hosts, were especially anxious to have Sara settle in the neighbourhood of Highgate and they were willing advisers in the matter of selecting a suitable house. James Gillman even accompanied Sara on a shopping expedition to Kensington, where house furnishings could be procured at more reasonable prices. Sara was delighted with her modest home in Hampstead, but there was one serious objection. Although the house was more comfortable and commodious than the quarters in Gower Street and was within walking distance of her father at Highgate, the change meant that Henry had frequently to be away from home for several days, in order to avoid the tedious and fatiguing journeys between Hampstead and Lincoln's Inn. As a result they began a correspondence almost unparalleled in tenderness. They were,

71

indeed, remarkably suited to one another, and their happiness reminds one of the love story of the Brownings. To similar intellectual interests Sara and her husband added rich congeniality and mutual understanding. Their love had survived the long, discouraging period of their engagement, and marriage brought an overflowing cup of happiness. They felt for each other that profound respect that lies at the basis of happiness in marriage. As we might expect, their letters were filled with deep emotion and love, with longing during absence, and with the comforting assurance of enduring affection; but more than all this, there was a sharing of intellectual discoveries, and co-operation and assistance in literary concerns. Henry constantly sought his wife's opinions and advice in matters of philosophical or literary interpretation and he came more and more to value her critical acumen.

Shortly after moving to Hampstead in the summer of 1830 Sara sent for her mother. Their separation, she wrote not long after her marriage, was 'the only material drawback to happiness'. Now at last, she could offer her mother a comfortable haven. Mrs. Coleridge, though she had been happy with Derwent, had longed to be with Sara again, and she gladly made her way to London. For the remaining fifteen years of her life she continued to be a member of her daughter's household, sometimes a trial as she grew older, but more often a comfort and a consolation to Sara. It fell, indeed, to Mrs. Coleridge to devote her life to others, and if she became increasingly querulous—'Jobish', Hartley once called her—her burdens were too heavy for human fortitude to bear uncomplainingly. Convinced that her marriage to Coleridge was a failure, as a result of his irregular habits, she tried by advice, warning, scolding, coaxing, and mournful entreaty to steer the destinies of her children. Yet each of them loved her, sought her advice, and forgave her for any emotional outbursts. Sara was particularly fortunate in having her mother with her to share in the duties of family life. Her mother, too, was 'happy in feeling herself so supremely useful'.

Marriage brought to Sara the enriching experience of

motherhood. A few days before the birth of her eldest child she wrote to Emily Trevenen, a middle-aged spinster, who became devoted to Derwent Coleridge and his family in Cornwall:

I am delighted to afford my mother a more comfortable abode [at Hampstead] than I could have done in London, and to enable the child we hope to be blessed with, to form some of these pleasing intimacies with nature which formed the delight of its parents' childhood.

To Sara's letter Henry added glad tidings of the baby's birth on October 7, 1830:

Mr. Gillman [who had taken charge of Sara during her confinement] says he scarcely ever saw a woman take the matter with such determined fortitude. . . . I have seen her smiling so sweetly on her little son by her side! The boy is dark, and as I think, plain, but quite right and tight in point of limbs and straightness.

Coleridge was in very feeble health at this time and in great anxiety over his daughter's confinement. 'Poor father at Highgate', Mrs. Coleridge wrote to Poole, 'has been very nervous about her, he will be now, relieved; for Mr. Gillman will have carried him the good tidings yesterday'; and she was desirous 'to know how he has taken the long-expected news'.[1]

Sara Coleridge was really an extraordinary mother. Deeply devoted to her baby, who was named Herbert after Southey's beloved son, she was able, nevertheless, to describe him quite objectively to her friends. 'He is not a pretty child', she wrote when he was only two months old;

he has a broad nose and one of those negative complexions which are akin to what drapers call indefinite colours. . . . Still his partial mama fancies that he will not a have a negative, indefinite phiz altogether; she flatters herself that he will have a manly and certainly not mean countenance and sees a something in his bright, dark grey eyes which she fondly imagines cannot but turn into a lively, intelligent expression, though lookers on might laugh at such fancies.

Early in the year 1831 Dora Wordsworth, then on a visit to London, had happy news to report to Rydal Mount. She

[1] Stephen Potter, op. cit. 163.

found Sara more beautiful and younger in appearance than before marriage, and little Herbert, '*as a baby* beautiful as she—fat and plump and sweet looking, with fine dark blue eyes'. Henry she thought more overjoyed, if possible, than the mother, and 'Mrs. Coleridge, too, happy and proud and anxious too—but . . . the happy and proud outweighed the anxious thoughts and feelings'. Her father's old friend, Coleridge, with whom she and Wordsworth had travelled to the Continent three years previously, she thought 'much changed for the worse—he is very feeble and moves about quite with an old man's step', but she was glad to add that 'his mind and countenance are vigorous and youthful, as ever'. Derwent was also in London on a visit from Helston, and Dora spoke of the reunion of Sara and her brother, for the first time since each had married, and wondered if they were as congenial as in childhood, now that they were both parents, with widely divergent interests.

On July 2, 1832, Sara gave birth to a daughter, christened Edith, after Edith Southey. Little Edith did not prove to be as attractive as Herbert. She 'is plump and fair of complexion, but not so comely, methinks, as my sweet Herbert, who is a dear villain of a boy', Henry wrote. Coleridge, who had learned of Sara's two successful confinements with great relief, was too infirm to see his daughter immediately after Edith's birth, but by August 9 they snatched 'a golden opportunity of a most sunny season of my dear Father's health, which we feared was far too bright to be lasting', and he came over to Hampstead to attend Edith's christening. The occasion was a gala one indeed; Coleridge was at his best and talked incessantly and with great vigour for most of the seven hours he was there.

Mrs. Coleridge, however, was unable to enjoy the festivities at Edith's christening because of her uneasiness about Hartley, who had temporarily deserted the Lake Country and had settled in Leeds. His mother, who knew only too well his inability to resist alcohol, especially under any sort of emotional stress, feared that he would fall in with intemperate companions. Her fears, as it happened, were unfounded, and Hartley conducted himself remarkably well. She and Sara assiduously kept such worries from Coleridge. Even when they learned of Dorothy Wordsworth's mental and physical prostration, they did not tell him—'were she to die he would not be told', Mrs. Coleridge wrote; for he was far too sensitive, too fragile, too liable to serious illness, to bear any bad tidings.

The coming of two babies proved to be too much for Sara's strength, and in the autumn of 1832 she suffered a serious nervous collapse. She had contracted puerperal poisoning at the time of Edith's birth, and in her weakened condition she wished pathetically that she could be given a three years' respite from child-bearing. She had such painful recollections of her last confinement that fears crowded in upon her—'the hopeful cheerful spring seems gone'. Her state bordered on hysteria. She suffered from insomnia, and her feelings were alternately animated or depressed. 'In my worst state of gloom', she noted at the time, 'I cannot shed a tear—I seem sealed up—a creature doomed to despair.' But tears, however violent, brought some relief. Being advised by her physician that a change of environment was necessary, in September she persuaded her husband to take her to Brighton, but she fretted continually about the expense involved in her stay at the coast. As a result of her disordered nerves, the sea air did her no good, and she returned to London no better than before. Even the joy of being reunited with her children was powerless to cheer for more than a moment her drooping spirits. In her dejection and insomnia she was forced to take drugs to quiet her nerves and to induce sleep; yet she struggled to avoid slavery to opium, and apparently took it only at night and at irregular intervals.

She bore her sufferings with Christian fortitude. 'Mortals', she once said,

are made perfect through suffering. . . . I shall have little enjoyment of life if this state of body continues; but I must try to bear my cross well—imitating the divine pattern which has been left us. In a few years, . . . it will signify little whether I have had health or sickness, joy or sorrow, in this life, but how I have borne and benefited by my trial will signify a great deal.

Her husband, too, was remarkably patient and tender. Sara said during her illness that ever after she would look upon him 'as a christened angel'. He pleaded with her to use as much will-power as possible in combating her disease. There were so many false improvements in her health that he sometimes found it difficult to be sanguine, even in her better days. Her long illness must have been a sore trial to him. Sara confessed that his life lacked only one thing to make it perfectly happy—a wife healthy and strong enough to take her place as the mother of their children. She brooded over the fact that her sickness meant a heavy drain upon their perilously small income and that a struggling young lawyer needed co-operation in his responsibilities.

By the year 1833 Sara began to improve in health, but before she had entirely recovered, she became pregnant again, and early in the following year gave birth to twins, named Florence and Berkeley, who died a few days after their birth. Henry was deeply moved and penned a poem upon them.

> O frail as sweet! twin buds, too rathe to bear
>   The Winter's unkind air;
> O gifts beyond all price, no sooner given
>   Than straight required by Heaven;
> Matched jewels, vainly for a moment lent
>   To deck my brow or sent
> Untainted from the earth, as Christ's, to soar
>   And add two spirits more
> To that dread band seraphic, that doth lie
>   Beneath the Almighty's eye;—
> Glorious the thought—yet ah! my babes, ah! still
>   A father's heart ye fill;
> Though cold ye lie in earth—though gentle death
>   Hath sucked your balmy breath,
> And the last kiss which your fair cheeks I gave
>   Is buried in yon grave.
> No tears—no tears—I wish them not again;
>   To die for them was gain,
> Ere Doubt, or Fear, or Woe, or act of Sin
>   Had marred God's light within.[1]

While this is not very good poetry,[2] the lines do show something of the tender nature of Henry Nelson Coleridge.

[1] Lord Coleridge, op. cit. 146–7.
[2] The reader may care to turn to Hartley Coleridge's poem on the same subject. See *Complete Works of Hartley Coleridge*, Muses' Library, 1908, 180.

During the first few years of married life Sara was too busy with domestic affairs to devote as much time to reading and study as she had formerly done. Mrs. Coleridge contrasted effectively Sara's life before and after marriage.

Reading, writing, walking, teaching, messing, mountaineering, and I may add, for the latter ten years of that state, weeping were her daily occupations, with occasional visiting—now house orders, suckling, dress and undress, walking, serving, homing visits and receiving, with very little study of Greek, Latin, and English, (no weeping) make up the role of her busy day—and her dear little soul lays down a weary head at night upon her peaceful pillow.

Shortly after Herbert's birth Sara amuses herself with Cunningham's *British Painters*, thus foreshadowing a great interest in art. A year later she takes up Shakespeare and Jonson again, seeing in the latter's *Addresses* models for Wordsworth, though she considers the '*Christian Warrior* . . . finer on the whole than any of them'. During her nervous collapse she attempts to read as an alleviation from her sufferings. In 1833 she examines both the French and Spanish versions of *Gil Blas* for purposes of comparison. Greek, she confesses, is too much for her. She scans the *Quarterly* and approves of the treatment of Harriet Martineau but deplores the ill-usage of Tennyson. Sidney's *Arcadia* she considers 'a good model of pure Saxon English in words and idioms', and Scott's *Napoleon* quite fascinates her, though 'bearing marks of haste like his other works'. A little later she turns to Mitford's biographies of Young and Parnell, as well as Henry Taylor's *Philip Van Artevelde* and Crabbe's *Life* by his son.

Her husband constantly urged her to 'improve her mind'. Shortly before Coleridge's death, Henry wrote to her:

I wish, sweetest Sara, that as your strength returns, you may take up some rather more substantial reading than that which has been your chief mental aliment.

She took heed of his exhortation, undertook an exhaustive study of Dryden, and soon became, in Henry's opinion, an authority upon that poet. She entered boldly into the field of science, examining such works as Nash's *Geological*

Sketches, the *Bridgewater Treatises*, and various botanical works, and wrote discerning comments upon them. She confessed, however, that she read botany, 'in order that I may wander among flowers in fancy, and feel that I have a numerous and lovely set of acquaintances: I want to know their features, every trick of their countenance'. She read much contemporary literature, often mentioning in her letters such writers as Harriet Martineau, Tennyson, Joanna Baillie, Mrs. Howitt, Maria Edgeworth, Moultrie, Thomas Arnold, Elizabeth Barrett, Patmore, and Carlyle.

Herbert and Edith proved to be a great delight to Sara. Like any mother she was thrilled as Herbert began 'to flutter the callow wings of his intellect', and her remarkable descriptive ability made possible many lovely records of him. We need not concern ourselves 'about Herbert's larning', she wrote humorously to her husband,

but I hear a sad account of his morals. All the naughty, indecorous words which his small stock of English speech affords, he, in his roguish moods, delights in repeating a hundred times over and he even flings them in the face of ladies out-of-doors who talk to him when he is not in a civil humour.

As a mere baby he could count to 12 and could spell a few words of one syllable. When shown Southey's *Colloquies of Sir Thomas More*, he exclaimed, 'Don't 'ike Tom More'. He delighted in being naughty. He kept at his daily lessons because he considered them 'rather as an amusement'.

Indeed everything is play with him in his lightheartedness and when he assures us with an air of happy roguery that he has been very naughty indeed and means to be very naughty again, and that nurse has been extremely angery (as he dwells upon the word) it is hard to impress him with a feeling that naughtiness is anything but an exciting variety of the pastimes of the day.

But for all his high spirits he was a precocious child.

Our boy's activity of mind is so Coleridgean! He is not content with playthings or hearing the daily hourly goings on—the facts of life. He must always be imagining some place or mountain or river or asking why Bonaparte or some such hero did this or that 30 years ago.

His sister Edith was equally adorable. When she learned
to say 'papa' for the first time, she 'repeated it a hundred
times, proud of her acquisition in the way of English speech'.
With true motherly instinct, Sara spoke of little Edith's lack
of beauty:

Poor little dear! How gladly would I transfer to her any rem-
nants there are of my former faulty sort of prettiness. . . . I fear
she may be fretted hereafter about her want of beauty—it is for
her sake—not for my own maternal vanity that I feel thus.

Mrs. Gillman somewhat tactlessly remarked to Sara, after
seeing the children at Highgate, that she 'thought Herbert
the most beautiful child she ever saw and . . . Edith . . . a
little dear, but not pretty', and Sara assured Henry that
'Our peskin girly shall have more money left her than Herby
if she turn out so much less pretty. She must be very
accomplished and we must let her learn the piano.'

Remembering the depressing occurrences which had so
often marred her happiness as a child, Sara determined to
bring up her own children in an atmosphere of tenderness
and kindness. Even when she was most wretched, she spoke
'lightly and sportively as long as Herbert was in hearing'.
She recognized the need for seriousness in important matters,
but she avoided 'violence and irritating words and looks and
tones', in handling her children.

This sort of demeanour may not excite any warm feelings of
gratitude at the time, but it gradually sinks into the mind and
consciousness never to be obliterated. . . . and in after years when
a boy so nurtured leaves his home and feels the difference between
that and the world in general, between his loving parents and
almost every other friend, if he has any sensibility at all, it will
start up with a lively conscious gratitude.

She felt, too, that a child should never be reproached for
want of affection:

I would never say, 'Alas—why don't you love me?'—but I
would say, 'My dear child, I trust you will obey me; if not I must
enforce obedience; you will learn why when you are older.' Love
is an emotion and cannot be compelled.

She was careful, however, not to carry the idea of gentle
treatment too far. She saw the folly of trying to appeal to

a child as to an adult. Do not attempt to lecture children, she suggested.

Punish a child for hurting his sister, and he will draw the inference that it is wrong, without a sermon on brotherly affection. . . . I would not tell a child to refrain from what is wrong because it *gives me pain.*[1]

In training her children to adjust themselves to the world in which they must live, she was especially concerned about taste and disposition. Both, she felt, were innate, but 'it is easier to direct the taste than to correct the disposition'. A taste for the beauty of nature or for the mental food supplied by books—this can be formed by habit; but 'generosity, patience, meekness, candour, truth . . . are not to be implanted and they are not so dependent as mere taste on opportunity for the field of their development'. Thus she laid stress on those mental and moral qualities which can be developed and trained; the more elusive traits of character she trusted to the subtle influence of environment and her own personality.

Sara and Mrs. Coleridge differed a good deal in their ideas of discipline. The elder woman, now a grandmother, tended to indulge little Herbert. 'I have a very *decided opinion,*' Sara wrote to her mother, when on a visit to Ottery with her husband and children,

and one that runs counter to all my present comforts and inclinations and therefore can only proceed from the verdict of my deliberate judgement, that whatever pain it may cost at the time it is our duty to bring Herbert, as far as we can, into more independent and manly habits. . . . In all your arguing, dearest Matercula, you overlook the general effect *on the mind*—the habits of endurance, patience, and self-control which are to be formed. When he is a man I hope he will control *himself*—it is a parent's duty to be to a child what he will be to himself when he is older.

Mrs. Coleridge, it seems, would not accede to the plan of having Herbert sleep alone, because he was afraid. 'Had I any such indulgence as that?' wrote Sara, reminding her mother of the past. 'Never . . . I was far more restricted than he and the *restraint was good for me.*' It would appear that the

[1] Edith Coleridge, op. cit. i. 66–7.

frayed nerves of both Sara and Mrs. Coleridge sometimes
gave way. Sara was fearful lest 'any impetuous or peevish
tones or words' should distress the children. If self-control on
the part of the adults were lacking, what good, she asked,
would religious instruction be?

As a young child Herbert began to stammer, an affliction
which rent the hearts of both his parents. Only her religious
feeling made it possible for Sara to bear this cross of sorrow
and to face the problem wisely. Quite in harmony with
modern ideas on the subject, she felt that the habit was due
to excessive sensibility and nervousness.

My great aim in correcting Herbert for hesitation is to do it
quite cheerfully and pleasantly, not frightening him about it, but
quietly teaching him to be more deliberate and to moderate his
impetuosity. . . . When Nurse stops him in stammering he is
very fretful and says, 'Do you think I can help it?' I think we
must take care not to tease him too much about it, or else discomfort and misery will be produced. If we call it 'dreadful' and
'horrid' and put on despairing looks, and talk of the pain it gives
us in mournful tones, I am sure we shall make the matter worse.
. . . Some *little* power the poor child may have over it, but alas!
how can we suppose that an act of the will can prevent hesitating,
in the common course of speech? . . . Besides, we shall not sufficiently distinguish between this and a moral trespass, if we do so,
and shall indeed be indulging our own impatience instead of
studying his good. . . . I always say to him calmly and gently but
with decision, 'Speak slowly, my dear'; instead of, 'Dear me!
Pray don't stammer so!' or any other impetuous or pettish expression.

By the employment of patience and understanding Sara
succeeded in partially overcoming Herbert's stammering,
though the slight impediment was diminished rather than
entirely outgrown.

Nor was the more formal training of the children neglected.
Herbert and Edith seem to have learned to read and to
write almost without effort. Thoroughly grounded in the
English classics as they grew ready for them, both children
began the study of Latin at a very early age. Sara was displeased with the Latin grammars then in vogue—especially
with the *Eton Grammar*—because they were on too high a

level for the child's mind and required too much explanation on the part of the teacher. She preferred an older
grammar. 'I think those old fellows who composed it were
not such blockheads (except as to hic haec hoc). They tell
their story very completely and in a very small space.' She
thought seriously of preparing a grammar herself, but did
not feel physically equal to the task. She did, however,
teach little Herbert according to a system. In helping him
with vocabulary she sought for definite meanings, and was
pleased when Herbert, after gazing intently at a map of
Cornwall, observed unassisted that it was a peninsula. She
wrote out cards with substantives from the *Georgics* on one
side and the English meanings on the other. Thus Latin
became for Herbert a game, and not a hated labour. 'His
declensions written on cards were his playthings.'

She used the same direct method in instructing Herbert in
geography—'Jog-free' as he called it. Here she ingeniously
traced the course of Napoleon's campaigns on the map, or
followed the Chosen People on their journey to the Promised
Land. It was something of a task, however. 'I am obliged',
she wrote her husband, 'to get up my geography and sacred
history even to instruct a chick of this age—four years old on
Tuesday.' She felt thwarted in not having a map of the world.
If she had one, 'When Herby looked for the River Amazon',
she insisted,

he would travel to it from England and would take in a general
view of geography whenever he learnt any particular place. Up
to years of adultship I had confused notions of geography from
having studied particular maps and not been shewn frequently
the grand divisions and relative situations of Seas and Continents.
This is what the merest child may learn to any extent by the
exercise of scarcely any faculty but memory.

When a physician, surprised at Herbert's attainments as
a child of four, warned against undue exercise of his intellect,
Sara explained that she did not insist on any voluntary
effort, and that a child looking at maps for sheer amusement
and running away the instant he felt a tinge of weariness
'could hardly be over head-worked'. Herbert was kept at
geography, Latin, or history by his natural interest. 'Put

works of simple natural history and geography into his head',
she insisted,

instead of sentimental trash. Give him classical Fairy Tales
instead of modern poverty-stricken fiction—shew him the great
outlines of the globe instead of Chinese puzzles and spillikins.
Store his mind with facts rather than prematurely endeavour to
prepossess it with opinions or sophisticate it with sentiment based
on slippery ground.

This is intelligent educational theory and shows that Sara
profited by her own experience in childhood.

Sara adopted the novel experiment of writing verses as a
means of amusing and instructing Herbert. To teach him
English history she wrote a poem, *Kings of England from the
Conquest*, of which the following extracts will give some idea:

William I surnamed *the Conqueror*   .   .   1066
> It happ'd in one thousand and sixty-six
> That William the Norman claimed this land:
> The laws of England he could fix,
> But could not his rebel sons command.

William II surnamed Rufus   .   .   .   1087
> It happ'd in one thousand and eighty-seven
> That William the second a king was made;
> In ten years more for the love of heaven
> Christians began the first Crusade.
> He died by an arrow sharply driven,
> Shot at a deer in the forest-shade.

John *Lackland*   1199
> One thousand one hundred and ninety-nine
> Did John to Richard the First succeed;
> Barons compelled the King to sign
> Magna Charta at Runnymede:
> The charter makes his *reign* to shine,
> But he was stained with a cruel deed.[1]

---

[1] 'He imprisoned and at last murdered his nephew Arthur, who was the son
of his elder brother, and had a superior right to the throne, in the opinion of
many.' Note by Sara Coleridge.

Edward I surnamed Longshanks . . 1272

One thousand two hundred and seventy-two
Edward the First a King was made;
Wales he did by arms subdue,
When he came back from the far Crusade;
He warred in bonny Scotland, too,
Wallace was into his hands betrayed.

. . . . . .

Henry IV *of Bolingbroke* 1399

One thousand three hundred and ninety-nine
Henry the fourth usurp'd the throne;
Against him Scots and Welsh combine,
Rebellions caused him many a groan.
  Dan Chaucer now began to write;
  A statesman and a poet he;
  He oft is called and with good right,
  The Father of English poetry.

. . . . . .

Mary I, or Queen Mary Tudor (vulgarly 'bloody Queen Mary'.) 1553

One thousand five hundred and fifty-three
Began Queen Mary's fiery reign;
The worst of counsellors had she,
And an evil spouse in Philip of Spain.

The meek usurper fair Jane Grey,
By others placed in Mary's way,
Just after Edward's dying day,
Did with her life the forfeit pay,
When came the Queen to sovereign sway.

. . . . . .

James II 1685

One thousand six hundred and eighty-five
James the Second took kingly state;
He chose for his Popish faith to strive
And so was obliged to abdicate,
In the famed Revolution of eighty-eight.

Queen Victoria   1837

> In eighteen hundred and thirty-seven,
> Fair Victoria became our Queen;
> May her reign by the grace of heav'n
> Still be prosp'rous and serene.

In order that Herbert might read as well as hear the verses she composed for his entertainment, Sara carefully printed them in ink upon small cards. Gradually she collected a considerable number of poems upon a great variety of subjects. There were lines upon spelling:

> Said Ronald, beginning to fret,
>   'These words in *ei* and *ie*!
> I ne'er could distinguish them yet,
>   They're terribly puzzling to me'.
>
>   .   .   .   .   .   .
>
> His father said thus in reply—
>   'The English words ending in *ceive*,
> Where *e* must be put before *i*,
>   Your memory ne'er can aggrieve.
>
> 'Those words we from Latin receive;
>   From *capio* all of them come;
> Their number is four, I believe,
>   And that is no very great sum.
>
> 'When this, my dear boy, you *perceive*
>   (A rule that will never *deceive*),
> 'Tis easy enough to *conceive*
>   What profit you thence will *receive*.'[1]

Or there were such lessons in geography as this:

> Tea is brought from China;
> Rice from Carolina,
> India and Italy—
> Countries far beyond the sea.
>
>   .   .   .   .   .
>
> Plantain and Banana
> Grow in hot Guiana;
> There the Chocolate is found—
> Parrots in the woods abound.[2]

[1] *Pretty Lessons in Verse for Good Children*, 1839, 37.
[2] Ibid., 14–16.

And lessons in Latin:

> A Father is *pater*, a mother is *mater*,
> A sister is *soror*, a brother is *frater*;
> A child should obey both his father and mother,
> And brothers and sisters should love one another.[1]

> *Acĭnus* means the stone of grapes,
>   And *asĭnus* means an ass:
> The boy that can't the difference see
>   May well for a donkey pass.[2]

> *Elephas* an elephant
>   *Leo* is a lion,
> That's a very noble beast
>   As you e'er set eye on.[3]

There were fables, moral tales, and instruction in proper names. Thus Sara Coleridge lectured, amused, and instructed her son in verse during a confining illness.

She was so successful in arousing the interest of her own child that her husband felt a collection of the poems should be published. Reluctantly, she gave her permission, and in the summer of 1834 a little volume appeared, quaintly entitled *Pretty Lessons in Verse for Good Children*. The book became an immediate success and before long ran through five editions. With her usual modesty in referring to her literary endeavours, Sara explained to her brother Hartley that these verses had been 'struck off for the occasion', to instruct Herbert and to amuse herself while she was ill. Her husband was less modest about her achievement. He wrote to her that she should be gratified 'by thinking how fruitful of pleasure and profit to your own children and to thousands of others your season of sickness has been'. He even doubted whether in good health she could have rendered Herbert 'more permanent good and present pleasure', and he thought she had done more for her son 'than mothers of unwearied strength and everlasting bustle'. He was vexed at having sold the copyright so cheaply— 'every one', he wrote to her of the volume, 'seems to be buying it and liking it'.

To a lesser degree Sara Coleridge did for her own times

[1] Ibid., 85.　　　[2] Ibid., 100.　　　[3] Ibid., 104.

what A. A. Milne in *Now We Are Six* has done so admirably
for ours. She anticipated the delicate poems of Christina
Rossetti—in fact Sara was a pioneer in children's verse. Ann
and Jane Taylor preceded her, but their poems were too
staid for children. To-day her poems seem a little old-
fashioned, but *Pretty Lessons* has been quite recently reissued.[1]
She does not write with the ease of Robert Louis Stevenson
or Walter de la Mare, yet she does catch something of the
spirit of childhood. The lessons, whether moral or scholastic,
are in Herbert's language. Children do not object to
didactic verse—in fact they like it; and they also enjoy the
stimulation of words and allusions they cannot quite understand. They are pleased, too, with anything which reduces
formal learning to the level of play. It is no wonder then,
that Herbert and hundreds of his youthful contemporaries
were delighted with Sara Coleridge's small volume. In her
Pretty Lessons, as in her educational ideas, Sara showed that
she understood children, and she was the forerunner of a
movement which has emphasized the right of the child to
enjoy the world in his own terms.

Success came fairly early to Henry Nelson Coleridge; but
despite his reputation among professional men, financial
rewards increased slowly. He supplemented his income
by writing for periodicals, and for a time seems to have
seriously considered a literary calling. He might have followed an academic profession, but his refusal to stand for a
Professorship of Humanities at Glasgow, a post which carried
an annual emolument of £1,000 and a house, indicated his
determination to continue his legal pursuits. His family
watched him with sympathetic interest. John Taylor
Coleridge, who saw a good deal of his brother and Sara, felt
that their income was wholly inadequate and urged his
father to assist them. 'I was thinking whether,' he wrote
early in 1833,

my Mother and you might not like to increase your annual
bounty. . . . Now I am quite sure no one of the other four, who
can all swim by themselves, but would rejoice and be thankful
to you if you were to double your annual gift to these two, who

[1] *Pretty Lessons in Verse for Good Children*, 1927.

87

need it much by no fault of their own. Henry *will* succeed, I have the most confident hopes, but it will not be yet awhile according to all present appearances, and help to him now would be most valuable. I am sure you will forgive me for mentioning this.[1]

During the last few years of his life Sara's father became extremely feeble. His mind remained clear and his conversational powers undiminished, but he no longer found it possible to leave Highgate very often or to receive visitors as frequently as he had formerly done. On his 'better days' he occasionally drove over to Hampstead to spend a few hours in the company of his beloved daughter, and she, too, paid many a visit to Highgate with her children. After Henry and Sara moved to Hampstead their chief delight was walking across the fields to the Grove to see Coleridge. Sara later said that one of the many blessings attendant upon her marriage was her communion with her father. After the closing months of 1832, her own ill health, along with Coleridge's decrepit condition, prevented regular meetings between father and daughter, a deprivation which she considered the major misfortune of her early married life; and it was, indeed, ironic that not long after fate had placed her in a home near him, illness should have kept them apart. 'Poor dear father', she wrote to Miss Trevenen, 'he is in a sad, weak, depressed state and has been so for some time. He keeps his bed a great deal. . . . . My father's state grieves my mind and mine has been an additional source of gloom to him, poor Man.' Through her husband and the Gillmans, however, she received almost daily reports of him. Henry looked upon his uncle with unbounded worship and veneration. This intimate association was a deep and abiding comfort to the ageing Coleridge, who looked to Henry as to a favourite son.

Poverty, which had hung like a black cloud over his entire life, clung to Coleridge to the very end. With the death of George IV in 1830, his annual pension from the Royal Society of Literature ceased. Efforts to gain an official pension from the government failed; and though Steinmetz,

[1] Lord Coleridge, op. cit. 311–12.

a younger admirer, gave him a legacy of £300, and though
John Hookham Frere endeavoured to make up the sum
formerly paid by the Royal Society, Coleridge still remained
dependent upon others for his support. In his extremity, and
feeling that the former editions had been much too dear, he
determined to issue a cheaper edition of his poems, a plan
heartily approved by Sara, Henry, and Mrs. Coleridge; but
because he was so weak, he was physically unable to do more
than supervise the task. Thus the burden fell upon Henry's
willing shoulders. Mrs. Coleridge felt the keenest concern
in this edition of her husband's poems. She wrote to Thomas
Poole, her old confidant of the Stowey days, telling him of
the project and begging him to send anything he had in his
possession. 'Henry,' she added, 'is collecting everything he
can to add to the Volumes. . . . It would be a great charity—
we hope that something may be made for him, for, of course
he must "sorely want it".'[1] A little later she thanked Poole
for transcribing the poems in his possession, remarking that
Coleridge had no other copy. Through Mrs. Coleridge's
assistance in gathering various unpublished poems, Henry
was able to include a number of new poems in the edition.
He entered enthusiastically into the work. 'Some new pieces
will appear', he wrote to Miss Trevenen, 'and as I hope, a
short autobiography in which the dates shall be correct, at
least'. No biography was included, however, when the
volumes were issued early in 1834, but Henry's contribution
was not merely editorial. He changed the title of one poem
from *A Trifle*, to *A Character*, and took an active hand in the
arrangement and in the text of the poems themselves.[2]

Although the ailing poet turned over to Henry most of the
responsibility for this edition of his poems, he must have
rejoiced at the opportunity to pour out his own aspirations
and disappointments in regard to his poetry. As he and
Henry worked together, he told his nephew how malevo-
lently and wrong-headedly the reviews had misinterpreted

---

[1] Stephen Potter, op. cit. 168.
[2] Even before the preparation of this edition of the poems Henry had ably
assisted his uncle in re-editing the *Aids to Reflection* in 1831. Coleridge had
sufficient confidence in his nephew's 'taste and judgment' to give him 'a Carte
Blanche for any amendments in the style'. E. L. Griggs, op. cit. ii. 433.

and misunderstood him, and explained in full the critical principles underlying his poetic productions. Henry listened, so well, indeed, that he became imbued with the very spirit and manner of Coleridge's genius.

Perhaps the greatest comfort in Coleridge's old age was his renewed association with his family. Mrs. Coleridge, whose bitterness towards her husband had vanished when she saw him again in 1822, shared with him the gratification of seeing their daughter happily married; and after her domestication with Sara at Hampstead, he saw much of her. Anxious to shield him from all family worries and to brighten his declining years, she talked over old times with him, delighted him by reading extracts from Poole's letters, and took their adorable grandchildren, Edith and Herbert, to Highgate. The spectres of the past had finally been laid at rest. Poor, wayward Hartley, their first-born, continued to be their common concern. He deeply affected them both, when just a year before the death of his father, he wrote a dedicatory sonnet to his first volume of verse; and because the poem expresses so poignantly the profound reverence felt by each of the Coleridge children for their father, it may be included here:

> Father, and Bard revered! to whom I owe,
> Whate'er it be, my little art of numbers,
> Thou, in thy night-watch o'er my cradled slumbers,
> Didst meditate the verse that lives to shew,
> (And long shall live, when we alike are low)
> Thy prayer how ardent, and thy hope how strong,
> That I should learn of Nature's self the song,
> The lore which none but Nature's pupils know.
> The prayer was heard: I 'wander'd like a breeze',
> By mountain brooks and solitary meres,
> And gather'd there the shapes and phantasies
> Which, mixt with passions of my sadder years,
> Compose this book. If good therein there be,
> That good, my sire, I dedicate to thee.[1]

The last years of Coleridge's life were the least embittered. Slowly a small group of admirers were beginning to read and appreciate his poetic and philosophical writings.

[1] *Complete Poetical Works of Hartley Coleridge*, 2.

Carlyle, still struggling himself for recognition, put the matter prophetically when in 1829 he remarked that

Coleridge's works were triumphantly condemned by the whole reviewing world, as clearly unintelligible; and among readers they have still an unseen circulation; like living brooks, hidden for the present under mountains of froth and theatrical snow-paper, and which only at a distant day, when these mountains shall have decomposed themselves into gas and earthly residuum, may roll forth in their true limpid shape, to gladden the general eye with what beauty and everlasting freshness does reside in them.[1]

Carlyle was right, Coleridge had to await 'the coming of a milder day', before his works were to command a sale commensurate with their worth, but in the autumn of his life he took his place as the foremost religious thinker of his day. Such men as Sterling, Maurice, Frere, and Hare were proud to call themselves his disciples. Emerson, James Fenimore Cooper, and other famous Americans made pilgrimages to Highgate. Coleridge had become, despite his brother's prognostication to the contrary, *venerable* to the fullest extent.

As his life drew to a close, Coleridge spent much of his time in the company of Joseph Henry Green, a surgeon with strong philosophical proclivities. Coleridge was determined to leave behind him a complete philosophical system—a treatise on the Logos—in order that he might share with posterity the results of a lifetime of metaphysical inquiry. In *The Friend*, the *Biographia Literaria*, and the *Aids to Reflection* he had given intimations of this system, while in many of his letters he had promised the completion of such a disquisition. As old age came upon him, however, he realized that he could hope to prepare only the materials from which another might actually issue a logical presentation of his ideas. To Green, therefore, Coleridge dictated a vast mass of fragmentary notes. After the poet's death Green continued to work over the materials until his own death, but his labours of twenty-eight years' duration resulted merely in an inconclusive, disorganized work—a metaphysical monstrosity

[1] Thomas Carlyle, *Critical and Miscellaneous Essays*, 1907, ii, 184-5.

some one called it—the *Spiritual Philosophy founded on the teaching of the late S. T. Coleridge*, which appeared posthumously.[1]

In the last days of July 1834 Henry was summoned to Highgate. He found Coleridge lying desperately ill, almost too weak to speak. Coleridge took final farewell of his nephew, and through him sent a last blessing to Sara and to her mother. Sara wished she might see her father once more, despite the fact that she was herself bedridden. She would have made the necessary effort and been carried over to Highgate, but Coleridge, as he sank lower, could scarcely bear any one's presence. As he lay dying, the fantastic story of his life passed in review before him, but in the 'peace that passeth understanding', all things now became 'reconciled and harmonised'. He asked to be alone that he might pass to his Maker purified and at peace. And so on July 25, 1834, the great spirit of Coleridge left his earthly being.

[1] It has been left for a contemporary philosopher to demonstrate clearly the justice of Coleridge's claims to have established a system. *Vide* J. H. Muirhead, *Coleridge as Philosopher*, 1930.

V

COLERIDGE IS DEAD

EVEN though Sara Coleridge knew that her father's death was imminent, it came, nevertheless, as a shock to her, but instead of giving way to unrestrained grief she took comfort in the manner of Coleridge's passing. 'There was everything', she wrote to a friend, 'in the circumstances of his death to soothe our grief', and she found consolation in his Christian spirit. Henry was the first to communicate the sad news to Hartley—'A great spirit has passed, a very great one—and what have not we lost!' A few days later Sara wrote a long letter to her brother. She described in detail the last days of her father, the circumstances of his death, the results of the post-mortem examination, and the funeral, and she agreed with Hartley that she and her brothers should strive to be a credit to Coleridge.

I hope too that we all may not only form but act upon the resolve which you have made to be what our father's spirit, if watching over us, would rejoice to behold us. Too often the inheritance of a great name inspires little more than an unfruitful pride—pride in the celebrity rather than in that which merited it, and it is valued as giving a degree of lustre and significance to those who have none that is unborrowed. Its due effect should be to inspire high aims . . . a desire to make the worthiest use of whatever talents may be intrusted to our charge, even though they be of the humblest description. It is very generally thought that in your case genius has been inherited or if genius be not transmissible, shared by the gift of nature. But *all* the children of genius who have lived at the fountain of that light which it is hoped may eventually help to enlighten the world should seek to prove the beneficial influence of it by their own character and bearing, and that though their powers may be of the common order, they have not thrown away their uncommon advantages.[1]

Not one of Coleridge's children was able to attend the funeral. Hartley, who had been an exile in the Lake Country

---

[1] E. Blunden and E. L. Griggs, *Coleridge: Studies by Several Hands on the Hundredth Anniversary of his Death*, 1934, 230.

for almost twelve years, could not endure the nervous strain of so sorrowful an occasion; Derwent could not leave Helston; and Sara was far too stricken to attempt it. The Rev. S. Mence read the service, to which a few of Coleridge's nephews, disciples, and friends came. Coleridge was buried in a vault in the Highgate churchyard, alongside the remains of Mrs. Gillman's sister. The Gillmans placed a sincere, though flowery, tablet in the Highgate Church. Coleridge was at rest.

Coleridge's will is a pathetic document, and the publication of so personal a record in almost all of the leading journals was intensely painful to Sara:

I shall be thankful when all the private, and public notices of our bereavement are over. There is something jarring to one's feelings in the latter, even when they contain nothing actually false. . . . religious considerations are the only ones which give deep and permanent comfort.

Joseph Henry Green, who was to publish Coleridge's 'great philosophical monster', was named sole executor; the disposal of Coleridge's books and full control over the publication of any new work from marginalia and other sources were in Green's hands. By the terms of his will Coleridge had carefully provided for his wife, but he was unable to leave any money to his children during her lifetime. The assurance policy, taken out when Sara was a baby, was worth £2,560. Mrs. Coleridge was to receive the interest upon this sum as long as she lived; after her death the interest was to be equally divided among Sara, Hartley,[1] and Derwent. There were a good many personal remembrances: the pictures and engravings were to go to Mrs. Gillman; mourning rings with Coleridge's hair to Lamb, Montagu, Poole, Josiah Wade, Lancelot Wade, and Sarah Hutchinson; the *Georgica Heptaglotta* to Sara; and an interleaved and annotated copy of *The Friend* to Derwent's wife. Special tribute was paid to Green and to the Gillmans, and Southey and Wordsworth were mentioned as those to whom Coleridge's children 'have a debt of gratitude and reverential affection'. Taking final leave, Coleridge added:

[1] The codicil to Coleridge's will altered this provision.

But with earnest prayer, and through faith in Jesus the Mediator, I commit him [Hartley] with his dear brother and sister, to the care and providence of the Father in Heaven, and affectionately leave this my last injunction—'My dear children love one another!'

It is a part of the irony of Coleridge's life that the first really significant appreciation of his poetry should have been delayed until his eyes had closed for ever, for Coleridge needed, if mortal ever did, the approbation and understanding of his fellow men. The *Poetical Works* was issued early in 1834, and Henry Nelson Coleridge prepared a long critique of his uncle's poetry, but unfortunately his review did not appear until the August number of the *Quarterly Review*—only a few days after Coleridge died. This review, published anonymously, proclaimed to the world that Coleridge was a truly great poet and entirely undeserving of the abuse frequently heaped upon him in the past.

Since the appearance of the *Lyrical Ballads*, indeed, Coleridge's poetic endeavours had been consistently misinterpreted, and even those critics who praised him did so without any insight into his real purpose. Because of personal animosity, Southey pounced remorselessly upon Coleridge's *Ancient Mariner*, calling it 'a Dutch attempt at German sublimity'. The *Critical Review*, in which his remarks appeared in 1798, was then the leading review, and set the tone for much of the criticism of the *Lyrical Ballads*. Nor had Coleridge fared better when his *Christabel* volume was issued in 1816. Inasmuch as *Christabel* had long been circulated in manuscript and had been unreservedly praised by such poets as Scott and Byron, Coleridge had been led to anticipate a more sympathetic reception, but he was to be sorely disappointed. Impelled, like Southey, by personal spite and sheer maliciousness, Hazlitt ridiculed the volume in both the *Examiner* and the *Edinburgh*. 'The thing now before us', he wrote, 'is utterly destitute of value. It exhibits from beginning to end not a ray of genius'.[1]

[1] *Edinburgh Review*, xxvii. 58–67. Despite the controversy concerning the authorship of both these reviews, a careful examination of the available evidence convinces me that they were the work of Hazlitt.

Coleridge is Dead

The harassed and maligned Coleridge recorded in his *Biographia Literaria* that since 1816 he had had from the reviews, 'with very few exceptions . . . nothing but abuse, and this too in a spirit of bitterness'. In contrast to such mistreatment as this, Henry Nelson Coleridge's article in the *Quarterly* was, as Walter Graham significantly remarks, 'the only adequate and just appreciation written during Coleridge's lifetime. [Henry] made specific comments which are still approved and repeated by students of Coleridge in our day.'[1]

Coleridge must have been gratified by his nephew's plans and undoubtedly offered his assistance as the article was being prepared; indeed, the masterful and wholly modern way in which Henry Nelson Coleridge criticized the poems and the clarity with which he analysed the critical principles underlying them afford strong evidence that he had not only become permeated with the ideas of his uncle but that he had also sought Coleridge's advice upon all controversial points.

The reviewer begins with an enthusiastic description of Coleridge's eloquent conversational powers and then turns to a consideration of the poet's technical skill, as demonstrated in an almost unrivalled handling of both English and classical metres. It is 'his remarkable power', the reviewer noted,

of making his verse musical that gives a peculiar character to Mr. Coleridge's lyric poems. In some of the smaller pieces, as the conclusion of the 'Kubla Khan', for example, not only the lines by themselves are musical, but the whole passage sounds all at once as an outburst or crash of harps in the still air of autumn. The verses seem as if *played* to the ear upon some unseen instrument.[2]

Henry Nelson Coleridge referred briefly to the 'fulness and individuality of thought'; but passed on to consider 'the uniform subjectivity' present in almost all the poems. 'The poet's intention', he said,

is that you should feel and imagine a great deal more than you

---

[1] Walter Graham, 'Contemporary Critics of Coleridge, the Poet', *Publications of the Modern Language Association*, xxxviii. 286–7.

[2] H. N. Coleridge, 'Coleridge's Poetical Works', *Quarterly Review*, ciii. 8 (August, 1834).

see. His aim is to awaken in the reader the same mood of mind, the same cast of imagination and fancy whence issued the associations which animate and enlighten his pictures. . . . No student of Coleridge's philosophy can fully understand it without a perusal of the illumining, and if we may so say, *popularizing* commentary of his poetry. It is the Greek put into the vulgar tongue.[1]

After deploring Coleridge's failure to produce 'a great heroic poem', and after a discerning estimate of the poet's dramatic achievement, Henry turned next to the most significant part of his review—a consideration of *The Ancient Mariner* and *Christabel*. The former, he wrote with genuine insight,

is, and will ever be, one of the most perfect pieces of imaginative poetry, not only in our language, but in the literature of all Europe. . . . It is a poem by itself; between it and other compositions . . . there is a chasm which you cannot overpass; the sensitive reader feels himself insulated, and a sea of wonder and mystery flows round him as round the spell-stricken ship itself. . . . [The poem] displays Mr. Coleridge's peculiar mastery over the wild and preternatural in a brilliant manner; but in his next poem, 'Christabel', the exercise of his power in this line is still more skilful and singular. The thing attempted in 'Christabel' is the most difficult of execution in the whole field of romance—witchery by daylight; and the success is complete. Geraldine, so far as she goes, is perfect. . . . The reader feels the same terror and perplexity that Christabel in vain struggles to express, and the same spell that fascinates her eyes. . . . We are not amongst those who wish to have 'Christabel' finished. It cannot be finished. The poet has spun all he could without snapping. The theme is too fine and subtle to bear much extension. It is better as it is, imperfect as a story, but complete as an exquisite production of the imagination, differing in form and colour from the 'Ancient Mariner', yet differing in effect from it only so as the same powerful faculty is directed to the feudal or the mundane phases of the preternatural.[2]

Such comments as these not only justly appraise the poems but also excite in the reader a desire to read them for himself.

The reviewer continued with a brief comment upon Coleridge's Odes (with a discriminating preference for

---

[1] Loc. cit. 14.   [2] Loc. cit. 28–30.

Dejection) and a general discussion of the many-sided nature
of the poet's mind. He called Coleridge 'the most imaginative
of the English poets since Milton', pointed out that it was the
predominance of the 'shaping spirit of imagination' which
set Coleridge apart from his contemporaries, and praised
him also as the 'poet of thought and verbal harmony'. He
admitted that there was obscurity in many of his uncle's
poems, but insisted that it was due to the originality and
individuality of the poet. He concluded his review by showing clearly why the full appreciation of Coleridge must await
the coming of a better day. It may seem remarkable that
Henry Nelson Coleridge should have perceived so clearly the
wide chasm between the critical standards of his contemporaries and the principles under which Coleridge wrote,
but his close association with his uncle for almost twelve
years had brought a full understanding of the philosophy and
mind of Coleridge, and enabled him to answer effectively the
long succession of oppugners who had barked at Coleridge's
heels for more than thirty years.

What part Sara had in this review we do not know, but
we can be sure that it expressed her own sentiments, and that
she was consulted frequently. Henry had boundless respect
for his wife's critical opinions, and during their married life
he constantly sought her advice on every occasion. 'I think
in all matters where the materials for a perfect judgement
are within your power', he once wrote to her, 'I would abide
by your opinion on a book as soon as by any person's I know:
indeed, I know not three persons whose opinion I would set
against yours under such circumstances'. In the same vein,
he remarked at another time: 'I have never met your fellow
among women—nor do any of the books I have seen con-
vince me that your superior in your own sex breathes in
England'. Sometimes Henry wrote even more affectionately
of his wife's attainments:

You are still, my Sara, a very lovely woman indeed. . . . I want
to have a great deal of discussion with you, my darling, about all
these literary matters. Every day I learn to respect your fine
judgement and unerring taste. I am most blessed in your love
and companionship.

This is high praise from a husband of five years' standing, and indicates most clearly how greatly Henry depended upon the co-operation of his wife. When to such comments we add those in which her womanly charm is equally emphasized, we cannot fail to appreciate Sara's share in every production of her husband.

But in sooth, sweet wife, it does give me the purest and yet most poignant pleasure to watch the gradual extension of your influence and estimation in our family and amongst all who become acquainted with you, . . . meet and just reward of your high accomplishments, your refined and acute mind, and more than all, your unfeigned and most genuine humility and modesty of spirit. I am thrice happy in being your loved husband.

On another occasion, in reply to an analysis of his own intellectual abilities, Henry wrote with an even greater acknowledgement of her powers of mind:

I believe you have described my mind very accurately, except that you praise me much too high in point of degree. In subtlety and continuousness of thinking I daily feel my vast inferiority to you—and scarcely less so in fancy and the combining power. I don't know what I can much boast of, . . . unless you will allow me a good, vivid, pure, and scholarlike style.

Following the decease of Coleridge, Sara and Henry were both filled with a desire to establish for her father a lasting reputation, and as far as possible, to 'popularize his work'. They felt that the publication of his philosophical and theological works, as proposed by Green, should be postponed until writings of a more readable nature had been presented to the public. They immediately set to work collecting biographical materials and transcribing Coleridge's letters and marginalia. Henry also began the preparation of his records of Coleridge's conversation for publication and in 1835 issued a two-volume work, entitled the *Table Talk of Samuel Taylor Coleridge*. It attracted a good deal of attention and soon ran into a second edition.

To the *Table Talk*, as she later confessed, Sara contributed only two or three items, and it was her everlasting regret that she had failed to pay sufficient heed when in her father's company. Nevertheless, she did offer advice to her husband in arranging and selecting his materials. The problem of omission bothered him especially; wishing 'to make the book popular', he sought Sara's judgement in regard to Coleridge's sceptical remarks concerning the authenticity of certain books of the Bible: 'Beloved wife—counsel me—you are deeply interested and will neither err from timidity or foolish recklessness. I shall abide ultimately by what you advise.' A week later he is still begging for further help: 'My dear, I mainly rely upon your fine taste and sober judgement in preparing this little work. *Your characteristic fault* (pardon me) is diffusion—splintering your thought into many bright fragments. I make this remark to you, my dearest Muse, with unfeigned diffidence, well knowing that you will not be offended. You are conscious of my reverential sense of your fine genius and cultivated mind.'

The *Table Talk* was perhaps the only editorial work in which Henry may have misinterpreted Coleridge. The attempt to reproduce Coleridge's opinions from fragmentary notes made of his conversations gave opportunity, it is true, for their modification. It is entirely probable that occasionally Henry recorded as Coleridge's ideas which were his own rather than his uncle's. Hartley Coleridge, whose somewhat Whiggish politics made him especially aware of Tory points of view, once wrote to Henry about certain opinions expressed in the *Table Talk*.

I must have expressed myself ill, for nothing could be more remote from my intention than to accuse you of misrepresentation or suppression in regard to the public opinions of ὁ μακαρίτης All I said was, that his was a many sided mind, that it had chanced that I had seen it under aspects probably less frequently developed in latter years, and though I well know that he never would have approved of the measures called reforms, . . . his conversation when I was last in the habit of hearing him authorized me to think that he did perceive the necessity of deep and vital changes, not in servile compliance with the spirit of the age,— (an odious phrase) but to approximate the practice of the constitution to its Ideal and final cause he certainly did hold, or I grievously mistook him, and though the government did work well according to the money getting commercial principles of the economists who assailed it, it did not work well morally, did not perform its duty to God or to the divine in Man, did not supply those demands of human nature, which are at once rights and duties. He did express strong indignation against the selfishness and short sightedness of the governing classes, a selfishness modified and mollified indeed by much kindness and good-nature, but not controlled or balanced by any clear principles. . . . I cannot, moreover, help thinking, that though at no time of his life a Jacobin or a revolutionist, he was in his youth at the period to which my earliest recollections of him extend, a great deal more of a republican, and certainly, much more of a philanthropist and cosmopolite, than he appears to have been distinctly aware of in his riper years. . . . He was, as far as his nature allowed him to hate any thing, a king-hater, and a prelate-hater. . . . He also . . . did even when I was last with him at Highgate, speak very harshly of the political subserviency of W. — and S. —[1].

In contrast to this somewhat rambling account of Coleridge's political views, it will be illuminating, perhaps, to include Sara's vigorous defence of her husband's editorial work:

One of my Father's Whig friends insinuates that if he had told his own story he would have told it more Whiggishly— . . . It is not true—Henry is a man of honour, though as some may think an illiberal Tory. . . . If Henry had wished to please his own party through thick and thin he would not have printed many of the opinions recorded in Table Talk.

In the midst of their labours upon the *Table Talk* Sara and Henry were rudely interrupted, however, for the death of Coleridge proved to be a battle summons for most of the leading magazines, who welcomed an opportunity to enrich their reviews of the *Poetical Works* of 1834 with biographical and personal details. Through mere chance Henry Nelson Coleridge spoke first in the *Quarterly Review*, but almost immediately the *Athenaeum*, *Blackwood's*, the *New Monthly Magazine*, the *Edinburgh Review*, *Tait's*, and *Fraser's*[2] burst

---

[1] G. E. and E. L. Griggs, op. cit. 188–90.
[2] *Athenaeum*, No. 353, p. 574 (Aug. 2, 1834); No. 355, 613 (Aug. 16, 1834); No. 364, 771 (Oct. 18, 1834); No. 365, 788 (Oct. 25, 1834); No. 377, 56 (Jan. 17, 1835); No. 424, 927 (Dec. 12, 1835); No. 425, 941 (Dec. 19, 1835). *Blackwood's Edinburgh Magazine*, xxxvi. 542 (Oct. 1834). *New Monthly Magazine*, Part III, 55 (1834). *Edinburgh Review*, cxxiii. 129 (Apr. 1835). *Tait's Edinburgh Magazine*, I, 509 (Sept. 1834); I, 588 (Oct. 1834); I, 685 (Nov. 1834); II, 3

forth with eulogy, condemnation, charges of plagiarism, defences of Coleridge against those charges—indeed, every sort of 'personal and private notice'. Under the guise of obituaries, the magazines laid bare what they could of Coleridge's life. He was pictured as an irresponsible drug addict, one whose wife and children were dependent upon the bounty of friends. No one ventured to question his greatness or his enduring reputation; friends and enemies alike placed him among the leaders of English thought in his generation. Unfortunately, however, Coleridge was vulnerable to attack from two sources—he had been careless in acknowledging his indebtedness to certain German writers, thus giving opportunity for charges of plagiarism; and his personal life had been sufficiently unconventional to give scandalmongers food for gossip. Thus, on the one hand, the reviews had much to say of Coleridge's moral weaknesses, real or imagined—his supposed idleness, his indulgence in opium, his unfulfilled literary promises; on the other hand, they set out to test the validity, consistency, and originality of his intellectual contribution.

De Quincey led the onslaught with four articles in *Tait's Magazine*, beginning in September 1834 and concluding in January 1835. His essays were cruelly malicious. In his younger days he had been an avowed disciple of Coleridge, as well as a warm personal friend of Mrs. Coleridge and little Sara's first sweetheart. As the intimate friend of the Wordsworths he had come to know many private details of Coleridge's life. More than this, De Quincey possessed rare intellectual powers. Any analysis he made of Coleridge's character and thought would necessarily be profound and penetrating. He was better equipped than any other living person, with the possible exception of Wordsworth, to set Coleridge before the world in brilliant colours. Unfortunately, however, there was in De Quincey's nature a malevolent streak. In his more prosperous days he had as a young man been Coleridge's benefactor; now, struggling to support himself and his family by his pen, he had con-

(Jan. 1835). *Fraser's Magazine*, x. 379 (Oct. 1834); xi. 50 (Jan. 1835); xii. 123 (Aug. 1835); xii. 493 (Nov. 1835); xii. 619 (Dec. 1835).

tinually to serve salable material to the public. Why he should have turned so venomously upon Coleridge one cannot guess. But let us examine briefly the four essays contributed to *Tait's*.

De Quincey gave a running account of Coleridge's life, mixing fact and falsehood. He treated rather fully the domestic infelicity of the poet. Although he did not know Coleridge until 1807, he examined Coleridge's early married life as if he were intimately acquainted with it. He spoke ungenerously of the mind and character of Mrs. Coleridge, whose 'face showed, to my eye, some prettiness of rather a commonplace order',[1] and contrasted her with Dorothy Wordsworth, whom he thought intellectually her superior. He went on to accuse Mrs. Coleridge of jealousy, letting his imagination run away in his description:

She felt herself no longer the entire mistress of her own house; she held a divided empire; and it barbed the arrow to her womanly feelings, that Coleridge treated any sallies of resentment which might sometimes escape her, as narrow-mindedness; whilst, on the other hand, her own female servant, and others in the same rank of life, began to drop expressions, which alternately implied pity for her as an injured woman, or sneered at her as a very tame one.[2]

There is just enough truth in this statement to make it painfully mortifying to Mrs. Coleridge, then in old age. Such ruthless disregard for the feelings of the living members of the Coleridge family was a violation of propriety no less than of common decency, and this too from one who claimed to be a friend. Equally false was De Quincey's statement that Coleridge 'first began the use of opium, not as a relief from any bodily pains or nervous irritation—for his constitution was strong and excellent—but as a source of luxurious sensations'; and equally misleading was his statement that Coleridge had gone to Malta merely from 'a desire to see the most interesting regions of the Mediterranean, under the shelter and advantageous introduction of an official station'.[3] In commenting upon Coleridge's intellectual contributions,

---

[1] *Tait's Edinburgh Magazine*, Sept. 1834, 515–16.
[2] Ibid. 517.   [3] Ibid., Oct. 1834, 593.

De Quincey was much fairer. He declared that Coleridge was both a poet and 'a philosopher in a comprehensive and a most human sense',[1] and he paid rare tribute to him as a political thinker:

> No more appreciable monument could be raised to the memory of Coleridge, than a republication of his essays in the *Morning Post*, but still more of those afterwards published in the *Courier*.[2]

The most insidious parts of De Quincey's essays, however, were those in which he laid bare certain instances of plagiarism in the work of Coleridge. Pretending to be friendly in the matter, De Quincey pointed out what he considered to be four examples of borrowing. Coleridge's poem, *Hymn before Sun-rise in the Vale of Chamouni*, he shows to have been in large measure a translation of Frederica Brun's German poem upon the same subject; *France: an Ode* is shown to be indebted in one passage to Milton's *Samson Agonistes*. De Quincey indicates that in *The Ancient Mariner* there are certain borrowings from Shelvocke's *Voyages*, and says Coleridge denied any indebtedness though Wordsworth admitted it. Finally De Quincey came to a 'case of real and palpable plagiarism'. Let us turn to his own words:

> In the 'Biographia Literaria' occurs a dissertation upon reciprocal relations of the *Esse* and *Cogitare*; and an attempt is made, by inverting the postulates from which the argument starts, to show how each might arise as a product, by an intelligible genesis, from the other. . . . Coleridge's essay, in particular, is prefaced by a few words, in which, aware of his coincidence with Schelling, he declares his willingness to acknowledge himself indebted to so great a man, in any case where the truth would allow him to do so; but in this particular case, insisting on the impossibility that he could have borrowed arguments which he had first seen some years after he had thought out the whole hypothesis *proprio marte*. After this, what was my astonishment, to find that the entire essay from the first word to the last, is a *verbatim* translation from Schelling. . . .[3]

[1] *Tait's Edinburgh Magazine*, Jan. 1835, 6.
[2] Ibid., Oct. 1834, 594. This may be the hint from which Sara Coleridge later developed her collection of Coleridge's political writings, entitled *Essays on His Own Times*.
[3] Loc. cit., Sept. 1834, 511.

Although De Quincey made the accusation of deliberate plagiarism, he had to admit that Coleridge was superior to Schelling, whom he had pillaged.

Had then Coleridge any need to borrow from Schelling? Did he borrow *in forma pauperis*? Not at all: there lay the wonder. He spun daily, and at all hours, for mere amusement of his own activities, and from the loom of his own magical brain, theories more gorgeous by far, and supported by a pomp and luxury of images, such as neither Schelling—no, nor any German that ever breathed, not John Paul—could have emulated in his dreams.[1]

To Sara and her husband these accusations came as a bolt of lightning. 'Yes,' she wrote after reading the first of these essays, 'I am grieved about De Quincey's paper. . . . [His] article makes me despise him for his weakness in betraying his own passions and his meanness in getting his bread by scandal.' She bitterly resented the depreciatory remarks upon her mother:

The impression which the account of my mother would have is that she is a mean-minded unamiable woman with some respectable qualities and that my father married from opportunity rather than much attraction of her's. My mother's respectability it did not rest with him to establish; her attractions he greatly under-rates and the better points of her temper and understanding are not apparent in his partial sketch.

With remarkable fairness she sought to analyse her mother's character and to understand the domestic infelicity of her parents. 'The sort of wife to have lived harmoniously with my father', she wrote to her husband,

need not have possessed high intellect or a perfect temper—but greater enthusiasm of temperament than my mother possessed. She never admires anything she doesn't understand. Some women, like Mrs. Wilson and Mrs. Wordsworth, see the skirts of a golden cloud—they have unmeasured faith in a sun of glory and [a] sublime region stretching out far beyond their ken, and proud and happy to think that it belongs to them are ready to give all they have to give in return. This faith, this docility, is quite alien to the Fricker temperament. . . . They are too literal and do not believe as I do that matters of imagination . . . can

[1] *Tait's Edinburgh Magazine*, Sept. 1834, 511.

work as many practical effects as what we see with our eyes and touch with our hands, and then my mother's very honesty stood in her way—unless at the same time she had possessed that meekness and forbearance which softens everything and can be conciliating by utter silence on all unpeaceful topics and the constant recurrence to soothing cheering themes. Neither had my mother that dexterity in managing the temper of others which is often a substitute for an even temper in the possessor. She has no power over her mind to keep the thought of petty cares and passing interests (the importance of which is often mere matter of fancy) in abeyance. She never compares on a wide scale the real importance of the thing with the degree of energy and time and vital spirit that she spends upon it; and though her talents are above mediocrity and her understanding clear and good—on its own range—she has no taste whatever for abstractions and formerly had less toleration for what she did not relish than now. But to say broadly or to imply unreservedly that she is harsh-tempered or narrow-minded (that is, of an ungenerous spirit) or more unintellectual than many women who have pleased my father is to misrepresent the subject. My father had a good opinion of her understanding and a very high one of her personal attractions.

As Sara read the successive parts of De Quincey's articles, she could not help admiring the literary excellence of his account, in spite of its intent to injure. She thought her father's genius and mode of discourse 'characterized . . . with eloquence and discrimination; and justice . . . done generally to the kindness of his nature'; but she went on to denounce De Quincey:

Upon other points the account is a libel though garnished with affectations of candour. No man can describe the domestic affairs of another without the risk of misrepresenting them—no man ought to expose the recesses of another's home to the public even if he could draw ever so fair a picture of it; that of De Quincey's, however, is an untruthful one, and even where the design is not wrong, which it is in many instances, there is a false colouring. If any feeling of delicacy and dignity remained unwithered in De Quincey's heart, he would have been the last man to institute an inquiry into the privacy of another knowing how little credit the investigation of his own would do him; but I believe, poor man! he is now utterly reckless, sensitive only where vanity is concerned, and ready to stoop to the readiest mode of supplying

his pressing necessities. It is truly grievous to see a man of such original refinement and of so high an order of intellect, stimulating and gratifying the depraved appetites of the Reading Public which his talents and the influence of his character as a gentleman would have enabled him in some measure to correct. . . .

With rare restraint Sara wrote to another correspondent that she would not consider a counter-attack upon De Quincey:

A friend of mine says, 'The little finger of retaliation would bruise his head'; but I would not have one whom I believe to have been so good a Christian as my Father defended by so unchristian a weapon as retaliation, nor would I have any one connected with me engaged in a warfare of personalities which I condemn so much when carried on by others. My Father has been much misunderstood and in many cases grossly calumniated. He was singularly regardless of his literary reputation as well as of his worldly interests, but I feel no doubt that his name will be held in honour hereafter, though as I firmly believe and hope he is now enrolled among the blessed and placed far above the desire of any earthly tribute.

She had less to say of the other writers upon her father. She was infuriated by a statement in *Blackwood's Magazine* (John Wilson, she believed, was the author) to the effect that Wordsworth was Coleridge's master:

He is a fool to speak of my father's *master*. . . . Wordsworth the master of Coleridge indeed! This is gross flattery of the living Bard. . . . He may say the one is a greater poet than the other if he will, but this, methinks, is an incorrect way of expressing the opinion: both as to reputation and enlightenment of mind I believe my Father conferred at least as much as he received in that quarter, for it was the nature of his genius to overflow on all around. Mr. Wordsworth is indeed 'on his own ground an uncomparable talker' but he did not give out all the riches of his mind with the same uncalculating profusion (without taking thought for a future work) as my Father was wont to do. Besides which their styles are not alike. One great man will gain something from another, but no man furnished my Father so largely as with justice to be called his master.

With the exception of Wilson's remark about Wordsworth being her father's master, she was not displeased with the article in *Blackwood's*; she rightly noted it echoed in many ways the tone, method, and conclusions of her husband's review in the *Quarterly*.

The article in *Fraser's Magazine*[1] Sara thought contemptible, and she accused the author, J. A. Heraud, of 'coarse presumption and arrogant vanity'. The whole article she considered to be 'eulogy mixed up with rough and as I think very stupid bantering'. Delicacy was certainly lacking in a man who could write:

One document has already surprised the general reader, having gone the round of the papers: it is the poet's will. What had he to leave? a man living, according to all accounts, on benevolence. Verily, his friends did well by him, and nursed his incomings and controlled his outgoings to good uses. By means of an assurance in the Equitable (effected by himself in early life), the widow and children of Coleridge will come in for the interest of 2665£. The means by which this was rendered possible were highly honourable, both to his friends and himself.[2]

The snapping and snarling of the reviews deeply wounded Sara and her husband. Apparently Coleridge was to be victimized in death as he had been in life. The malevolent and contumelious attacks upon him demanded a complete vindication of his character and a full examination of his intellectual independence. Temporarily they must hold in abeyance their plan to publish his works, and step forward to defend him against a swarm of ravenous enemies. They must be prepared to answer argument for argument, to refute upon intellectual grounds any charges of dishonest borrowing, as well as to tell the truth about his personal affairs. Nor was it an easy task. Henry Nelson Coleridge was a struggling young lawyer and he could not give his whole attention to it. Sara, though greatly troubled by the slanderous accounts of her father, was physically incapable of doing so. Hartley promised assistance in the form of an essay in the *Quarterly Review*, but he never succeeded in writing it. Sara and Henry immediately began to examine Coleridge's German sources, but they realized that the question of Coleridge's plagiarisms from Schelling was too involved a

[1] *Fraser's Magazine*, xi, No. 61 (Jan. 1835).   [2] Loc. cit. 50.

task to be exhaustively undertaken at this time and that any adequate answer on their part would require years of study. In their anguish, however, they determined to reply as fully as they could to De Quincey and to include their defence in the *Table Talk*, which was now ready for publication. Here Henry Nelson Coleridge answered De Quincey as convincingly as he could. The actual parallels between Coleridge and Milton, Shelvocke, and Frederica Brun he did not deny, but he disagreed with De Quincey as to Coleridge's intention. Of the words borrowed from Milton and used in *France: an Ode*, Henry insisted, Coleridge merely 'meant to deny any distinct consciousness of their Miltonic origin'.[1] In like manner Henry said he preferred to believe Coleridge's statement that he had no recollection of any indebtedness to Shelvocke in writing *The Ancient Mariner*.[2] 'What Mr. De Quincey says about the Hymn in the Vale of Chamouni is just', Henry conceded, but he went on to add:

This glorious composition, of upwards of ninety lines, is truly indebted for many images and some striking expressions to Frederica Brun's little poem. The obligation is so clear that a reference to the original ought certainly to have been given, as Coleridge gave in other instances. Yet, as to any ungenerous wish on the part of Mr. Coleridge to conceal the obligation, I for one totally disbelieve it.[3]

Henry felt that silence regarding De Quincey's main charge—Coleridge's plagiarism from Schelling—would imply acquiescence; since he was unprepared to answer the attack himself, he turned to Julius Hare's almost unassailable defence, which had been published in the *British Magazine* in January 1835, and with Hare's permission included a portion of it in the Preface to *Table Talk*. Hare begins:

The dissertation in the *Biographia Literaria* 'on the reciprocal relations of the *esse* and the *cogitare*' is asserted to be a translation

[1] *Table Talk of Samuel Taylor Coleridge*, i, p. xlix.
[2] Alexander Dyce on noting 'the announcement of a *new* edition' of the *Table Talk* wrote to Henry Nelson Coleridge: 'When my truly honoured friend, Mr. Wordsworth, was last in London, soon after the appearance of De Quincey's papers in *Tait's Magazine*, he . . . made the following statement— . . . "The idea of shooting an albatross was mine; for I had been reading Shelvocke's Voyages, which probably Coleridge never saw." '   [3] *Table Talk*, i. 1.

from an essay in the volume of Schelling's *Philosophische Schriften*.
. . . the Opium-eater is indeed mistaken in the name of the book;
but that is of little moment. . . . The dissertation, as it stands in
the *Biographia Literaria*, vol. i. pp. 254–61, is a literal translation
from the introduction to Schelling's system of *Transcendental
Idealism*; and . . . Coleridge's additions are few and slight.[1]

De Quincey had falsely declared that Coleridge had prefaced this 'literal translation' with a statement that it was
entirely his own and that he had thought out the whole
hypothesis years before he had read Schelling's own argument. Hare shows conclusively that Coleridge had not said
a single word about the originality of this essay one way or
another and that it was not prefaced by any remark. Hare
points out that in the earlier part of the *Biographia Literaria*
Coleridge had made a general acknowledgement of his
indebtedness to Schelling. 'This, no doubt,' Hare says, 'is
the passage which the Opium-eater had in his head; but
strangely indeed had he metamorphosed it.'[2] Had Coleridge
wished to purloin from Schelling, Hare insists, 'he never
would have stolen half a dozen pages from the head and front
of that very work of Schelling's which was the likeliest to fall
into his reader's hands; and the first sentence of which one
could not read without detecting the plagiarism',[3] nor would
he have bestowed such high praise on Schelling as to excite
his readers to know more of him. Hare then continues:

But, even with the fullest conviction that Coleridge cannot have
been guilty of intentional plagiarism, the reader will, probably,
deem it strange that he should have transferred half a dozen
pages of Schelling into his volume without any reference to their
source. And strange it undoubtedly is! The only way I see of
accounting for it is from his practice of keeping note-books or
journals of his thoughts, . . . with a sprinkling . . . of extracts and
abstracts from the books he was reading. If the name of the
author from whom he took an extract was left out, he might
easily, years after, forget whose property it was; especially when
he had made it in some measure his own, by transfusing it into
his own English.[4]

---

[1] *Table Talk*, i, pp. lv–lvi.
[2] Ibid. lviii.   [3] Ibid. lx–lxi.   [4] Ibid. lxii–lxiii.

Hare concludes by saying, 'I readily acquit him of all suspicion of ungenerous concealment or intentional plagiarism.'[1]

Hare's conclusions are substantially those which later were to form the basis of Sara Coleridge's own defence of her father in her edition of the *Biographia Literaria* in 1847.

The laceration of the feelings of the Coleridge family was not, however, yet over. During his life the poet had rather guilelessly made intimate friends of men neither intellectually nor culturally his equal, and upon his death several of them, desirous of reaping some share of the reputation which was rightly his, determined to publish biographical and personal accounts as well as letters. The first to appear before the public was Thomas Allsop, one of Coleridge's younger disciples, who in 1836 issued a volume entitled *Letters, Conversations and Recollections of S. T. Coleridge*. A more impudent, imprudent publication cannot be imagined. During his early residence at Highgate Coleridge seems to have been misled by obvious flattery into overestimating Allsop's feeble intellect. Unwisely he laid bare to Allsop the secrets of his life—a tendency Coleridge always manifested—and when it is recalled that the period of intimacy with Allsop coincided with the tragic outcome of Hartley's Oxford career and with Derwent's 'caterpillarage', one cannot blame the Coleridge children for resenting Allsop's publication. Few names were mentioned, to be sure, but the references to Coleridge's children were unmistakable. The trite moralizing in the work, the naïve pretensions to learning, and the stupid commentaries by Allsop himself certainly placed the work beneath contempt. Sara agreed with Hartley, when he said:

I owe Master Allsop a licking. To be sure, he has the excuse of idiocy, which De Q. could not plead. How could [my father] unbosom himself to such a man? Alas, the wisest of us are not invulnerable to flattery.[2]

In 1837 a still more offensive publication appeared. Joseph Cottle, who had first published the *Lyrical Ballads*, came forth with *Early Recollections: Chiefly relating to the late*

---

[1] Ibid. lxv.   [2] G. E. and E. L. Griggs, op. cit. 203.

Samuel Taylor Coleridge. Cottle felt it incumbent upon himself to tell the story of Coleridge's opium habit and to make known the fact that De Quincey had once bestowed a gift of £300 upon Coleridge. This work rivalled Allsop's in stupidity. Small wonder that Sara thought her father had been sadly 'misbiographized'! 'Cottle's vanity . . . amounts to a great folly and leads him to do things which he ought to despise.'

In 1838 James Gillman, upon whom old age and its attendant debility of reason had crept unawares, published his *Life of Samuel Taylor Coleridge.* Gillman's book, unlike those of Allsop and Cottle, reflected upon the unfortunate biographer alone—Coleridge came off very well. Sara was not displeased with the book:

> Though our friend is not adept in the art of bookmaking, yet we feel much gratified by the warm affection for the subject of his memoir which pervades the whole of it and are pleased that such a record of a good man's love, respect, and admiration for my dear father, after such long and intimate knowledge, should become public.

She was fully aware, however, of Gillman's incapacity as a biographer:

> A friend of Henry's writes to him thus: 'How could you trust S. T. C.'s Life to Mr. Gillman! all men say he is an ass.' Alas! we were sorry enough to trust him, poor man! . . . A surer way to blur the bright face of his newly bought fame and credit through my father's name he could hardly have hit upon than to bring out this absurd hodge podge of stale and vapid ingredients, just to shew how long an unwise man may live with a wise one without catching any of his wisdom. But Mr. G. was not always so unwise. Poor man! he is now in a state of anticipated senility and feebleness of mind.

Immediately following the appearance of the *Table Talk* in 1835, Sara and Henry resumed their earlier plan to present Coleridge to the public in agreeable form. Into Henry's plans to rescue Coleridge's works from oblivion Sara entered whole-heartedly, and she was as unwearying a worker as her husband. Even in times of sickness when she was confined to her bed, she was busy transcribing and editing, and the fact that so many of Coleridge's works were published and reissued during the nine years until Henry's death was in great measure due to Sara's active co-operation. While this editorial work was not characterized by the meticulous attention to detail now pursued by modern scholars, it was undertaken conscientiously. If for the sake of clarity Henry Nelson Coleridge sometimes gathered together in a single passage fragments widely separated in Coleridge's note-books and marginalia, and if he occasionally added finishing touches to a sentence or a paragraph, one should remember, before condemning him, that he was endeavouring to set Coleridge before the world in the best light. As a member of the family, too, he felt an unquestioned right to make minor changes, corrections, and interpolations in editing Coleridge's manuscripts.[1] Had Henry deliberately falsified opinions then we should have just cause to censure him. As a matter of fact, the sum total of his textual tamperings amounts to very little. Sara concurred with Henry's editorial procedure, and she recognized that the fragmentary state in which Coleridge left his unpublished works rendered neces-sary an intelligent handling of them.

The various editions of Coleridge's works which appeared during Henry's lifetime were issued under his name, but Sara was a willing collaborator; she became so well versed in editorial procedure that within a few weeks of her husband's death she was carrying on alone with the editing of Coleridge. In 1839 Henry Nelson Coleridge issued the fourth edition of the *Aids to Reflection*, with the author's last corrections; and in the fifth edition of 1843, augmented to two volumes, he added materials likely to help the reader. In 1836 he issued the first two volumes of the *Literary Remains of Samuel Taylor Coleridge*, the third and fourth volumes following in 1838 and 1839. This work, drawn as it was from Coleridge's note-books, from marginalia, and from other elusive sources, rescued for posterity a vast amount of really valuable material. In 1837 he published the third edition of *The*

---

[1] Coleridge's confidence in Henry Nelson Coleridge's 'taste and judgment' led him to grant 'a Carte Blanche for any amendments in the style'. E. L. Griggs, op. cit. ii. 433.

Friend. To Coleridge's essays were added a 'synoptical table of contents', and an appendix containing passages from the 1809 *Friend* which were not included in the second edition. In 1839 he reissued the *Constitution of the Church and State* and the two *Lay Sermons* in one volume with a valuable introduction. In 1840 he issued the *Confessions of an Inquiring Spirit*. With ill health coming fast upon him, he dedicated the last years of his life to a new edition of the *Biographia Literaria*, which had not been reissued since its first appearance in 1817. He proposed to write an introductory memoir for that work, and to accompany the text with whatever critical apparatus should prove necessary. Henry assembled a vast store of letters, notes, and miscellaneous Coleridgeana, but he did not live to add an edition of the *Biographia Literaria* to his long list of editorial works.

Surely these conscientious and laborious efforts, which Sara and Henry entered into with such deep filial piety, were the best means of permanently establishing Coleridge's reputation.

VI

DOMESTIC LIFE

IN the autumn of 1836 Sara journeyed with her husband
and children into Devonshire, to visit the Coleridge
relatives at Ottery St. Mary. During this visit, however, she
was far from well. The journey homeward proved to be too
much for her, and at Ilchester she completely collapsed.
She had to remain at an inn there for several weeks, her
husband returning to London without her. This derange-
ment of her nervous system was her most serious illness since
her marriage. She showed a tendency to dejection, suffered
from insomnia, and often wrote hysterical letters to Henry.
When he suggested that she should exert the effort necessary
to make the journey to Hampstead, she replied almost
bitterly, 'If I reach Hampstead paralyzed or dead what will
it signify that husband, mother, and children are there—
what good will my return do then?' The very thought of
travel led to sleepless nights and fear-haunted days, and
she was forced to take drugs to alleviate her terrors. She
recognized her own symptoms with remarkable lucidity,
but she was powerless to overcome her obsession. 'O this
Devonshire visit', she wrote in an imaginative strain,

has been a black vulture which . . . came . . . to cast his grim
shadow over me, and give me a sight of his beak and claws. Now
he holds me down upon the ground in his horrid gripe; . . . if I
ever get alive out of his clutches I will drive the monster away
and when he comes near me again he shall be received on the
prongs of a pitch-fork.

After several weeks Henry, realizing the uselessness of allowing Sara to remain at Ilchester a prey to morbid fears of
travelling and grief-stricken at being separated from her
family, took matters into his own hands, went to Ilchester,
and insisted that she should return home with him in a bed-
carriage. She made the journey successfully, but it was several
months before she fully recovered her strength and spirits.

During her illness Sara remained intellectually clear and

keen and she wrote with critical discernment upon what she
was reading. While her malady rendered her incapable of
assuming household responsibilities and enjoying any social
intercourse whatsoever, and while it made her a prey to
morbid but self-invented fears, her mind remained unaffected. Her nervous system, not her rational being, was
temporarily deranged. As a matter of fact, her illness seems
to have stimulated her imagination, and during the months
of convalescence she composed her beautiful fairy tale,
Phantasmion, the composition of which, she said, did much to
assuage her days of misery. Just as Coleridge composed his
greatest critical work, the *Biographia Literaria*, during the
period of his most abject slavery to opium, when he seemed
almost oblivious to moral responsibility, so his daughter
created her fantastic story during a period of nervous
and physical debility. Both father and daughter found relief
from suffering in literary exertion, as an escape, perhaps,
from reality. Henry Taylor once remarked that Sara's eyes
shone with the same lustre as her father's, and more figura-
tively, some one else said, 'Her father had looked down into
her eyes, and left in them the light of his own'.[1] It is fruitless
to attempt a comparison between Coleridge's immortal
masterpieces and his daughter's long-since forgotten book;
suffice it to say, however, that Sara inherited from her father
not merely the love of metaphysical inquiry but also a
measure of poetic imagination.

When *Phantasmion* appeared anonymously in the summer
of 1837, Sara was not sanguine of its success. 'It was Henry's
partiality, not my presumption,' she wrote to one of her
friends, 'which brought *Phantasmion* to light.' She would
never 'have put together such a string of waking dreams', she
said, had she not been confined to her couch and withdrawn
from 'natural objects'. She wondered if her friends would
agree with her husband that the tale was worth printing,
and she explained that she had begun it for Herbert's amusement, without any design of writing a full-length book.
When her fairy tale outgrew the proportions of an educational device for her son, she confessed, she would have

[1] Edith Coleridge, op. cit. i. 49.

abandoned it entirely, had not her husband urged her to complete it. She questioned, too, whether the reading public still had any taste for such fantastic tales as hers; 'works of this kind', she wrote, 'are now out of fashion, though Sir Walter Scott and Charles Lamb, Coleridge, Southey, and Wordsworth all stuck to them manfully, preferring them to modern substitutes.' She certainly intended no allegory, but considered it 'no defect in this attempt of mine that it contains neither allegory, nor general moral'. The book was not intended exclusively for mere children. '[Its] likers, if any,' she wrote,

[will be] among the youthful boys and girls in teens or under— those in whom fancy is a more active power than judgment, and whose own state of mind lends a glow and a novelty to that which seems too fantastic, yet not over-original to them who have had more experience in life and literature.

To Derwent, who had apparently objected to 'the disproportionateness of the machinery to the events and people of the tale', and who had complained of a want of moral, Sara wrote, acknowledging the justice of his first charge but answering the second:

Now I fairly admit that the tale in question was written to illustrate no one general truth; I thought it sufficient for the soul and individuality of the piece that there should be upon the whole a unity of conception and feeling throughout. . . . If you ask me, however, what advantage a young person could possibly derive from such a tissue of unrealities, I should say that every work of fancy in its degree, and according to the merit of its execution, feeds and expands the mind; whenever the poetical beauty of things is vividly displayed, truth is exhibited, and thus the imagination of the youthful reader is stimulated to find truth for itself. . . .

There is no fear of . . . [children] . . . mistaking the people or events of fairy tales for realities, but they may and should perceive the truths and realities both of the human mind and of nature which may be conveyed under such fictions. . . . Tales of daily life, where the ostensible moral is strongly marked, in my opinion, have generally less of this merit, than fictions where the scene lies more out-of-doors, and the materials of which have more to do with the general, than with the petty and particular.

Phantasmion, like *The Ancient Mariner*, has no end but pleasure, and Sara was frankly puzzled by her critics' attempts to discover some allegorical significance in her story. Her tale abounds in supernatural occurrences. Except for his devotion to virtue, his unyielding courage, and his love for Iarine, her youthful hero is powerless to act unaided by superhuman beings. Nevertheless, the story of *Phantasmion* keeps up a show of reality. Phantasmion's emotions are human ones. Even the unearthly beings in the tale are but personifications of nature in her many-sided aspects. Natural laws are transcended rather than violated. When Phantasmion flies, it is with the wings of an eagle or of insects. When various persons in the story are miraculously healed of wasting sickness or of deathly wounds, the medicines are made of earthly herbs. It is worth noting, too, that only the living are restored to health; the dead are never reanimated. Sara Coleridge succeeds, then, in winning from her readers 'the willing suspension of disbelief', transporting them for the duration of her story to a region where the ordinary limitations of time and space disappear into nothingness. The world of *Phantasmion* is in many ways the counterpart of the real world. One finds there good as well as evil men; but whereas in the living world right triumphs, if at all, only through the slow process of time, in the kingdom of Phantasmion and the surrounding countries supernatural agencies accomplish at once, or only after a brief period, the achievements of centuries. And that is as children would have it. *Phantasmion* is a more successful work than *Pretty Lessons* because it breaks away from the bonds of didacticism and anticipates, in some measure, such immortal stories as *Alice in Wonderland* and *The Water Babies*.

The style of *Phantasmion* is full of charm and grace, and the descriptions are minute and colourful. The diction is 'pure mother English', as Coleridge had said of Sara's youthful translation from the Latin. There is in the book, as she admitted, 'over-depth of colouring, and prodigality of beauty', but these faults she thought she 'could not afford to lose, being substitutes for better things'. Thoroughly at home in the flowers and trees, the mountains and lakes, she makes her story seem alive by the picturesqueness of the landscape. She wrote feelingly, too, of the animal world, from the roaming tiger and gentle deer to the bees and beetles. London may have deprived her of the rural scenes she loved so well, but the memories of Keswick remained—delicately reproduced through the lenses of her fantastic imagination.

Sprinkled through *Phantasmion* are a series of lovely lyrics. Gone now are the moral lessons of *Pretty Lessons*. In their place we find songs, lyrical poems, and beautiful descriptions, many of them exquisitely wrought. Such lyrics as that which follows bear witness to her poetic ability.

> The winds were whispering, the waters glistering,
> A bay-tree shaded a sun-lit stream;
> Blasts came blighting, the bay-tree smiting,
> When leaf and flower, like a morning dream,
>   Vanished full suddenly.
>
> The winds yet whisper, the waters glister,
> And softly below the bay-tree glide;
> Vain is their cherishing, for, slowly perishing,
> It doth but cumber the river side,
>   Leafless in summer-time.[1]

Hartley Coleridge thought *Phantasmion* set his sister 'above all female writers of the age—except Joanna Baillie',[2] and an American critic who admired the tale to an extravagant degree wrote of it:

Nothing has appeared in this species of writing to be for one moment compared with 'Phantasmion', since Fouqué produced his inimitable 'Undine.' . . . It has the patriarchal simplicity, the beautiful truthfulness of primitive ages; while it is at the same time enriched and ennobled by the refinement of a more advanced period. . . . Do you ask what is its grand characteristic? It is beauty,—beauty, truly feminine, beauty of conception, character, and expression.[3]

The *Quarterly Review* was equally eulogistic:

'Phantasmion' is not a poem, but it is poetry from beginning to end, and has many poems within it. It is one of a

---

[1] *Phantasmion*, London, 1837, 177.
[2] G. E. and E. L. Griggs, op. cit. 264.
[3] Quoted by Edith Coleridge, op. cit. i. 42–3.

race that has particularly suffered under the assaults of political economy and useful knowledge;—a Fairy Tale, the last, we suppose, that will ever be written in England, and unique in its kind. It is neither German nor French. It is what it is—pure as crystal in diction, tinted like an opal with the hues of an everspringing sunlit fancy.[1]

In general, *Phantasmion* was rather indifferently received, nor has it ever been much read.[2]

Not long before the appearance of *Phantasmion* early in the summer of 1837 Sara and Henry moved from Hampstead to a larger house in Chester Place, Regent's Park, London. Not only had Henry recently inherited some money but he had prospered in his profession as well, and the constant frugality of the earlier years of marriage was now no longer necessary. As early as 1835 he had written to Southey that he had made £600 clear for the year and intended removing from Hampstead; two years later he recorded his income as nearly £1,000. Until Sara recovered from her nervous illness, however, no move could be considered. Regent's Park, of course, was a much more advantageous location for both Henry and Sara. It brought Henry much closer to Lincoln's Inn, and it gave them increased opportunity for social intercourse. Her own description of their new home will be of interest:

Our house is small, though much more capacious than our cottage at Hampstead, and the back part is noisy, which grieves me not a little on mama's account; ... but we have some pleasant neighbours in the adjoining terraces, and the Park with its miles of greensward, clumps of trees, and bleating sheep, is more rural

---

[1] *Quarterly Review*, cxxxii. 411 (Sept. 1840).

[2] In 1874 Lord Coleridge reissued the volume, hoping to awaken an interest in it, but his efforts were disappointed. Herbert Wilson, reviewing the book in the *Examiner* of Apr. 11, 1874, sums up the matter: 'Lord Coleridge's estimate of his relative's work is exaggerated. ... "Phantasmion" indeed is a beautiful conception of a rarely-gifted mind; but hardly less rare than such minds as that of Sara Coleridge are the minds which, in these fuller and busier times, will be able to appreciate her story. ... Like the "Arcadia", "Phantasmion" is too refined for the general run of readers. ... There are of course fairy tales and fairy tales, and we incline to the opinion that there ought to be one at least for every year of our allotted three score and ten. "Phantasmion" would come in suitably enough for the spare moments of, say, our fiftieth year. We certainly should not think of putting it into the hands of an ordinary child.'

and pleasanter to roam in than we expected to find it. . . . But there is no water near us, running or at rest; and this to me, who have in my early days, luxuriated so in water, is a great want. . . . Among the advantages of this new residence I ought to have mentioned its proximity to a new Church in Albany Street, where we have a most excellent and zealous minister in Mr. Dodsworth.

Chester Place was to be not only Sara's home during the remainder of her life, but the home of her children for many years to come.

From the time of their settlement at Chester Place Sara's health improved; but she suffered three miscarriages in the years following her nervous collapse of 1836, her frail constitution being unequal to the task of frequent childbirth. Though only two children survived infancy, she was pregnant seven times in her thirteen years of married life. In the summer of 1840 she gave birth to a baby girl, christened Bertha Fanny, but the child survived only a few days. Sara, not yet recovered from her trial, first learned of its death by the broken sobs of her husband leaning over the crib in the next room.

The loss of her father drew Sara much closer to Hartley. Remembering perhaps Coleridge's last injunction in his will—'My dear children, love one another'—and painfully aware that in many ways her brother needed to be shielded and encouraged, she turned to him with almost maternal tenderness. Coleridge, who for years had never laid his head on his pillow without a prayer for his beloved first-born, must have known, as he lay dying, that Sara would watch over Hartley. She seems, indeed, to have understood Hartley's weaknesses; and if she wrote to admonish him, it was never about his personal life, but always concerning his failure to produce literary work compatible with his high gifts. She took unlimited pride in his published writings, slight as they were, and bitterly regretted the weakness of will which so thwarted and frustrated the full expression of his genius. And it is worth remarking, too, that Sara shared fully Hartley's utter disregard for worldly reputation, for she was completely devoid of any worldly ambition for herself.

Her relations with Derwent were, of course, on a different

plane. Self-sufficient almost to the point of arrogance, he
did not need her sisterly protection. Whereas Hartley rarely
ventured, and then most humbly, to disagree with her in
intellectual matters, Derwent never hesitated to express his
views. He and Sara clashed frequently over theological
matters and certainly they were in disagreement on many
occasions. With some annoyance she wrote in her diary:

Had a long debate on Baptism [with Derwent]. He is in an odd
position. Whatever I think on the matter—*that* he is resolved not
to think. He has a view of his own, or could have if he chose to
take the trouble. What the view is he never seems to know.

Derwent once suggested that Sara's letters were too long
and a waste of time, but she retaliated by showing the uselessness of his amateur interest in architecture. Both Sara
and Hartley were displeased with Derwent's affected
manners, and she thought Christabel a ridiculous name
for her niece. She disapproved of Derwent's 'smart dinners'
and the clever sprinkling of foreign words in his conversation. When Derwent visited him in 1843, Hartley
noted, too, his brother's fine manners and thought him 'the
happiest mixture of Divine, Philosopher, Poet, Man of Business, and fine Gentleman' he ever saw. 'The quantity of
French phrases wherewith he tambours his conversation
would have made Papa blaspheme outright without reverence to the cloth'.[1] Yet withal there was understanding
between Sara and Derwent and certainly nothing ever led
to an open quarrel. Derwent's wife and children were an
especial delight to Sara and she wrote of them and to them
constantly. In 1841, when Derwent became Principal of
St. Mark's College, Chelsea (the first Training College for
National Schoolmasters, in which Henry had been interested
as early as 1838), Sara saw Derwent and his family frequently.

The fact that Derwent occasionally acted toward Sara in
a rather high-handed manner must not, of course, blind us
to his real merits. He was a steady, practical, successful man,
and if he did not have Sara's brilliance or Hartley's genius,
he had good sense and an honest, open nature. His ability,

[1] G. E. and E. L. Griggs, op. cit. 268.

too, as a teacher and as an editor must not be overlooked.
During the last years of her life Sara found in him a refuge
and comfort. From the point of view of Sara's feelings, one
of the unkindest things he did—and it certainly was not pre-
meditated—was in sending her a Coleridge letter to himself,
wherein Coleridge rather thoughtlessly spoke of Mary as
dearer to him than a daughter. Sara was engaged in collecting Coleridgeana and had asked for letters, but Derwent
need not have sent those likely to cause his sister unnecessary
pain. 'Some of those letters', she wrote to Henry,

ought never to have been sent to us. D. has not acted by me as
I have ever done by him on many subjects of this kind. An
'unseen daughter-in-law elect more closely at the heart'. . . but it is
better not to look *this way*, and I believe he [S.T.C.] had [a]
hundred moods after this. . . . I slept ill and brokenly last night,
haunted by the S.T.C. letter, which however was written before
D.'s marriage.[1]

'It was your father's habit', Henry replied,

in letters and speech to be entire and excessive to the immediate
object—he no doubt, had a mode in his own mind of harmonizing
all his views and sayings . . . but the records remaining seem
really to impeach his sincerity to strangers' eyes. You, however,
may well rest on what he subsequently wrote of you in his will
and in the Sotheby Virgil. He wrote those letters . . . while you
were at Keswick and there was a prejudice, afterwards worn off.

With the Wordsworths, Sara remained on intimate terms
and when they were in London they came out to see her. In
the summer of 1837, she reported that

Mr. Wordsworth looks well after his Italian tour, which he says
has added something to his thought, [and] much to his imagery,
though it is rather late in the day for him to make much use of it.

---

[1] The unpublished letter from Coleridge to Derwent reads: '. . . and now
you and Mary; and Sara and—for her sake and *since so it is*—Henry—but you
and my Unseen Daughter-elect more closely—are at my heart—and tempt me
to the unworthiness of self-wishing, that instead of a voluminous System of
Philosophy and Divinity, on God, Nature and Man etc.——' At this point the
manuscript breaks off. Sara has endorsed it: 'The unseen dearer than the
seen! [I] grudge no love that he bestowed on dear D and M—but there is an
expression of *alienation* painful of course—There was a bar between his heart.
Well he had many moods.'

Sara followed the course of Dora's engagement and marriage to Edward Quillinan with great interest, being fully informed of the details by the Wordsworths, Dora, and Miss Fenwick. Sara felt that the parents were too unyielding in their attitude toward the whole matter. 'It is strange', she argued,

that Mr. and Mrs. Wordsworth do not see how much the least of two evils their consenting to Dora's marriage with Mr. Quillinan would be than letting her pass her life in regret and uneasiness. . . . Their dreams are now over that she prefers single blessedness—and they must see that she is not likely to make any other match.

Sara attributed the objections of the Wordsworths to the fact that Quillinan was a Roman Catholic, though she admitted that his precarious financial affairs must have been a contributing factor.[1] She understood the feelings of both Wordsworth and Dora, and may have been partly instrumental in encouraging the poet to modify his attitude.

Sara objected rather strongly to the exaggerated estimates Wordsworth made of his daughter. 'Everybody admires Dora', she wrote to Henry,

even on a cursory acquaintance, but it requires to know her well, and also to understand her father's mode of language and turn of thought well to understand what he means by *capacity of mind*, and 'genius', which he once assured me she possessed.

She was, indeed, less pleased with the ageing poet than with her memories of the past. The 1836 edition of his poems she read with interest, delighted more in 'old acquaintances in manuscript' than in the poet's recent pieces. In retrospect she looked back on the Wordsworth household of her youth:

The latter years of that family have not been like the earlier ones. . . . Then there were April showers, and vernal gusts of pettish weather. But now there is a settled dullness—no Lyrical Ballads—no Excursions—no White Does of Rylstone issue from that quarter now—No gladsome Miss Wordsworth and cheerful Miss Hutchinson to say alternately sharp and kind things: no naughty but mirthful Willy at the door—the careless children

[1] Recently Mr. E. de Selincourt has presented the whole story of Dora's marriage. See 'Wordsworth and His Daughter's Marriage', *Wordsworth and Coleridge . . .*, E. L. Griggs, editor, 1939, 62.

turned to anxious men and women—the bard shorn of his vigour
by age, and of his gentleman-like courtesy of manner. For on
both points I remember him different from what he now is.

The Wordsworths loved and admired Sara, but occasionally one catches a slight trace of jealousy in their remarks
about her. Reluctantly they were forced to admit that she
was the intellectual superior of their own children; and
indeed, with the possible exception of Hartley, she stood head
and shoulders above the younger generation of Coleridges,
Wordsworths, and Southeys. As early as 1809 Dorothy had
mentioned that Sara had 'nothing about her of the natural
wildness of a child';[1] and twenty-five years later Dorothy
could speak of Sara's illness as 'fanciful despondency'. But
such comments as these were not common, and though both
Wordsworth and his wife were occasionally to be impatient
with Sara in the future, when she undertook editorial work
in real earnest, in general they spoke and thought of her with
the tenderest feelings.

Sara never forgot how much she owed to Robert Southey,
and during his wife's mental illness she often mentioned him
with deep affection. 'As to my Uncle,' she wrote in 1837,
his heart has long been in Heaven—he is cheerful—even playful in
the daily intercourse of life, but you cannot converse very seriously
with him for any length of time before you are made fully sensible
that his most cherished hopes and most deep-felt longings are not
concerning the things of this world. Indeed he never acts as if
earthly blessings and possessions had any great hold upon his
mind.

When Southey, bereaved of his first wife, married Caroline
Bowles in 1839, there occurred in the Southey household
a series of distressing and disgraceful quarrels. Eventually
Mrs. Lovell and Kate Southey were turned out of Greta
Hall. To Sara the unjust conduct of the second Mrs.
Southey in the role of stepmother and the mistreatment of
Kate Southey by her sisters were particularly grievous. By
espousing Kate's cause Sara permanently alienated her
childhood companion, Edith Southey Warter. She agreed

[1] E. de Selincourt, *The Letters of William and Dorothy Wordsworth. The Middle Years*, i. 343.

with Wordsworth that Kate should put her version of the affair in writing, that ultimately an unprejudiced judgement might be formed by friends of the family. She felt keenly the contention among her cousins, who were almost like brothers and sisters to her, three of her children having been named for them, and she deplored the lot of poor Aunt Lovell, who was now aged and penniless.

Sara continued to give detailed attention to the education of her children. Until Herbert was nearly nine years of age she taught him at home, but in 1839 she sent him to a school at St. John's Wood. He was not particularly happy—'I am so out of the world out there at St. John's Wood', he used to say! Sara laid her finger on the difficulty, however. The school was unable to give him instruction on a sufficiently high intellectual level, and she feared he would not only fail to progress but would actually forget what he already had learned. Sara was especially gratified when in June 1840 Herbert was entered at Eton, under the guidance of his uncle, Edward Coleridge. He was admirably equipped to take a leading place among his schoolfellows. His natural brilliance had been carefully directed by his devoted mother, who, even in sickness, had made his training her primary concern. His earliest instruction, as we have seen, was as much play as work for him. *Pretty Lessons* and *Phantasmion* were, indeed, tender efforts to develop his unfolding intellect. Yet Sara did not fail to awaken in her son a yearning for the rich stores of knowledge which still lay outside his ken, nor did she neglect his moral education. Thus Herbert went to Eton with a knowledge of Latin, a solid foundation in Greek, and an uncommon fund of English, mathematics, history, geography, and botany.

Herbert was, nevertheless, a perfectly normal child, with a small boy's pride and wants. The following letter shows him at eleven years of age.

My dear Mamma

I have just come from trials for the Remove, which I hope I shall get. Fancy what we had—a difficult bit of Caesar to translate, which I construed with Papa at Dover, and a few rotten questions. Why, bless you, I rattled 'em off in 3 minutes. Please, dear Mamma, may I have one of those large Album books, bound in leather, to write all my verses in and copies I shall be sent up for good for, and such things as that? You promised in the Pretty Lessons, when I was a yarker of a boy, you would grant me such things as that; it will only cost 7s 6d. If you will kindly say 'Yes,' I shall be much obliged. . . . I do not seal with wax because I am out of wafers, but because it is more noble, and in imitation of Nelson, who would not seal his letter with wafer because the Danish King might think him funny. . . . Tell Nurse to make me a Christmas treat of a center-bit, and not of cake, or humbug like that. I hope when Edith begins Prosody it will be when I am at home, for then I shall have the pleasure of seeing her use Uncle's verses.

. . . P.S. Pray don't forget to tell me about the Album in your next.

Concerning Herbert's stubborn determination, Sara wrote many years later of his dislike of school:

I can see him now stumping off to his uncomfortable Preparatory School with large teardrops in his large bright eyes, but never lingering for a moment. He bore the discomforts of that training place with a doleful doggedness, the tyrannies and trials of Eton with a taciturn gruffness.

Sara instructed Herbert even after his entrance at Eton, and throughout his education he sought her advice. In 1843 she is helping him with Latin. He had to render certain portions of Milton into that language. 'I only helped negatively', she says, 'by putting aside what was not grammar—not sense—not poetry—not Milton'; but she admits that putting Milton into Latin is 'impossible to do otherwise than *miserably*—unless by a freer translation than is allowed'. She delighted, too, when she and Herbert translated Greek together. 'Herbert', she wrote,

triumphs greatly when he can find out a better meaning for a line of Euripides than Mama. He translates Greek mighty well for his age—but is fond of rushing on, and taking up with half meanings which by no means content me.

Sara devoted even more effort to Edith, who never received any formal education. Though she would have liked a governess for the child, Sara said she would 'still read her Latin and Greek—and read the Bible with her'.

She believed firmly that constant reading of the Bible should be encouraged in children.

Let a child read his Bible in short portions consecutively from the time that he is 5 years old—let him go over the same ground every successive stage of his growing life, and he will find it new, always find something which he did not perceive before added to what he formerly saw there. . . .

While her children were carefully taught the basic principles of religion, morality, and social intercourse, these things were never heedlessly imposed upon them. Children, Sara believed, should be guided not ruled, directed not checked. Blessed with two children who inherited more than ordinary talents, she recognized the challenge their superiority presented. Her direction was not haphazard. Instead, she planned in detail each aspect of their work.

Sara's children did not inherit her love of poetry, a deficiency she tried in vain to overcome. She wrote to a friend that Herbert's want of poetry stood somewhat in the way of his success at Eton, and she went on to speak of her daughter:

If Edith takes up a poem I think it is for the sake of the story it contains, not for its imagery and poetic tone. The productions of Wordsworth which I used so to dwell upon in childhood and youth my children call 'seedy' and dull.

In many ways the death of her father marked a definite change in the life of Sara Coleridge. It intensified, for one thing, her preoccupation with religious and philosophical problems, and from then on her letters reflect more and more her metaphysical turn of mind. She kept constantly before her the need for religious thinking. 'Intellectual pursuits', she once wrote to her husband,

are of inconsiderate value if they do not lead to religion. They may be better to a certain degree than mere sensuous delights: they may be more exalted, yet still they are of the 'earth earthy' —they may be more lasting, yet still they are brief and transitory—they may refine but they cannot glorify. We must not forget that the most unintellectual person may attain to Christian goodness through God's grace which is incalculably superior to all which cultivated intelligence alone can give or lead to.

She became well informed about the controversies surrounding the Oxford Movement. Thoroughly Protestant at heart, she could admire Newman for his sincerity as well as his reasoning powers, but she abhorred the Romish tinge of his writings. She objected to Newman's idea that God does not work 'our Salvation through our active forces or faculties but in some mysterious way'. She declared that 'such distorted and extreme views can only arise out of a spirit of opposition which besets the writer under the disguise of a zeal for truth.' Ultimately, 'Newman's scheme is a house divided against itself and contains the materials of its refutation from *within*.' She disliked the 'party spirit' of Newman, Pusey, and Keble; surely, she argued, there cannot be the unanimity of opinion among them which they publicly pretend. Religion to her was a personal, intimate matter; the Church, she believed, was of less significance than the faithful heart, and the emphasis upon apostolic succession, stressing as it does the divine character of the Church and the clergy, irritated her. 'We are better content', she wrote, 'with the Reformation effected by Cranmer, Ridley, Luther and their fellows than by any which can be substituted by Froude, Newman, Keble and Co.' Occasionally she thought her own intellectual curiosity in religious matters too worldly.

Never again, dear friend, will I read a Resurrection Sermon on a Sunday—at least, unless I am greatly improved in mastery over my own mind. It summons before me such a crowd of controversies, conflicting opinions, metaphysical objections (not to Scripture, but to the writer's interpretation of it)—party feelings, domestic affections, for I always imagine what my Father would have said on the subject, what Hartley did once say on the subject, what Henry now says to me on the subject, what objections to my objections Derwent would bring upon the subject, in short it makes me think so many earthly things such a waspish throng; I am like one sitting in a boat with his face to the stern and fixing his eye upon the glorified West, while the vessel carries him away fast to the eastward.

Several years after Coleridge's death, Sara, recognizing her 'bent for theological topics', said she would like to prepare a book of extracts from her father, 'as he did from Leighton, and to write comments upon them. This could begin in some things I have already written and if the book were read it could do good to S. T. C.'s works and in some degree tend to familiarize and popularize them'.

There are very definite resemblances between Sara Coleridge and her father. They shared the same intellectual curiosity, particularly in theological inquiry, and in each the passion for truth was basically religious. Like her father, Sara wrote at great length, in a rambling discursive style, without sufficient discipline and self-control, but she often showed the same flashes of insight so characteristic of him. Like him, too, she possessed a fine taste and critical acumen. She inherited from him a sickly constitution and she used opiates as he did to quell the horrors of sleepless nights and waking dreams. She had Coleridge's happy faculty for making friends, and while she did not possess his amazing conversational powers, her talk was witty, sparkling, and profound, and she was eagerly sought after at public gatherings.

She always felt a sense of intimacy with her father and could declare not long before her death:

Indeed, he seems ever at my ear, in his books, more especially his marginalia—speaking not personally to me, and yet in a way so natural to my feelings, that *finds* me so fully, and awakens such a strong echo in my mind and heart, that I seem more intimate with him now than I ever was in life.[1]

On another occasion Sara remarked that she felt a complete sympathy with her father because of 'his literary difficulties. Whatever subject I commence', she said,

I feel discontent unless I could pursue it in every direction to the farthest bounds of thought, and then, when some scheme is to be executed, my energies are paralysed with the very notion of the indefinite vastness which I long to fill. This was the reason that my father wrote by snatches. He could not bear to complete incompletely, which everybody else does.[2]

She tried to follow her father's attitude towards suffering:

We should look *beyond* the imagined calamity and see what good may spring out of it. From my own experience I can truly

[1] Edith Coleridge, op. cit. ii. 315.   [2] Ibid. i. 193.

say that my nervous trials have been the source of some of my most valuable mental acquisitions. . . . If suffering is the occasion to us of self-knowledge and strength . . . still more if it is an occasion of God's grace—it must be accounted a blessing—without that self-knowledge and grace—ease of mind and body is but a snare. . . . I know this, that I look back with no regret to any of my past miseries—though none but myself knows how severe they were—and that I would not if I could that any of them had not been. . . . You may perhaps derive a something of strength and comfort from [these] words of my dear father—. . . 'We must look the more deeply inward and learn to draw up[on] that inner mind over which the body has no power.' And certainly a habit of distinguishing what flows from our moral and rational part from that which has its source in the earthly receptacle is the best defence against the despotism of deranged nerves which . . . I have yet met.

She began to express herself in aphoristic fashion, writing somewhat in the manner of Coleridge. 'My turn of thought may be like my father's', she wrote to her husband,

as my face and constitution are—though the power of genius was peculiar to his individual spirit. But had I been born out of reach of his voice and writings, my style would be essentially the same. I never try to imitate my father, but when I have finished a sentence I often laugh inwardly at this filial likeness of manner and aim—though the execution and degree and force of thought are so different.

In an effort to explain Coleridge's religious ideas Sara began in 1839 her *Essay on Rationalism*, which was published as an appendix to the fifth edition of the *Aids to Reflection* in 1843. Concerning this essay, Hartley remarked:

Dear Sara's treatise on Rationalism is a wonder. I say not a wonder of a woman's work—where lives the man that could have written it? None in Great Britain since our Father died. Poor Henry was perfectly right in saying that she inherited more of her father, than either of us; and that not only in the amount but in the quality of her powers.[1]

A little later, in describing himself and Derwent in relation to their father, Hartley asserted that 'Sara is the inheritrix of his mind and of his genius. Neither Derwent nor I have

[1] G. E. and E. L. Griggs, op. cit. 267.

much more than the family cleverness, which with hardly an exception accompanies the name of Coleridge.'[1]

But if she was like her father in many respects, she differed greatly from him in others. If she lacked the strange hypnotic power that won for Coleridge the immediate reverence of every one who met him, she succeeded better than he in holding her friends throughout her life. No sordid quarrels or misunderstandings marred her associations. 'I have never outlived any deep-seated attachment or lost one of my friends, except by death', she once remarked. She had not, of course, Coleridge's philosophical power, nor was the vein of creative imagination strong within her, but she was remarkably sensitive to beauty and pain. She did not produce literary works, it is true, in any way comparable to the creations of her father, but whereas he was indolent and could not consistently apply himself, she was endowed with a full share of perseverance and industry. Had she chosen to do independent critical or philosophical writing, for which she was admirably equipped, she would have undoubtedly been successful; but she preferred to devote her life to editing her father's works. It was, of course, her similarity of mind and temperament which made her the best of the early editors of Coleridge. If she noticed in herself and in her son the same 'dread of change both as to persons and things', as in her father; if, during her last years, as she humorously remarked, even her shuffling gait was like his; she also became increasingly conscious of her intellectual heritage. And of that heritage she was never unworthy.

[1] G. E. and E. L. Griggs, op. cit. 275.

VII

THE DEATH OF HER HUSBAND

FROM the time Sara settled in Chester Place she seemed to have overcome at last the nervous weakness which had so frequently overpowered her. She even conquered her old fear of travel and in September 1841 accompanied her husband on a ten days' tour of Belgium, her only venture away from her native land. Foreign scenes and places delighted her. She wrote in ecstasy of the cathedral in Antwerp and of the paintings of the Flemish masters. Rubens's *Descent from the Cross*, she wrote to Hartley, 'is the most beautiful painting I have ever seen. . . . It makes the Vandykes beside it appear cold, prim, and passionless.' She was led by the divine service in the cathedral to 'many serious reflections—not only on the defects of such unintellectual worship, which has all the outwardness of old Jewish ritual without its inwardness and meaning, but on the weakness of human nature and its aptness to elude every form of religion devised to entice it into heart and soul worship'. She was not sure, indeed, that she thought Rubens as religious a painter as Van Eyck, but of his 'boldness and dash' there was no question. She returned to London refreshed and stimulated by her journey.

And it was fortunate that she and Henry had made this excursion together, for not long afterwards he began to show symptoms of the spinal paralysis which was to strike him down. Never robust in health, he had as a young man been forced to travel to the West Indies for his health, and from 1837 he had occasionally been unwell; but his unquenchable good nature, his high spirits, and his sparkling wit obscured his physical condition. There were times when he took brief holidays in order to conserve his strength. These things Sara knew, but she was hardly prepared for the major collapse which occurred in May 1842. From then on, Henry gradually lost the use of his legs, until towards the end of that year he became hopelessly bedridden.

Sara once wrote to Henry that the only blot on their married happiness was ill health. So complete and so gratifying was her married life that she hardly dared look to the future, and at times she had premonitions of disaster. Separation from her husband, even for short intervals, she deplored. 'My love,' she confided to him in 1838, 'three days of you is much to lose out of the years that we may humanly expect to live together. You do tease certainly—but there are prickles and bristles and dingy moss on the *Rosa Centifolia,* and yet what flower on earth could be substituted for the double moss rose? As little would I substitute any living creature for you, or fancy you more lovable than you are by any addition or subtraction.' Sometimes, recognizing the transitoriness of life, she dwelt on the fullness of marriage.

I feel more than ever as if other sources of enjoyment were falling away—as if they more and more gained the colour of life from your presence so that if that were withdrawn the remainder would be like the skeleton leaves which are seen to shiver in the trees in the gloomy vestibule of winter. . . . Seventeen years in which the affections have been interlacing themselves with one object—and that during the flexible period of life. What in this mortal term can ever replace such an interlacing or unlace all its tendrils!

Henry was equally devoted to Sara. During her frequent illnesses he remained tender and affectionate, and his patience never once gave way. There is no trace of irritation over Sara's inability to take much part in society, despite the fact that he was inordinately fond of social gatherings. Occasionally in his efforts to encourage Sara to help herself, he took a firm stand—as when he insisted that she should return to London with him from Ilchester—but at such times he always accompanied his insistence with tenderness. He gloried, too, in Sara's beauty, and during the last years of his life, when the long struggle with poverty was over, he showered her with finery. She thought him 'very extravagant, having spent I don't know how many pounds on a Honiton lace veil and an ermine muff and a boa for a wife who does not make a smart call once in six weeks'.

For Sara, Henry was a tower of strength. How quickly and easily her morbid fears vanished under the warmth of his radiant good humour! Whatever blows fate might have in store for her, to him she could turn for comfort. 'My beloved', she once declared in an outburst of feeling,

I think of you with the deepest love, and am drawn nearer to you by all the events of life; if others disappoint my hopes I seem the tighter bound to you; if kindness and friendship abound, I rejoice in it as a common good with you; yet think what a nothing it is compared to your love—the great source of heartfelt happiness. God bless you, dearest.

There was between Sara and Henry a mutual respect for each other. We have seen how they worked together to forward Coleridge's reputation, from the publication of *Table Talk* to the collection and editing of unpublished manuscripts and the reissuing of works already published. Henry realized that his wife was not only a willing labourer in this cause but also one whose intelligence and judgement he could trust. She was proud, too, of his achievements. When his *Introduction to Homer* appeared, she said,

I am more than ever charmed by that book of yours, and my desire that you should give it a brother, and continue leisurely and enjoyably to practice original composition exceeds my desire for your having more than a competent share of law business— exceeds even my desire for the putting forth new editions of Samuel Taylor Coleridge.

At Easter in 1842, Sara and Henry made their last journey together. They set off for Oxford, in the hope that a change might be beneficial to his rapidly declining health. But all was in vain, and a few weeks later he became too ill to continue his legal practice. From then on there were no interludes of health, and even the hope they both fed on was slowly extinguished.

The story of Henry's illness is almost too harrowing to repeat. Sara gathered an unsuspected strength from the hidden resources of her being and mastered herself. At first she hoped for Henry's complete recovery. Slowly she came to realize that even if he survived the present collapse, he could never expect to resume his profession. 'At times I tremble', she confided to a friend,

to find how strong and vital my hope is that he will *not die but live*. . . . To have him out of danger, is all that my hopes and thoughts are fixed on now; how our lives are to be shaped hereafter, in consequence of his illness should he never return to his profession, I do not know, but any shape appears lovely which looks out beyond the present danger and uncertainty.

Towards the end of 1842 it became only too evident that Henry could not survive even in a state of semi-invalidism. The nature of his complaint, affecting as it did the lower spinal cord, not only caused paralysis, but, as it crept upward, would have brought on insanity, had he lived. That calamity Sara could not endure. Thinking perhaps of Mary Lamb, Mrs. Southey, and Dorothy Wordsworth, Sara could write as she watched her suffering husband:

I now feel quite happy, or, at least, satisfied. Could I arrest his progress to a better sphere of existence by a prayer, I would not utter it. When I once know that it *is* God's will, I can feel that it is right, even if there were no such definite assurances of rest and felicity beyond this world. I cannot be too thankful to God, so far as my own best interests are concerned, that He is thus removing from earth to heaven my greatest treasure, while I have strength and probably time to benefit by the measure, and learn to look habitually above; which now will not be the spirit against the flesh, but both pulling one way, for the heart will follow the treasure. Thus graciously does the Blessed Jesus condescend to our infirmities, by earthly things leading us to heavenly ones.[1]

As the Christmas season drew near, Sara thought of the happy festivities of past years, and realized that this would be her last in Henry's company. As she heard the Christmas carollers singing in the street outside, she wrote in a contemplative mood:

Never before did I hear them [the waits] with so heavy a heart and yet this is not all heaviness—it is a seriousness which I do not wish to exchange for the feelings of youth when this world is a sort of heaven. In childhood we think of the realms above—then comes a season when this present life is all engrossing; we feel

---

[1] Edith Coleridge, op. cit. i. 261–2.

that if it is not perfect Paradise, this is because some unlucky cloud, which ought not to have come in our way, has cast a gloom over our particular allotment. Madame de Staël, I think, says that in youth we look upon happiness as our right—in after years we are glad to receive it, when it comes, as a boon. But there is in music a special melancholy and this periodical music knits together all our past years as with a running thread—so that they are all brought together before the mind. I am particularly full of our sorrow.

To her friends Sara wrote with outward calm, but into her diary she poured the anguish of her heart. On January 21, 1843, five days before Henry died, she recorded,

He looks worn—but his countenance is quiet—though with more ghastliness about it. He talks a little—slowly and at intervals. He embraced and kissed me this morning. . . . O my beloved —how thou sleepest—Alas is this the prelude to the sleep of the grave? . . . Even thus I would fain keep thee ever by me.

Next day she wrote:

He bade me to pray. I knelt and prayed earnestly that God would cleanse him from all sin and unite him for ever to Christ. He joined fervently.

During these last agonizing days little Edith was ill with whooping-cough, but at Christmas time, while Herbert was home from Eton, Henry had not asked to see the children. Sara noticed, however, that he enjoyed hearing them play in the room above, but she was not anxious for the children to see the emaciated spectre who had once been her joyous husband. She insisted that Herbert should return to Eton in January, wishing to spare him and Edith any unnecessary suffering.

Henry retained his mental faculties to the end, which was of inestimable comfort to Sara. During the last days of his fatal illness he engaged in a painful correspondence with William Pickering, regarding the terms of publication of Coleridge's writings. From the time of Coleridge's edition of his *Poems* in 1828, Pickering had continued to issue Coleridge's works.[1] At first the business arrangements seemed

---

[1] Excepting the *Church and State* (1830) and the second edition of *Aids to Reflection* (1831), both of which were published by Hurst, Chance & Company; and the *Table Talk*, which Murray issued in 1835.

satisfactory. The author was to pay the expenses of publication entirely, to give five per cent. commission on the sale of all copies, and after that one-half the net profits to the publisher. Under such an agreement Pickering assumed no financial responsibility, but was hardly more than an agent. In 1828 Coleridge accepted these terms, and as they began to issue Coleridge's works, Sara and Henry merely continued the old arrangement. As time went on the Coleridge publications met with an enthusiastic reception, three thousand copies of the *Poems*, two new editions of the *Aids*, and other volumes being disposed of in a few years. It seemed to Henry, therefore, that the time had come when a modification of the original agreement should be made. Wasting away, he requested Pickering 'to divide the net profits for the future in the proportion of one-third to yourself and the other two-thirds to the estate', especially in order to benefit Mrs. Coleridge and Hartley. When Pickering absolutely refused, Henry 'now too ill to think of trying any point at law', asked him to state what sum he would demand for the transfer of the entire stock of Coleridge's works to Edward Moxon, who 'had no hesitation to accept the new terms'. Pickering's offer was so exorbitant that Henry was unable to extricate the Coleridge works from him, and there, much to Henry's sorrow, the matter rested.

On October 25, 1842, Henry dated his preface to the fifth edition of the *Aids to Reflection*, and as long as he could, he continued to work on the new edition of the *Biographia Literaria*. The welfare of Sara and their children was his major concern, and before he died he called her to him and talked over their financial affairs. He was pathetically anxious to leave his family with adequate protection.

Gathered round their dying kinsman were Henry's brothers: John, who was henceforth to take charge of all Henry's family affairs; James, who performed for Henry the last offices of the Church; and Edward, master of Eton College. Henry's sister Fanny had preceded him to the grave. The tenderness and affection bestowed upon him by his brothers and their warm sympathy for her helped Sara to endure her suffering.

At length the fatal hour drew near. Sara 'kissed his beloved face—over and over again in his last unconscious
hours'. In the morning of January 26, 1843, Henry passed
away—'So ends the great charm of this world to me', Sara
recorded. 'He has made all things bright to me for 20 years—
perhaps too bright. It is time to look at the brightness that
can never fade.'

As she sat beside the body of her husband, Sara turned her
thoughts to Herbert. What of his future, deprived now of
the guidance and inspiration of a father? With her eyes
steadily on duty, as always, she wrote to Herbert, that he
might remember this saddest of all days.

My dear Boy—

My most beloved and honoured husband, your excellent father,
is no more in this world, but I humbly trust in a far better. May
we all go where he is, prepared to meet him as he would have us!
God bless you! Live as your beloved father would have you live.
Put your trust in God, and think of heaven, as he would wish you.

May we all meet above! May we all join with him the Communion of Saints, and be for ever with the Blessed Jesus! Your
good uncle James was with me at the last.

I make an effort to write to you, my dear boy, from beside the
remains of the dear, blessed, departed one. For you alone could
I do this; but it is due to his son, our child.—Your loving mother,
Sara Coleridge.[1]

Next day Sara saw Henry's remains in the coffin. To her
diary she confided: 'After two o'clock a heavy black cloud
came over me. It seemed as if the prop of my spirits had
fallen away and all was crushed into flatness. I am better
now—but very low. I am resigned to the blackness and desolation of feeling that I must go through. God's will be done
in all things. The Lord gives and the Lord hath taken away.
Blessed be the name of the Lord.' Later she stood beside the
coffin, which was placed in the dining-room. The past
crowded into her mind. 'How often at the head of that little
dinner table', she wrote,

have I seen him radiant with smiles and glowing cheeks—and full of
wit and glee! Now his cold remains in their double coffin occupy
the spot once the scene of so much lifesome gaiety and gladness.

[1] Edith Coleridge, op. cit. i. 265.

Henry was to be buried in the Highgate churchyard. It was at Highgate, Sara recalled, that she had first met him twenty years before. She desired, too, that he might lie near her father. Coleridge having been interred in a common vault, it was at first impossible to place Henry immediately beside him, and a private vault was purchased. The funeral occurred on February 2. She insisted that Herbert should accompany her, for she hoped his memories of the sad occasion would help in the future to guide him towards Christian principles. John Taylor Coleridge found her 'in a beautiful state of mind. I never saw so much feeling with so much composure and such deep principle. If she acts hereafter as she now evidently resolves, she will be a treasure to us.'

When all was over and the last of the mourners had departed, Sara sought for those values which could make her life endurable. She found them in her responsibilities to her children and her aged mother; but more than that she found them in her Christian faith. The last entry in her journal relative to Henry's death reveals resignation, fortitude, and in a measure, hope.

My health will perhaps gradually return. My happiness, such as it *was*, is gone forever. But I have begun at least to set my affections on things above, and I console myself with bringing it home to my thoughts—that the blessing taken from me I *could* not expect but to part with after a few years—and that the loss of it *now* has turned my thoughts and wishes toward a better world with an earnestness which nothing but such a deprivation could have produced, and this before I have lost my full powers of mind whereby to make my peace with God and prepare myself for that better world—while I am yet a sojourner here.

Among the many letters of condolence, Sara probably treasured most the one from Hartley to his mother, dated January 28, 1843. 'I am glad', he wrote,

that Sara is *tearful but calm*, those were good James' words. Tears are a great relief. She has been wonderfully supported—I do not fear, that she will bear up for a while, for recent affliction has a sort of excitement. I only fear for the ebb of her spirit which may take place some months, or perhaps a year hence. But she has her children, God bless them, and though they must needs in-

crease her anxiety, they will prevent her sinking into herself in
moody retrospect—making her duty to look forward.

> For who hath aught to love and love aright
> Shall never in the darkest strait despair.
> For out of love, exhales a living light
> A light that speaks in promise and in prayer.[1]

Hartley, better than any one else, realized what Henry had
meant to the family in the past. Several years earlier
Hartley had written a sonnet to Henry:

> Kinsman, Yea—more than kinsman, brother, friend—
> O more than Kinsman, more than Friend or Brother
> My Sister's Spouse, Son to my widowed mother,
> How shall I praise thee right and not offend?
> For thou wert sent a sore heart-ill to mend:
> Twin-stars were ye—Thou and thy wedded Love
> Benign of aspect, as those Imps of Jove
> In antique Faith commissioned to portend
> To sad sea-wanderers peace. Or like the Tree
> By Moses cast into the bitter pool
> Which made the tear-salt water fresh and cool—
> Or even as Spring, that sets the boon Earth free,
> Free to be good, exempt from winter's rule
> Such hast thou been to our poor family—[2]

Scarcely less comforting were Wordsworth's letters. The
first, written to John, during Henry's fatal illness, shows how
affectionately Wordsworth remembered the sweet child who
once played with his own children and who later rambled
over the hills in his company. Of Henry, the poet remarked:

> Your brother will be a great loss to his Profession, to the World,
> and to his relatives and friends, and, above all, to his dear and
> excellent wife.

'Toward Sara', he went on to say,

> I have much of the tenderness of a Father, having had her so
> near to us and so long under our eye, while she was growing up,

---

[1] G. E. and E. L. Griggs, op. cit. 260.

[2] Ibid. 218. In enclosing this sonnet to Henry, Hartley had written in deep
feeling: 'I could not thank you in prose for the great reconcilement you were
the means of effecting—the peace and comfort and universal charity you gave
to the last days of τοῦ Μακαρίτου. You caused him to die in good will with all
men.'

and afterwards when her circumstances brought her by necessity habitually to our thoughts. God will support her, for a more excellent creature is not to be found.[1]

During the months following the death of her 'beloved friend, my cousin-husband, certainly nearer and dearer to me for being cousin, as well as husband', Sara took a mournful pleasure in visiting the Highgate churchyard. The vault in which Henry lay was all that she could desire, but the sight of Coleridge's coffin, beginning to rot from the dampness of the 'promiscuous vault' in which it was deposited, greatly troubled her. When she learned from the sexton that there was a veritable pilgrimage to Highgate, including visitors from America, who asked to be shown Coleridge's final resting-place, she felt that the state of disrepair reflected on the family pride, and determined to remedy matters. Her fondest wish—that her husband lie beside her father—had not been possible earlier; why not now enlarge Henry's vault, she asked, and remove Coleridge's remains there? Inasmuch as the Gillmans had taken charge of Coleridge's funeral arrangements, Sara sought Mrs. Gillman's permission to make the change. Accordingly, a new coffin was provided to encase the old one, and Coleridge's remains were placed beside Henry's. Almost morbidly Sara made plans for her own and her mother's interments in the same tomb. She and members of the family debated, too, the nature of the inscription to be placed on Coleridge's coffin. Derwent suggested one in Latin, but Sara preferred the simplicity of English, and she had her way. The expenses, running to nearly £100, were mainly borne by Sara. Derwent provided the new oak coffin for Coleridge's remains, and John paid a small amount. Poor Hartley pathetically asked that he, too, might be allowed to contribute his share, but Sara, protective as ever, would accept nothing. The many questions connected with the family vault helped to occupy her mind, and she remarked:

It is a great pleasure and comfort to me to be busy about these sepulchral affairs. Griefs of this kind ought not to be put aside, but to be soothed and sanctified and thus converted into instru-

[1] Lord Coleridge, op. cit. 148–9.

ments of spiritual good and links with the assembly of Saints in Heaven.[1]

Sara bore her sufferings with Christian resignation, and though she was never to recover from the overwhelming sorrow of Henry's death, she eventually won peace of mind. In a letter written to Hartley two years later, she shows how fully she had become reconciled to her loss:

Sometimes I feel glad that it has been my lot to know my husband only in his prime of life—never to see him worsened and weakened by years and infirmities. For some time after my loss of him I felt my bereavement most painfully in a double way. I was deprived of him I loved best on earth, who had been most to me, . . . and sympathized most nearly with me; not only had I lost *Henry*, but I was without a husband and lover—one to whom I was everything and who was everything to me. Nobody was now left who loved me more than all the world beside, took an interest in whatever concerned me, and saw my whole mind and person through a glorifying golden mist. I seemed to be laid bare—reduced from poetry to prose—with no help-mate and protector whom I had not to *thank* for help and protection as a favour, not a thing of course. This underside of sorrow has now for some time been wearing away. I dream of Henry's return, and have sad disappointments in waking. But I am reconciled to being without a *lover*—though never to losing *him*;—(it was ever the lover more than the protecting husband that I missed)— I feel content with singleness and begin even in some respects to prefer it, which I once thought impossible. But then a singleness with children—that is far different from old maidism.

[1] The vault, on which Sara lavished so much loving care, remains to-day just as she left it. She and her mother now lie beside Coleridge and Henry. Unfortunately, however, the growth of the school connected with the church necessitated building the chapel over the vault. The Coleridge tomb now lies beneath this structure in semi-darkness, a dreary, damp, and forbidding place.

VIII

SETTING COLERIDGE'S HOUSE IN ORDER

DESOLATE as Sara may have been after the death
of her beloved husband, she did not give way to self-
pity, but found much to fill her time. Her aged mother and
two young children were absorbing responsibilities, and the
task of editing her father's works now lay mainly in her
hands, Derwent being too preoccupied with his clerical
duties[1] and Hartley too undependable to contribute very
much.

Because Sara's life was thenceforth divided among three
major interests—her editing of Coleridge, her intellectual
activities, and her personal concerns—it has seemed best to
depart from a mere chronological account of her activities.
She made four separate contributions to Coleridge scholarship. She wrote an *Essay on Rationalism* as an outgrowth and
expansion of ideas contained in the *Aids to Reflection*; she
prepared for publication the second edition of the *Biographia
Literaria* (1847); she edited the *Notes and Lectures upon Shakespeare* (1849); and she collected and published Coleridge's
fugitive contributions as *Essays on His Own Times* (1850).
Let us glance first at her *Essay on Rationalism*.

For several years she assembled materials for a formal discussion of rationalism and baptismal regeneration, and before
her husband died she had written a long essay on the subject.
She inserted it (out of deference to his dying wishes) as an
appendix in volume ii of the fifth edition of the *Aids to Reflection* in 1843. In a prefatory note written not long before his
death, Henry Nelson Coleridge remarks that his wife's essay
appeared to be so much in harmony with the principles of the

---

[1] It should be noted, however, that Derwent Coleridge later undertook a
number of editorial labours. In 1852 he collaborated with Sara in editing
Coleridge's *Poems*, and in the same year he issued *The Dramatic Works*; in 1853
he published *Notes on English Divines* and *Notes, Theological, Political, and Miscellaneous*; and in 1854 he brought out the seventh edition of the *Aids to Reflection*.
To this imposing list should be added his editions of his brother's, Moultrie's,
and Praed's works.

from an open book, and not dream over it, idly. We can know nothing beyond what is revealed,—and the apocalypse of the present dispensation, with all that rustling of divine mysteries which we hear just beyond it, is in itself warm and throbbing with humanity,—and I feel this more and more deeply—I feel too more and more certainly, that to pass *beyond*, we must pass *through*,—through the grave to the resurrection,—and to speak it reverently, to God, through the flesh—this, for the poet, as for the man actually!—To spring from the earth, the foot must press on it strongly. I think it so much, that I class world-knowledge, life-knowledge, very high among the poetical writer's necessary preparations, and look down on my own deficiencies in this respect, with profound sadness, whenever I am on the sad subject of my defects in general.[1]

Of her own poetic achievements Elizabeth Barrett spoke most diffidently:

You have written very kindly to me,—and if you had not, I should be particularly loth to appear to *you*, as given to the mean-ness of affectations—But also, before *you* who have, as you say, lived all your life among true poets, (such poets!) and who bear the name of perhaps the greatest of them,—I cannot help saying that I shrink from the assumption of any sort of poet's rank myself,—I should feel afraid of my own words—Only I see higher than I climb—and I love more than I can see—think so meet of me, if you can.

The friendly tone of Elizabeth Barrett's letters to Sara Coleridge might have led to an intimacy between the two women; it seems likely that Elizabeth Barrett's engagement and marriage to Robert Browning completely occupied her attention until their departure for Italy a year later. When the Brownings returned for a brief visit to London in the summer of 1851, however, Sara and her daughter were introduced to them by John Kenyon, Mrs. Browning's cousin and one of Sara's old friends. John Kenyon had invited the Brownings, Alexander Dyce, Sara and her daughter, and several other distinguished guests to dinner, and for Sara, who had long been an intelligent and astute, if not an

[1] In the interests of greater clarity, the editor has made minor changes in the punctuation of the passage given above.

indulgent reader of Mrs. Browning's poetry, the occasion was a significant one. Her description of the Brownings, contained in a letter to John Taylor Coleridge, gives an interesting and enlightening picture:

[Mrs. Browning] struck me as cold and self-involved at first and very plain, with a small ungraceful figure, and a wide mouth. . . . Her eyes are fine, and there is something about their deep, subdued expression, the pallid cheek and plaintive voice which made me think of Goethe's Mignon—what she might be grown into full womanhood and maturity. They have a little sprite of a two year old boy, with yellow ring curls, a small but interesting child. Browning is clever, good-natured, and chattery. He ran on in a poetical, ignorant way about Italian pictures, exalting Razzi and Pacchiarotto to a level with Raphael. . . . I do not think Browning quite as much the gentleman, as his wife is the lady. He takes rather too much notice of her in company and shews his pride in her too openly perhaps. But this is not all of what I mean—there is an indescribable tone and manner a little below the mark of what we call social refinement. . . . [Mrs. Browning's] Sonnets from the Portuguese, a feint name, for they are all about herself and her husband—his charms and graces set in a strong light—are much admired by lovers of poetry. On my saying to Mr. Kenyon that they reminded Edith and me of Shakespeare's Sonnets, he said Landor had made the same remark.

After dinner the ladies retired to themselves. They discussed Fanny Kemble's Shakespearean interpretations. Sara, who had noticed Mrs. Browning's pale cast of countenance and a deep cough, apparently spoke of her own use of drugs for medicinal purposes and learned that Mrs. Browning also used morphine to alleviate her suffering.

A week later Sara called upon the Brownings at their lodgings, but they soon departed for Paris and Italy and she never saw them again. Undoubtedly Sara's death in the following year and the continued residence of the Brownings abroad prevented a warm intimacy between these two gifted women. Each respected the other; each had dedicated her life to intellectual pursuits; and both of them moved easily in cultivated circles. Sara was, one suspects, unduly critical of Browning, but with further intimacy she might have come to understand the rich resources of his personality. She seems never to have read his poetry; in fact, she mentions it but once, when she wrote scornfully of someone who had ranked Browning among the leading figures of the day.

Among Sara Coleridge's friends was William Ewart Gladstone, whose early theological publications (*The State in Its Relations with the Church*, 1838, and *Church Principles Considered in Their Results*, 1840) are often obscured by his later political career. She talked over with him her son's progress at Oxford and the prevalent system of competitive examinations. 'I have seen', she remarked, 'what was undesirable in the feelings of boys toward each other—a proneness to contemn and judge harshly—but I never witnessed any evil arising from emulation, and Mr. Gladstone the other day confirmed my opinion on this point by his experience both of school and college.' She discussed with Gladstone the sermons and poetry of Keble. 'Mr. Gladstone . . . seemed quite or nearly to agree with me on the merits of the book as poetry and said [Keble] could never "quite come up to the mark".' Gladstone, Sara found, was much closer in spirit to Coleridge than to the Anglo-Catholics. She was pleased with Gladstone's personality. 'How obviously in . . . Mr. Gladstone amiability is interfused with intelligence and refinement of thought. . . . He does not look very well. . . . I thought him so smooth, comely, and youthful when I met him seven or eight years ago at Sir R. Inglis'.'

With Sir Francis Palgrave, the historian, Sara Coleridge was on friendly terms and she occasionally saw and conversed with such literary figures as Bryan Waller Procter (better known as Barry Cornwall), Henry Hart Milman the historian, and Alexander Dyce, the scholar and editor of the Elizabethans. Of Macaulay she did not wholly approve, remembering perhaps that he was intimately connected with Derwent's 'caterpillarage', during undergraduate days at Cambridge. In 1837 she wrote that she had met Macaulay, 'a clever, agreeable man, though rather fond of shewing off in conversation'. She was indignant over the 'audacious utilitarianism of his remarks on Bacon's philosophy', and cited phrases from the *Essay on Bacon* to demonstrate

Macaulay's materialistic spirit. 'He speaks of Bacon', she concluded,

as the finest and greatest of intellects, predicts that he will be honoured to the end of time, and then endeavours to shew that this wisest of men was a mere utilitarian. Surely no man who believes in the immortality of the soul and a future state of existence to which this life is but a vestibule could possibly propound such doctrines, which seem to say that the soul is made for the body rather than the body for the soul.

She rather anticipated modern criticism of Macaulay as a historian:

Macaulay's History [Volumes one and two, 1848] has had, and is still having, an immense run. It is certainly a fascinating book, but in some respects perhaps too fascinating and attractive to be thoroughly good as history. Dry matters are skipped, and many important events are rather commented on than narrated. And yet every true history that is to be a useful and faithful record must contain much that is heavy to the common reader.[1]

Though Sara did not attribute 'high creative power' to Macaulay, she was rather pleased with his appearance. In many ways he seemed to resemble her father. In 1849, after seeing him again, she wrote:

[Macaulay] was in great force, and I saw the likeness (amid great unlikeness) to my father, as I never had seen it before. It is not in the features, which in my father were, as Lawrence says, more vague, but resides very much in the look and expression of the material of the face, the mobility, softness, and sensitiveness of all the flesh,—that sort of look, which is so well expressed in Sir Thomas Lawrence's beautiful unfinished portrait of Wilberforce. . . . The eyes are quite unlike—even opposite in expression, —my father's in-looking and visionary, Macaulay's out-looking and objective. His talk, too, though different as to sentiment and matter, was like a little, in manner, in its labyrinthine multiplicity and multitudinousness, and the tones so flexile and *sinuous*, as it were, reminded me of the departed eloquence.[2]

Sara once met Thackeray at a dinner party, but she did not realize at the time that she had seen the distinguished novelist. In 1849 she was introduced to Harriet Martineau, who 'has

[1] Edith Coleridge, op. cit. ii. 235.   [2] Ibid. ii. 276-7.

more ruddy comeliness about her than I expected . . . [She has] nice, clear, light grey, open eyes and a comfortable, chatty manner. Her countenance is strong, but expresses power without genius, enthusiasm, or refinement.' Sara did not find Mrs. Gaskell particularly interesting—'She has sweet expression, [and is] good looking, but with no elegance of form or face.' Joanna Baillie, whom she thought the only poetess of her day furnishing 'the genuine article from her brain-warehouse',[1] Sara saw frequently. She recognized Miss Baillie's loss of creative power in old age, but admired her nevertheless. 'Our great poetess,' Sara wrote to Miss Trevenen in 1833,

or rather the sensible, amiable old lady that *was* a great poetess thirty years ago, is still in full preservation, as to health. . . . Yet if the authoress of 'Plays on the Passions' does not now write or talk like a poetess, she *looks* like one, and *is* a piece of poetry in herself. Never was old age more lovely and interesting; the face, the dress, the quiet, subdued motions, the silver hair, the calm *in-looking* eye, the pale, yet not unhealthy skin, all are in harmony; this is winter with its own peculiar loveliness of snows and paler sunshine; no forced flowers or fruits to form an unnatural contrast with the general air of the prospect.[2]

Sara often attended the social functions given by the Wedgwoods, and she was particularly fond of Erasmus Darwin, who occasionally accompanied her to art exhibitions. 'He is', she remarked, 'a most pleasing man, a grandson of *the* Dr. Darwin, his name Erasmus too.' She knew Severn, the artist, and greatly admired his pictures of Keats and Byron. She once met Francis Newman, the theologian's brother. She recorded her impression of Francis Newman in a letter to Aubrey de Vere:

He seems to me from all I have read, heard, or seen of him, his brother on a somewhat smaller scale. He has the same sort of countenance and manner, which is not shy or taciturn yet essentially reserved; all that is said seems meted out beforehand so far as it is to go, and no farther; the smile is sweet yet seems too intentional. I like more overflow and self-abandonment to the subject of discourse; but then I was bred up amongst poets, who

[1] Ibid. i. 128. [2] Ibid. i. 61–2.

are enthusiastic, overflowing people for the most part, and let their thoughts run away with them now and then, as the dish ran away with the spoon.

For John Gibson Lockhart, who took over the editorship of the *Quarterly* after John Taylor Coleridge resigned as editor in 1825, she had the greatest personal esteem. 'You can't think', she once wrote to Mary, her sister-in-law,

how Lockhart reminded me of the ghost of Hamlet's father—what with his stately figure, his fine cast of features, his white hair, pallid thin face, and extreme stillness and taciturnity and high reserve, he might act 'the buried majesty of Denmark' with nothing done to him.

She read with great pleasure Lockhart's *Life of Scott*.

Of John Murray, her first publisher, and the publisher of her father's *Christabel* and the *Table Talk*, Sara was particularly fond during her early married life. The Murrays used to call frequently at their cottage in Hampstead, and John Murray generously gave her a good many of the books he published. Moxon, whose wife Emma was the adopted daughter of Charles and Mary Lamb, Sara numbered among her closest friends. He supplied Sara with books, encouraged her in editorial labours, and in every way performed the offices of a good friend as well as of a business associate.

During the time when Sara was editing her father's works she saw a good deal of Henry Crabb Robinson, but she was not entirely pleased with him. 'Mr. H. C. R.', she noted in her diary,

with all his talent and quickness appears to me very ignorant and ill informed on some points as to men and things and books—as to what is really contained in them. He talks so much that he cannot take in aught from others—he reads very much on one side and praises up to the skies whatever echoes his own preconceived notions.

Henry Taylor, author of *Philip Van Artevelde* and an admirer of her father, was on terms of friendly intimacy with Sara Coleridge. From him she borrowed books, and he frequently enlightened her on political subjects. One suspects, for instance, that the clarity of her remarks in *Essays on His Own*

Times about Ireland and the poor laws may have been partly due to information gathered from Taylor. 'Mr. Henry Taylor', she wrote in 1847,

was kind enough to sit part of an evening with me lately. . . . From him I obtained more notion of the objections to the government outdoor relief measure for Ireland than I had derived from any other informant. I still hope that some good may come from the proposed change and interference.

Aubrey de Vere was the warmest friend of Sara's widowhood, but the story of her relations with him belongs to her personal rather than her intellectual life. De Vere did, however, afford her a clear and sympathetic view of the Anglo-Catholic Movement. His final acceptance of Roman Catholicism was, of course, a great disappointment to her. She knew Keble, 'who has a sweeter countenance than I thought he had', and she heard Newman preach at Oxford. William Dodsworth, one of the lesser leaders among the Anglo-Catholics who turned to Rome after the Gorham judgement in 1851, she often heard preach at Christ Church, St. Pancras, London, and with him she engaged in a spirited correspondence on theological problems. He apparently read her *Essay on Rationalism* with some disfavour, for there is preserved an immense letter to him. Only the first paragraph need be included here:

I feel truly obliged to you for reasoning with me on what I have written; you will permit me to explain why I cannot think your arguments conclusive against the views I have ventured to put forth, but you must be pleased to recollect that my motive for arguing is, and has been, the desire to vindicate not my Father only, but all who think with him on the points in question: that I have never dreamed of winning over to his theology those who have deliberately adopted a different one.

Dodsworth occasionally quoted from Coleridge in his sermons. 'This respectful tone about my Father of course gratifies me', Sara wrote: 'and I fancy that Dodsworth's writing less party-spiritedly than Newman about reason may in some measure proceed from his greater congeniality with the mind of S. T. C.'

To J. C. Hare and F. D. Maurice, two of her father's most devoted disciples, Sara was strongly drawn. After Coleridge's death Green assigned the task of editing the theological works to Hare and Sterling; they wished immediately 'to start with a volume of theology, containing amongst other things six letters on Inspiration'. Sara and Henry, however, persevered in their attempt 'to widen Coleridge's public first', by works less controversial in nature, and Hare and Sterling apparently withdrew. In 1840 Henry published *The Confessions of an Inquiring Spirit*, the volume being reissued nine years later by Sara. Though Hare did not edit any of Coleridge's works, he made a thorough study of Coleridge's indebtedness to Schelling, and Sara found him of invaluable assistance in her editorial labours. She paid him the highest tribute by dedicating *Essays on His Own Times* to him, 'in token of her grateful sense of his affectionate reverence for the name and memory' of Coleridge. Maurice, as the leader of the Broad Church Movement, seemed to her the 'most vigorous' writer 'to be found at the present day among the youthful race of theologians'. She thought his views 'completely based' upon the writings of Coleridge, but, she remarked, 'this takes nothing from his merit; every writer takes a foundation from some preceding one'. In one of his letters Maurice expressed his deep sense of obligation to Coleridge, a sentiment almost coincident with Hare's opinion:

I am a very indifferent critic about any work of Mr. Coleridge's, as I can never divest myself of a feeling of peculiar obligation and reverence which attaches to anything he says, even when my judgment happens to disagree with it. I hope his contemporaries will be duly grateful to you for your editorial labour, but I do not think they can feel what we of the younger generation do, whose minds have been in a great degree formed by his writings.

J. H. Green's association with Sara had begun even before Coleridge's death. Later, as co-workers on behalf of Coleridge's posthumous reputation, they saw much of one another. Green, in choosing for himself the editing of the philosophical remains, had selected the most difficult task, and Sara readily forgave him for lack of co-operation or for delay. There were times, however, when she disagreed rather strenuously with him. Concerning his views of baptism, she once re-marked:

Green attempts to disjoin me from my father on this point, which is very shabby in the extreme. I shall point out to him, that if he objects to my Anti-High-Churchism on this point he may *object to S. T. C.* unless he can shew that I go beyond his warrant, which I am sure he can not.

At another time she complained bitterly of having

to fight the S. T. C. battle *alone*—every one of my name is against me. Derwent *will* not agree with me. He will not. He must have a view of his *own*. I do not pretend to a view of my own. But it is plain enough both Green and he are not well pleased that I should be the Guardian of my Father's doctrine. Whatever view I take—*that* will not be the view they patronize.

Towards Green, of whose unchanging devotion to Coleridge there was never any question, however, Sara retained a warm affection; and she endeavoured to show her appreciation of his almost filial regard for her father by dedicating to him, 'the approved friend of Coleridge', her edition of *Notes upon Shakespeare*.

2. AMERICAN ASSOCIATIONS

Several articles have been written about Coleridge's influ-ence in America,[1] but the actual part played by Sara Cole-ridge has not been fully investigated. Coleridge had been strongly drawn to America and her institutions. As a young man he evolved (in conjunction with Southey) the Pantiso-cratic scheme, which called for emigration to the banks of the Susquehanna River. More than a decade later he wrote a glowing eulogy of George Washington for the *Courier*. One of his most beloved friends in middle life was the Ameri-can painter, Washington Allston. He saw clearly the danger of discord among the States of the Union; 'the Union', he declared, 'will be shaken almost to dislocation whenever a very serious question between the states arises'; and he looked

[1] See Alice Snyder, 'American Comments on Coleridge a Century Ago', in *Coleridge: Studies by Several Hands*, ed. by Blunden and Griggs, 1934, 201 f. In a footnote on p. 201 Miss Snyder lists the important studies concerned with Coleridge's influence in America.

upon 'the states as splendid masses to be used, by and by, in the composition of two or three great governments'.[1] But Americans, though they read and admired *The Friend* and *Table Talk*, were not concerned with Coleridge's political ideas. It was his poetry, his criticism, and particularly his theology with which they were engrossed. Because of the lack of any copyright agreement, Coleridge's works frequently appeared in America in pirated editions, but in some cases the editors communicated with Coleridge or with his heirs. In 1829 the Rev. James Marsh, President of the University of Vermont, wrote to Coleridge at great length; Marsh explained that he had issued an American edition of the *Aids to Reflection* and that he had added a preliminary essay by way of explanation. The peculiar state of theology in America, Marsh insisted, made necessary a special introduction to the *Aids*. Five years later John Wheeler, also of the University of Vermont, wrote to Gillman of American issues of *The Friend* and the *Lay Sermons*, and inquired about the publication of Coleridge's posthumous works. In 1839 Marsh wrote enthusiastically to Henry Nelson Coleridge, declaring that not only Coleridge's works, but those of Hartley and Sara as well, were then widely read in America; a year later he declared that Coleridge's 'views indeed are taught . . . in all our colleges and theological schools'.

Marsh belonged to the liberal tradition and stood in much the same position as Maurice; Dr. John McVickar of Columbia College, New York, championed the High Church Movement and in 1839 went so far as to issue a separate edition of the *Aids* along with an introductory essay refuting Marsh. Both Marsh and McVickar communicated their views to Henry Nelson Coleridge, who endeavoured not to give patronage to either party, but his sympathies lay with Marsh, and it is significant that Marsh's preliminary essay was included in the 1839 edition of the *Aids*.

Henry Reed, Professor of English in the University of Pennsylvania, was a devoted student of both Coleridge and Wordsworth. Not particularly interested in Coleridgean metaphysics, he gave special attention to the poetry. In 1836

[1] *Specimens of the Table Talk of . . . S. T. Coleridge*, ii. 100.

he wrote to Hartley Coleridge, sending a critical article which he had published on Hartley's poems, and speaking of his proposed edition of Wordsworth's poetry. Reed went on to declare that he was indebted, 'both intellectually and morally', more deeply to Coleridge than to any other author. In 1843 George Allen (of the University of Delaware) sent a description and eulogy of Reed to Henry. 'If I wished to give you', he wrote, 'the best impression of the best class of men from this our too democratic Republic I would send you Mr. Reed.' Allen told Henry that Reed bought everything bearing the name of Coleridge and that only recently Reed had sent him *Pretty Lessons*, *Six Months*, and Derwent's *Sermons*. In 1849 Reed applied to Sara for permission to publish an edition of Coleridge's poems, explaining that he wished to have any financial remuneration payable to the Coleridge heirs. Sara gave him the permission he sought, but graciously insisted that the Coleridge heirs did not expect any pecuniary advantage from American publications.

Much of the correspondence between Reed and Sara Coleridge has survived. Reed wrote of his editorial work. He sent her such things as his edition of Gray and his review of the *Wordsworth Memoirs*, and an intellectual correspondence sprung up between them. He once sent her the first edition of *Descriptive Sketches*, the very copy, indeed, which Dorothy Wordsworth had given to Coleridge and which Reed had bought at a sale. Sara wrote at great length on literary matters and prepared innumerable notes on his memoir of Gray. In 1851 she sent Reed a large engraving of Wilkie's portrait of Hartley Coleridge as a child. Reed had earlier found a great likeness of his son to the engraving of this portrait in Derwent's *Memoir and Poems of Hartley Coleridge*. 'When I received my copy of Hartley Coleridge's Poems', Reed wrote to her,

we were startled . . . by the likeness in it [the engraving] to our little boy—a child of five years of age. It was observed, without my pointing it out, by the different members of the family and others to whom the print was shewn. It is in the eyes and eye-brows—and there the coincidence of expression is truly remark-able. The resemblance again struck my eye yesterday as the little fellow stood before me—with an expression a little more pensive than common as he was musing under a maternal remonstrance at some excess of playfulness he had been indulging in.

Knowing how much Reed valued Hartley's poetry, Sara once wrote to him:

Seldom has a poet had so poetical a son as S.T.C. had in Hartley. Not one poet of this age beside, has transmitted a spark of his fire to his offspring; but it is curious that Hartley excelled most in the sonnet, in which my father excelled least of all the poetic forms that he attempted.[1]

Not long before she died, in one of the last letters she wrote, Sara bade Henry Reed farewell. After telling him of her malady, she added, 'Farewell, my dear Sir, . . . I *may* not be able to answer any more letters from America—a land in which I shall never cease to take an interest—but I shall ever hear with pleasure of you and yours, as long as my powers of thought remain'.[2]

Reed never had the privilege of meeting Sara Coleridge, but in 1854 he visited England. He perished, as someone reported, 'in the Arctic on his return from a pilgrimage to the graves of Sara Coleridge and William Wordsworth'.

Another American correspondent was Ellis Yarnall of Philadelphia, whom Sara had met in 1850. Reed had given Yarnall a letter of introduction to Sara, and Yarnall, after his return to America, wrote frequently to her. He said much of American customs and scenery. In many ways he deplored the lack of culture in America, but he was also enthusiastic about his own country. On July 2, 1851, after telling Sara that his perusal of her edition of the *Biographia Literaria* made him the more proud to have known her, he launched into a description of his visit to Wisconsin. He succeeded in arousing Sara's curiosity, for upon receiving his letter she hunted for the places he mentioned on a map. 'This is a part of our country', Yarnall wrote,

necessarily cut off from intercourse with the busy world. . . . The London 'Guardian' of June 11th has just been handed to me. . . . The Railways . . . enable us to whirl off a thousand miles or so whenever we are disposed. From Chicago at the foot of Lake Michigan one will shortly be able to travel in 48 hours to New

[1] Edith Coleridge, op. cit. ii. 378.   [2] Ibid. ii. 466.

York. Already that distance is travelled in the shortest time that any other like space on the face of the earth can be gone over. The last 3 years in the U.S. has been a period of prosperity and progress quite unexampled. . . . The fertility of the soil and the energy of the people are of course the two great sources of our national wealth. Slavery, over a great portion of our Country has, however, a most depressing and injurious influence. . . . For this great evil no man living can be said to be responsible nor has any one yet been found wise enough to propose a plan at all practicable for its removal.

A few months later Yarnall wrote again. He had acquired the Gillies' portrait of Wordsworth (painted at Rydal Mount in 1839) and he was delighted with it. He wished particularly to learn Sara's opinion of the portrait. Yarnall went on to speak of the *Memoir* of Hartley Coleridge. He thought Derwent had done 'his work in a masterly way. I doubt whether there is in modern English literature a more interesting biography. . . . I felt almost as if I had known him, and I closed the book with a saddened heart as if it was the record of the life of a familiar friend.' He told Sara of a forthcoming American reprint of the book—

a wide circle of readers will thus be obtained, but there will be no return of the sort which authors certainly are entitled to—Alas for the absence of international copyright!

From literary matters Yarnall turned again to his country for a subject. 'We are on the whole', he confided,

a well governed people and there is great security of life and property here, and there is prosperity unbounded, and continual growth. We are without your vexatious difficulties in the conveyance of land, and we are freed from many old-time abuses. But we lack a correct taste in literature, and a learned atmosphere around our colleges—we have neither fellowships nor cloistral shades. You speak kindly of what you call our refinement without conventionality, and of our having books and of the fair face of Nature which is spread before us. You wish we had more pictures by the old imaginative masters—heartily do I echo this.

On another occasion Yarnall undertook to explain to Sara the origin of the American Thanksgiving Day:

This is Thanksgiving Day—a Puritan festival, instituted in New

187

England as a substitute for Christmas which the sad fanaticism
of the 'Pilgrims' led them to refuse to observe, and so large has
been the influence of that part of the country on the rest that in
nearly all of the States the Day is set apart by annual proclama-
tion of the Governor of each, for special observance; . . . business
everywhere is suspended and churches are filled in the mornings
as if it was Sunday—and surely as a people we have cause to be
thankful.

Yarnall possessed excellent powers of description and his
pictures of America must have proved very illuminating to
Sara. As a final example of his letters, let us cite another
passage from the letter written on Thanksgiving Day, November 27, 1851.

[Several years ago] I ascended the Mississippi as far as the
Falls of St. Anthony—a voyage from St. Louis of 800 miles. From
Prairie du Chien to the Falls, a distance of 300 miles, the country
on both sides of the river was in the possession of the Indians—the
Chippeways on one bank and the Sioux on the other. Civilization
had not yet taken away from the region its beauty and peculiar
charm; all was solemn and still—the river clear and placid flow-
ing at its 'own sweet will.' It is not, you know, until the Missouri
rushes into it that the Mississippi becomes turbid and rapid in its
course. . . . The rich . . . calm of the river as you go northward,
contrasts strangely with the boiling mud of the stream as it
descends toward the gulf. . . . At the time of which I speak there
was a greater charm about it [the Upper Mississippi] than there
is now: the occasional Indian canoe, or the Indian villages with
their strange groups of blanketed red men, women, and children
—their gravity and silence—all this can no longer be seen. The
land has been purchased of these tribes by the U.S. Government
and our hardy western immigrants are fast peopling it—the
territory of Minnesota will soon be the 32nd of the United States.

Yarnall's letters were of great interest to Sara, and she
answered them as well as she could; but she confessed that
the labour of writing to her American friends seriously taxed
her rapidly waning strength. She must have been flattered,
however, by the downright admiration shown to her by
both Yarnall and Reed.

The pilgrimage of many Americans to Coleridge's grave at
Highgate afforded Sara definite evidence of her father's

reputation in America, and Mrs. Bancroft, wife of the American Ambassador, once reported to her the tremendous popularity of Coleridge in America. Emerson, who had been somewhat disappointed when he met Coleridge, returned to England in 1848 and Sara was introduced to him. 'Whatever his writings may be,' she recorded,

and I have not that clear feeling about them, that they are truly religious, that I have about Carlyle's, . . . he is himself a very pleasing person. A smiling intelligence and quiet simplicity are the characteristics of his face. He is as little like an American, except in accent, as Carlyle is like a Scotchman, except in accent. We talked of the different Constitutions of our country and his. When I urged the advantages of our limited monarchy, the greater freedom, which he admitted, and the absence of those defects which amateur republicans impute to all monarchies, he only said the question was whether our state arrangements did not *cost too much*.

Sara did not like Emerson's writings as she did Carlyle's and she thought him 'clearly a *Pantheist* in the irreligious sense'. Mr. Bancroft, the American Minister, however, insisted otherwise:

[He] told me of an Essay of . . . [Emerson's] . . . on the over mind [Oversoul], which proves that he believes in a Supreme Mind and Moral Being to which the mind of man owes homage and allegiance. I am very glad to hear this. The fewer clever, high-minded, and thinking men [who] are Pantheists, the better; and that Emerson has very noble sentiments cannot be doubted from the impression he makes on persons who are themselves of no vulgar cast of mind.

3. LETTERS AND JOURNALS

When Edith Coleridge's *Memoir and Letters of Sara Coleridge* appeared in 1873 there was an enthusiastic round of applause from the reviews. The work was apparently widely read, since four editions appeared within a year. While certain reviewers deplored the fact that Edith had seen fit to exclude almost everything of a personal nature from the volumes, thus stressing the mind and thought rather than the character and temperament of her mother, and while other reviewers found Sara's combination of Tory politics, Broad Church theology, and disciplined critical views somewhat unpalatable, they were unanimous in praising the forceful, intelligent, and occasionally epigrammatic way in which Sara wrote. The mass of unpublished letters still extant not only strengthens the effect of Edith's publication but also adds the picture of a charming and lovable personality. Partly because she lived in a day when there was less visiting between friends separated by more than a few miles, and partly because ill health often shut her off from social intercourse, she wrote innumerable letters. She corresponded regularly with John Taylor Coleridge, especially after Henry's death, as well as with her brothers and Mrs. Derwent Coleridge. She wrote occasionally to the Wordsworths, the Southeys, and other friends in the Lake Country. She kept up a correspondence with a number of acquaintances living in or near London. Her letters are written with ease and unaffectedness, but with even greater prolixity and diffuseness than her formal writing. Unlike her father she did not wear her heart on her sleeve, nor did she reveal, like her brother Hartley, a self-condemning conscience; but she was always truthful, frank, and unassuming. To her less personal friends she wrote with more reserve. Her letters form, indeed, a remarkable commentary on her generation. They touch on almost every subject. The strong intellectual note which runs through all of them was due to her dedication of herself to learning. She discussed the theological obscurities of the Oxford Movement, the philosophy of the German metaphysicians, or the political theories of her father with the same ease with which most women of her day wrote of their domestic affairs, the dress of their friends, and the activities of their social circles. She loved controversy and thoroughly indulged in it; she seldom disciplined herself, frequently wandering far from the subject at hand; and she had a great fondness for figurative language. In spite of these faults, however, her letters are stimulating, and sprinkled through them are many passages worthy of quotation. Along with Sara's letters mention should be made of her diaries. Here she wrote even more intimately. Let us examine a few passages from her letters and journals, in order to gain some further insight into her mind and character. Speaking of the effect of children upon their parents, Sara remarks of her son at nineteen years of age:

Herbert is in full bloom now. What an interesting age is his, . . . how full of perfection in one way—of promise in another. Yet like all bright things of earth it inspires melancholy in the thoughtful mind, except so far as we are cheered by faith. For the second spring which it is given to us parents to enjoy seems to pass more rapidly than the first, and there is no other in expectation. Grandchildren are not our second selves as children are.

In the early days of her widowhood Sara wrote of Edith:

I often think of dear departed Aunt's remark on her—'the most elegant little girl in her motions I ever beheld'. She certainly has that charm. As I enter the mouth of the gully [near Margate] she bounds down it and is gone to the bottom and far far on to the edge of the receding sea over sand and black seaweed, as if by a *single impulse,* like a bounding ball, or as a swallow sweeps the sky all at once within a certain sphere. Her form is solid, but her *run* is swift, smooth, and buoyant, as if she were made of cork, and her little body is full of lithe vigour and easy strength.

Sara was always sensitive to the external world, and she frequently pauses to describe natural beauty. She wrote to Edward Quillinan that she would be delighted to see him, 'before you go back to the land of lights and shadows, whence you so seldom emerge into the glare of London'. Struck one evening by the peculiar effect of the moonlight, she wrote in her journal:

The moon's bright crescent shown in the pale serene above a large bank of soft blue cloudage broken into vultures' heads and bold projections; the waters were bluish grey. Swansdown clouds shaded as with Indian ink overhead. The sky above the eastern horizon—yellowish rose colour among the clouds.

On the subject of poor relations, a state which Sara understood only too well, we may expect a keen observation:

The stinginess toward certain poor relations and silence respecting them shews that their poverty, like pitch, clings to those who let it come too close to them, and where it clings, [defiles?] and darkens.

She thought the shopkeepers of London rather vulgar people. Once at Broadstairs she lived in rooms just below a middle-class family on vacation. Delighted with the sea and the general surroundings, she found her fellow boarders intolerable, the undisciplined children being especially annoying:

Yesterday afternoon I began to think it went quite beyond bounds, and all my self-remindings that I had loud-voiced chatterers of my own, did not bring me to feel complacently on the subject of so much rattling up and down stairs, incessant slamming of doors, and squeaking and squabbling. . . . Their 'pa' and 'ma' keep a shop in Oxford Street; and now that I am able to make some calm, disinterested philosophic reflections on all that I have observed in this family, I am confirmed in my old opinion that the inferior London shop-keepers are an ill-managing class. I *suspect*, at least, (I will not venture to say more), that they have more luxury with less in proportion of real respectability, that they partake more of the *civilization* of their times with less of the *cultivation*, than almost any other portion of the community. . . . The extravagance and recklessness that go on in the families of tradesmen in London is beyond what the rank above them even dream of. . . . They represent the *bad* spirit of this age more completely than almost any other large class amongst us; but, I believe, they are to be pitied more than blamed, having great temptations to all they do amiss.[1]

Sara's attitude towards the lower classes was hardly democratic, and she deplored Harriet Martineau's attempts to teach them political science.

[Miss Martineau] wants women and children and the lower classes to pursue her favourite study—a study that of all others demands matured intellect and general information and a man's knowledge of society for its basis! . . . I would have a poor man read the Bible and go to Church as much . . . as he can, because he will thereby learn what concerns him even more than his worldly business, what he is daily and hourly called upon to practice, and what no one else can do for him. For my own part, the more I read on this subject, the more I see that I can't possibly understand it, and that it is entirely out of the way of my experiences and reflections and the topics that naturally present themselves to a woman's mind; and if the ploughmen and [those?] who hold forth on Political Economy had even advanced as far

---

[1] Edith Coleridge, op. cit. i. 311–13.

as myself in general information, they would see their ignorance as clearly.

Sara did not possess her father's comprehensive understanding of the scientific controversies of the early nineteenth century, but she did not fail to observe the advancement of science. Her love of flowers led her to master the elements of botany, and when the *Bridgewater Treatises* appeared in 1834, she enjoyed particularly Roget's essay, 'On Animal and Vegetable Physiology'. She was less pleased with Thomas Chalmers's article, 'On the Adaptation of External Nature to the Moral and Intellectual Constitution of Man', and gave full vent to her love of figurative language in commenting upon the method of argument:

And, oh! when the wordy Doctor does get hold of an argument, what a sputter does he make with it for dozens of pages. He is like a child with a new wax doll, he hugs it, kisses it, holds it up to be admired, makes its eyes open and shut, puts it on a pink gown, puts it on a blue gown, ties it on a yellow sash; then pretends to take it to task, chatters at it, shakes it, and whips it; tells it not to be so proud of its fine false ringlets, which can all be cut off in a minute, then takes it into favour again; and at last, to the relief of all the company, puts it to bed.[1]

Sara prided herself upon her truthfulness, and one is constantly struck by her downright honesty. She did not flatter her literary relatives and friends by undue praise of their writings. Concerning her honesty she once wrote to Aubrey de Vere:

What you say of my sincerity is but just. I remember Hartley saying emphatically, and with a grave look, that I was *very truthful*. This was true then—and is still true now. A love of truth has grown with my growth. But I am too truthful to pretend that I can tell my friends always and on all subjects the *whole* truth, and all at once. I tell them nothing but the truth, and from the character of what is said, discerning persons will soon feel the general estimate made of them.

In speaking of a sketch of Henry Nelson Coleridge in

[1] Ibid. i. 169.

Moultrie's *Dream of Life*, she showed an astonishing open-mindedness:

> But you will want to know . . . whether I am satisfied or dissatisfied . . . with what is said of my Treasure in Heaven. Well, I will say frankly that, though the sketch is true as far as it goes, I think that *comparatively with his college compeers* my Henry's powers of mind and literary genius were higher than Mr. Moultrie has ranked them. High *creative* powers are not possessed by Macaulay —were not, I think, by Praed—To Henry they are expressly denied in the Poem; and again it is expressly said or at least intimated that his was *not* a profound mind. Very true—but I doubt whether his mind possessed less original power upon the whole, . . . than most of his contemporaries at Cambridge. A profound mind in the sense that my Father's was profound, is not commonly found even among the highly gifted of the age.

The same fundamental sincerity led Sara to denounce Landor's unfair treatment of Coleridge and Wordsworth in his dialogue between Southey and Porson in *Imaginary Conversations*:

> S. T. C. is also brought in for to be knocked down—a witticism of his misinterpreted (as to the feeling through which it was conceived and uttered) and moreover misquoted—a sting added to the gay insect and its wings torn off. My Father never said that Southey's verses *sound* like dumb bells, but that such verses as some of his (though the application to my Uncle was only in private) bore the same relation to metre that dumb bells do to music—both being for exercise and pretty severe too. A saying of which Landor would have been proud enough, had he said it; and *I* say, who shouldn't say, that it is a specimen of pure wit.

She had but little toleration for most of the adverse literary criticism then appearing in magazines:

> Very few people will take the pains to censure a work unless they are moved to do so by some evil motive or stimulus: by self-love, jealousy, pride, or positiveness. Literary censure like poetical advice, admonition, and reproof, is too often a mere void or venting spleen, anguish-overbearing temper, which seeks to keep down and stifle all expressions of opinions contrary to their own.

Ill health quite naturally received much comment by Sara Coleridge. When she learned that the tumour in her right breast was in reality a cancerous growth, she noted pathetically in her journal: 'Thus a shadow is cast over my life which I must seek to convert into spiritual sunshine. Heaven should open up on me as earth closes. I pray that it may be so! My dear dear children!' Her physical condition influenced even her reading. *The Scarlet Letter*, she wrote:

is striking, but I think unnatural, and too full of unrelieved gloom and perturbation to suit my present *sere and yellow leaf* taste. We begin to look for brightness without when the light within us is waning.

Sara Coleridge was not only an excellent judge of people, but she was articulate in descriptive power. Her description of Mary Lamb and Dorothy Wordsworth, for example, gives a pretty clear picture of both women:

I see that Mary Lamb is dead. She departed, eighty-two years old on May 20. She had survived her mind in great measure, but much of the *heart* remained. Her mental decay was far less sad and unpleasing than poor Miss Wordsworth's; it was a dulness of the faculties, but no unhappy moral symptom was exhibited. Perhaps her nature was more faultless; indeed I believe this to have been the case. She had a very pure, perfectly sweet, meek, humble, unselfish nature; in dear Miss Wordsworth great good qualities and high intelligence kept down or made up for, or neutralized (while her mind was sound) much that was faulty and unpleasing; she would have been selfish always, but for the counter-action of warm affections and a fine understanding. Miss Lamb had a very fine feeling for literature and was refined in mind though homely, almost coarse, in personal habits. Her departure is an escape out of prison to her sweet soul more especially; to put off the clay of the flesh must be to the sanest an escape from a body of death.

Although Sara was not an artist herself, she was as fond of commenting upon art as she was of criticizing literature, and her letters are sprinkled with numerous comments on painting. She disagreed with Ruskin's insistence upon truth in artistic representation. The painter, she said, sought to produce in the spectator a strong emotion, not a full consciousness of the various details in the scene depicted. She admired Turner, but not to the extent of disparaging the work of Poussin and Claude. She often discussed portraits.

Here she tended to analyse the character and personality of the subject. Thus, for example, she wrote of a portrait of Byron:

I regaled my eyes as usual on that grand portrait of Lord Byron. What a seeming *ideal* it is—What a noble air it has in the head and neck and the manner in which they rest on the shoulders. If the poetry that came out of this Poet Lord had been of as high an order as that which rested upon him, he would have taken a permanent first rank. As it is, his portrait is a better poem, I think, than any contained in his books.

Sara was more at home in speaking of literature. Commenting upon Hartley's prose style, she wrote:

in Hartley . . . there are occasional eccentricities of thought, which borrowing a soft peculiar hue from neighbouring perfections harmonize in some measure the whole, and hardly appear like blots, but which if looked at in themselves are the irregular offshoots of weakness.

Lamb was a great favourite with her, and though in general she did not give evidence of a sense of humour, his irrepressible wit delighted her. She once noted in her journals a story some one had seen in one of Lamb's letters:

W. W. [Wordsworth] has just been here and says he could write as well as Milton if *he had a mind*. So you see it is only the mind that makes the difference.[1]

4. REVIEWS

In 1848 Sara wrote two reviews for the *Quarterly*. John Taylor Coleridge suggested that she should undertake a review of Tennyson's *Princess*,[2] and though she was engaged in a translation of the *Agamemnon* of Aeschylus she accepted the task. Her negative opinion of the *Princess* as a work of genius led her to write a review of an 'intermediate cast', and as such displeasing to Tennyson's detractors and admirers alike.

---

[1] The gist of this quotation is contained in a letter to Manning in E. V. Lucas's edition of the *Lamb Letters* (ii. 51), but Wordsworth speaks of Shakespeare, not of Milton. 'Wordsworth, the great poet, is coming to town, . . . He says he does not see much difficulty in writing like Shakspeare, if he had a mind to try it. It is clear, then, nothing is wanting but the mind' (Feb. 26, 1808).   [2] *Quarterly Review*, lxxxii (Mar. 1848).

But the remuneration of twenty-five guineas was more than she expected, and she considered it 'money easily earned. I wish I could make as much for all of the same sort of thing that I write in a year.' Thus she readily acceded to Lockhart's request for a review of Dyce's *Beaumont and Fletcher*.[1] She set earnestly to work, not only examined the volumes from a scholarly point of view but also read critically every play in the edition, and submitted a long critique of ninety-nine pages to Lockhart.[2] The published review was, of course, reduced in length, but Sara recognized that this time the money was not easily earned, for she gave weeks of almost uninterrupted labour to the task. She felt, indeed, her shortcomings as a reviewer:

I have by nature no review-writing qualifications. I cannot easily adapt myself to place and occasion. I am carried away by my *subject*, and cannot help going too deep into it, and travelling too widely all about it, into all its inmost recesses and round all its extensive environs. I ought either to think less, or to have more executive and *arrangeative* power. My father hardly ever wrote for reviews. He could not brook interference with his productions which it would have subjected him to.

Elsewhere Sara is even more explicit:

They who write for a Review ought to let the Review speak with and through them—ought to look on it as an individual having its own character to keep up, its own conscience, opinions, responsibilities, need of consistency,—not as a mere dead receptacle for various essays of various thinkers. The fault has been . . . that the Review has been a mere weathercock . . . or an automaton through whose mouth persons of most opposite opinions on politics, poetry, religion, literature, ventriloquized.

5. LITERARY CRITICISM

But it is time to speak of Sara Coleridge's literary criticism *per se*. At the outset it is necessary to remark that, except for these two reviews and one or two critiques in manuscript, Sara never attempted formal criticism. We have, therefore, to examine her letters and journals, in the hope of finding in

[1] Ibid., lxxxiii (Sept. 1848).
[2] For a fuller examination of both these reviews see pp. 207–10.

her desultory remarks, thrown out at random over a period of twenty years, evidences of a critical system or, at least, of principles and consistency of opinion. Such a task is not an easy one. Sara seldom thought it necessary to express more than her personal reactions to what she read, and yet, when all her remarks are pieced together, there emerges a considerable body of literary criticism. From Coleridge, Southey, and Wordsworth she gained a certain perspective in critical judgement at an early age, and her later comments are really elaborations and extensions of her youthful opinions. We are justified, therefore, in considering her criticism as a whole, instead of carefully examining it year by year.

As a young woman Sara began a course of religious reading which took her over a vast territory, from the Bible and the early Church Fathers, through the tangled controversies of the Reformation, down to the multifarious tracts, essays, and disquisitions of the Oxford and Broad Church Movements. But this reading was seldom for literary purposes; it arose from both intellectual curiosity and a truly Coleridgean preoccupation with divine truth. Of far more importance in an estimate of Sara as a critic are her scholarly interests in the classics and foreign literatures. At an early age she studied Latin, Greek, German, French, Spanish, and Italian literature, not so much for pleasure as for self-development. When Herbert began the study of Greek, she became his best teacher, and throughout his years at the University she read Greek with him. Only two or three years prior to her death she remarks that she and Herbert are enjoying the *Phaedo* together. She possessed, therefore, an extensive acquaintance with both ancient and modern literature. In writing of what she read, she was fond of comparisons between authors, and her wide reading developed a toleration for all kinds of literature and a remarkably catholic judgement. She could appreciate the excellence of authors as diverse, for example, as Dryden and Wordsworth, or Jane Austen and Scott.

Not only was Sara Coleridge an extensive reader; she was also a careful one. Her acquaintance with foreign languages made her sensitive to matters of diction, expression,

and style. She read and criticized Elizabeth Barrett's translation of *Prometheus Bound* with the eye of an amateur philologist.
She noted innumerable examples of faulty diction in Keats's
Endymion and praised the pure English of Sidney's *Arcadia*.
She thought Wordsworth's alterations in his early poems
infelicitous and considered Landor's *Gebir* an example of the
impossibility of catching the classical spirit merely by imitating the form.

Inasmuch as Sara was so absorbed with the mind and
teaching of her father, she accepted in part his critical conclusions. She once remarked, in speaking of Jeffrey as the arbiter
of taste and criticism in the early nineteenth century, that
the principles expressed in the *Biographia Literaria* would still
be accepted long after Jeffrey and the reviews were turned to
dust. She resented, as we have noted, John Wilson's calling
Wordsworth 'Coleridge's master', for though she ranked
Wordsworth next to Shakespeare and Milton, she believed
her father's poetic genius to have been highly independent
and individualized. She insisted that just as Coleridge's
religious thought greatly influenced the theologians of her
day, so he 'was in great measure the head and founder . . . of
the Shelley-Keats-Tennyson school in the more sensuous part
of his poetry; but . . . he combined more of the intellectual
with this vein than his successors'. Her inborn reticence, her
feminine reserve, and her regard for convention led her to
question the outspoken, sensuous nature of certain of her
father's poems. She once confessed that she had never placed
Coleridge's poems in the hands of her daughter, and she said
she would not think of reading the poetry of Coleridge aloud
in the company of Aubrey de Vere, as she had done the
poetry of Wordsworth.

It was but natural that Sara should have adopted from the
Biographia Literaria the theory of imagination and the closely
allied idea of organic unity. 'Mrs. Hemans', she wrote to her
husband, 'takes a theme, and this she illustrates in fifty
different ways, the verses being like so many wafers—the
same thing in blue, green, red, yellow. She takes descriptions
from books of natural history or travel, puts them into verse,
and appends a sentiment or a moral, like the large bead of

a rosary at the end of several white ones. But all these
materials have undergone no fusion in the crucible of
imagination.'[1] Keats, she felt, lacked solidity—'his path is
all flowers, and leads to nothing but flowers'.[2] The third
stanza of the *Ode on a Grecian Urn* she disliked; it 'is stuff of
fancy, not of the higher *imagination*'.[3] The perceptive aspect
of imagination she found lacking in *Endymion*. '[Keats] turns
the outer world into a sort of raree show, and combines
shapes and colours as fantastically and lawlessly as the
kaleidoscope. . . . Reading the Endymion is like roaming in
a forest of giant jonquils.'[4] She remarked that the later
poems of Wordsworth 'have more *fancy* [than his earlier
ones], but surely not more imagination, latent or patent'.[5]
Dryden's imagination she considered one-sided; it 'was fertile
and energetic rather than grand or subtle'.[6] Sara probably
did not perceive, any more than her contemporaries did, the
psychological implications of her father's distinction between
imagination and fancy; she preferred rather to consider
imagination as the fusing power of the poet's mind, the soul
of poetry. When properly functioning, the imagination
harmonized the varied representations of nature, breathed
into them the spirit of truth, and held in order the creative
faculties. Goethe's *Faust*, she believed, lacked totality of
impression; it was not 'a symmetrical whole, but a dual
consisting of two halves',[7] despite the author's attempt to
give it unity. 'Shakespeare's judgement was commensurate
with his genius', Coleridge had affirmed. Sara believed this
true of all great works of art; thus the earlier odes of Wordsworth are '*organic* wholes; . . . [The *Immortality Ode*] is in some
sort an image of the individual spirit of which it is an efflux'.[8]

Coleridge's *Biographia Literaria*, then, gave Sara a fundamental principle for the criticism of poetry, but it was a
principle to be imposed only by one who possessed a rare
sensitivity to beauty. The theory of imagination stripped of
its philosophical and psychological implications might have

[1] Edith Coleridge, op. cit. i. 161–2.
[2] Ibid. i. 339.   [3] Ibid. i. 339.   [4] Ibid. i. 343.
[5] Ibid, ii. 37–8.   [6] Ibid. i. 80.   [7] Ibid. i. 192.
[8] Ibid. ii. 409.

become an excuse for arbitrary and prejudiced judgements; for Sara it was a constant reminder of the high pretensions of poetry. In spite of her severe censures, she was passionately fond of the poetry of Keats; likewise she enjoyed the work of her lesser contemporaries; but she always maintained that the ultimate test lay deeper than mere enjoyment and sensuous gratification. Nor was this all. She could not accept, it is true, the senses as exclusive guides in matters of poetic excellence; in the same manner, she refused to permit the intellect and moral nature to assume control. Thus the sacred poetry of Keble, despite its author's high sincerity, cannot take a high place in literature. She preferred Crashaw to Herbert and Vaughan, because his 'sacred poetry [is] more truly poetical than any other except Milton'. Miss Barrett's *Seraphim* failed, she thought, in its attempt to describe Heaven; Milton and Dante alone could treat such a subject successfully.

On the question of the relation of form to matter Sara accepted her father's insistence that they were essentially one. She did not ignore, however, the obvious necessity of separating them for purposes of critical analysis. The poetry of her friend Aubrey de Vere, for instance, however much she might like it for personal reasons, was lacking in power of expression. To a young friend, to whom she later sent a long letter on prosody,[1] she wrote, 'Poetry is more of an *art* than people in general think. . . . They imagine that Poetry must flow forth spontaneously, like the breath which we breathe, without volition or consciousness. . . . Art alone will do nothing, but it improves and educes the natural gift.'[2] She scolded a young friend for 'uneven numbers' and criticized the hexameters of Longfellow's *Evangeline*. She constantly complained about Mrs. Browning's poetical defects and unpleasing prosody:

She has more poetic genius than any other woman living [in 1851],—perhaps more than any woman ever shewed before, except Sappho. Still there is an imperfectness in what she produces; in many passages the expressions are very faulty,—the images forced and untrue,—the sentiments exaggerated, and the

[1] Ibid. ii. 131–4.   [2] Ibid. i. 307–8.

situations unnatural and unpleasant. Another pervading fault of Mrs. Browning's poetry is rugged, harsh versification, with imperfect rhymes, and altogether that want of art in the department of metre, which prevents the language from being an unobstructive medium for the thought. Verse and diction are the bodily organism of poetry; this body ought to be soft, bright, lovely, carrying with it an influence and impression of delightfulness, yet not challenging attention by itself. These defects in poetical organism are inimical to the enduring life of the poetry; the same or similar thoughts will reappear in better form, and so supersede the earlier version; whereas, if poetic thoughts are once bodied to perfection, they will remain and exclude all future rivals. There is fear with regard to many of our present producers of poetry, lest the good that is in them should be swamped by the inferior matter, which gives a grotesque air to their compositions at large.[1]

So much for the insistence on technique in poetry. Sara was equally convinced of the high spiritual function of poetry. She questioned Wordsworth's reading of Nature in the *Prelude*; surely, she argued, Nature was not the only moral teacher of the poet. She preferred the poems of Crabbe to Tennyson's *Dora* and like poems, because 'Crabbe's tales were all taken from real life. But this "Dora" is a poet's dream. Crabbe's people say strong things—not just what the poet would have them say. Tennyson's Farmer becomes very soft all at once—and William says on his death-bed just what dying men . . . seldom say—but what people imagine in such a case, when they make it all very fine for their own edification and amusement.' Beyond this kind of realism, however, Sara Coleridge asked that the poet should 'see life steadily and see it whole'. She would have accepted Matthew Arnold's definition of poetry as a 'criticism of life'. She condemned the didactic tendencies in modern poetry, but she could not forbear passing moral judgement on Byron. His 'imaginary personages . . . are not reprehensible for that they represent men as worthy to be admired in spite of great vices, but because they tend to produce admiration of the very vices themselves,—to detach it from virtue altogether, and place it on inferior objects. . . . Such representations are essentially mean and worthless'.[2]

[1] Edith Coleridge, op. cit. ii. 447–8.   [2] Ibid. ii. 199.

Thus far we have been concerned with certain criteria or principles inherent in Sara Coleridge's remarks, and certainly this is as far as we may safely go in setting up a critical system. We can, however, see something of the nature and breadth of her critical powers by a brief examination of some of her conclusions; and we shall be able to appraise the consistency of her opinions, the limitations of her intellectual outlook, and the acceptability of her criticism in terms of modern scholarship. Let us begin with the four topics on which she wrote at length: a comparison of the relative merits of Dante and Milton, a subject with which she frequently dealt in her letters; an examination of the poetry of Wordsworth; and the two reviews, previously mentioned, one of Tennyson's *Princess* and one of Dyce's edition of Beaumont and Fletcher.

Sara Coleridge greatly preferred Milton to Dante, agreeing with her father that the character of Satan was 'deeply philosophical, as well as poetically sublime in the very highest degree'.[1] She felt that one might rightly condemn the characterization 'in reference to a high pure philosophical Christianity', but it should be considered 'poetically and dramatically'. If one is to grant 'the very idea of a personal evil Being, the adversary of God', then surely Milton's creation of Satan is sublime. The fault, theologically considered, lay 'in the gross idolistic system' to which Milton adhered. Dante's Lucifer, she found, had 'all that contrariety to reason which you find in Milton's "Satan", without one particle of the sublimity. He is a fallen angel too, but every bit of the angel is well done out of him, and how he ever could have been aught of the kind is inconceivable'.[2] The whole of the *Inferno*, she declared, 'treats of disembodied spirits, not angelic beings that may have a *kind* of bodies merely, but *souls divested of their bodies*, yet to these Dante assigns corporeal pains, and every attribute of matter'. Turning to the *Paradiso*, she found Dante's representations of the Deity 'in general not so deroga-

[1] Edith Coleridge, op. cit. ii. 89. For Sara's comparison of Milton and Dante see ii. 83–94.
[2] It is worth noting, perhaps, that Sara Coleridge's remarks concerning the anthropomorphism of Milton and Dante are directed less against the poets than against the 'Antiquarian High Churchman'.

tory as Milton's', and less 'broad and bold', but withal 'most insipid and fatiguing'. She admired Dante in his 'plainer part'. The description of 'old *Graffiacane* with a grappling-hook in his hand [was done] to the very life'; but she preferred less the sweetnesses in the *Paradiso*—'he makes a baby of himself too much beside Beatrice, it puts one in mind of Gulliver and Glumdalclitch'. Although Sara rated the *Inferno* above the other parts of the *Divina Commedia*, she contrasted Dante's utter lack of a 'genial, expansive tenderness of soul', with Milton's 'sympathy with human nature, with fallen finite nature'. There was in Dante too much 'triumphant delight and horrid mirth' over the tortures of his sufferers, too much 'spitefulness' in his work. She found Dante's poem 'least abounding in grace, and loveliness, and splendour' of all the world's greatest poems. Nothing in it, she maintained, could compare with 'the address to Venus at the beginning of Lucretius' great poem', and Goethe's *Faust* has many passages more 'brightly beautiful'. Sara Coleridge in her judgement of Dante was unable to disentangle successfully his poetry and philosophy from his theology, which she thoroughly detested; and there was a strain of tenderness in her nature, amounting almost to sentimentality at times, that made her reject the awful justice of Dante's sublime poem.

In her estimate of Wordsworth Sara was much sounder. Believing as she did that his poetry carried a message of profound truth, and a solidity lacking in Keats and Shelley, she found much in his work to uplift and 'to chasten and subdue'. In youth she accepted Wordsworth as a matter of course; during the distressing years of her engagement she turned to him for solace and comfort, especially to his *White Doe of Rylstone*, the heroine of which endured sufferings so like her own; in middle life she watched with deep satisfaction his growing influence and popularity, climaxed by the laureate-ship in 1843; and as she lay dying she examined Christopher Wordsworth's *Memoirs*, enjoying the picture drawn therein of the poet, but deploring the uncritical nature of the work and resenting the editor's treatment of Coleridge and obscuration of herself and Hartley. She brought to her analysis of

Wordsworth a sympathetic and personal understanding. Her letters are filled with allusions to his poetry, and on one or two occasions she treated it at length. She preferred his early poems, and she rated the *Prelude* higher than the *Excursion*. She endeavoured to rank his shorter poems in order of merit. Among 'the meditative strains, sedate in character, and in which solemnity and tenderness mutually succeed or flow into each other',[1] she placed *Tintern Abbey* and the *Old Cumberland Beggar* first; among the 'lyrical compositions, more rapt and fervid than the former, and equally exalted in spirit', she chose the *Immortality Ode* and the *Song at the Feast of Brougham Castle*; among the elegiac poems, she placed *Peele Castle* and *Laodamia*, though she considered neither equal to those cited above; among the 'poems containing some history or incident', she selected *The Leech-gatherer*, with *The Female Vagrant* and *The Brothers—Michael* gets only third place; among the 'poems, reflective and pathetic', she thought *The Two April Mornings* and *The Fountain* the best; among the 'poems of sentiment, imaginatively presented, distinguished by exquisiteness of expression, in which the language seems more especially one with the thought, or inseparably incorporated with it', she chose *Three Years She Grew in Sun and Shower*, *The Highland Girl*, *To H.C.*, *Six Years Old*, and others. From these classifications she went on to mention the lighter poems (*The Cuckoo*), those of reflection (*The Gypsies*), the descriptive poems (*Yew Trees*), and 'poems of the ballad character' (*Lucy Gray*). The sonnets are kept in a class by themselves, and she selects as the best *I Am Not One*, *Earth Has Not Anything*, *Lady*, *the Songs of Spring*, and the *World Is Too Much With Us*. This table of Wordsworth's poetry is of great interest as showing the fine sensitiveness of Sara's mind. It is accompanied by a good many miscellaneous notes on certain poems. The table concludes with a group of later poems, of which *Lines on a Portrait*, *On the Longest Day*, and *The Triad* receive special mention.

Laodamia and *The Triad* Sara commented upon in some detail. In the former she observed 'both a coarseness and a

[1] Edith Coleridge, op. cit. ii. 39. The classification and ranking of Wordsworth's poems will be found on pp. 38–52.

puerility in the design and the sentiments'.[1] She went on to declare that 'in this poem Mr. Wordsworth wilfully divested himself of every tender and delicate feeling in the contemplation of the wife and the woman, for the sake of a few grand declamatory stanzas, which he knew not else how to make occasion for'.[2] She could find no true moral in the poem, felt that Wordsworth coarsened Laodamia's character, and compared the poem with *She was a Phantom of Delight*. *The Triad*, though Sara was herself eulogized in it, she considered second-rate—

It is just what he came into the poetical world to condemn, and both by practice and theory to supplant. It is, to my mind, *artificial* and *unreal*. . . . The poem always strikes me as a mongrel—an amphibious thing, neither portrait nor ideal, but an ambiguous cross between the two. Mr. de Vere, before he knew me, took it for a personification of Faith, Hope, and Charity, taken in inverse order—a sufficient proof, I think, that it is extravagant and unnatural as a description of three young ladies of the nineteenth century.[3]

In a critique on Wordsworth's *Lines Left Upon a Seat in a Yew-tree* Sara wrote more at length and possibly for publication.[4] In the *Quarterly Review* for November 1837 there appeared a review of the Wordsworth poems of 1836 and 1837, and her essay is in the main an objection to certain remarks of the reviewer upon the *Yew-tree Seat*. Insisting that 'in Wordsworth as in Shakespeare and every truly great and popular poet there is a something which the understanding alone will not recognize, and which may be felt by persons of very little power and compass of thought', she believed a person like herself might 'enter into the spirit of certain poetical compositions more fully than some who are greatly . . . superior in power of mind'. Therewith she turned to berate the reviewer, who had questioned the applicability to the general reader of the moral lesson on pride which concludes the poem. 'In addressing one whose heart has been kept pure by the holy forms of young imagination' Wordsworth, she declared, did not mean some one eminently

---

[1] Edith Coleridge, op. cit. ii. 53.   [2] Ibid. ii. 55.
[3] Ibid. ii. 410.   [4] No such published critique has come to light.

endowed. 'Imaginativeness', she insisted, 'can hardly be called an uncommon quality, and more or less of Imagination belongs to all.' She supported her contention that Wordsworth's appeal in the *Yew-tree Seat* was an elevating lesson for all readers, by referring to his address to Dorothy in *Tintern Abbey*, and by noting his emphasis on 'the inestimable privileges of our early years . . . [as] . . . the source of perpetual benedictions' in the *Immortality Ode*. She then proceeded to analyse the *Yew-tree Seat*, defending Wordsworth's condemnation of pride and contempt. She went on to quote Biblical authority for compassionate sorrow rather than contempt for fallen humanity, and the latter part of her essay is mainly devoted to a digression on moral goodness rather than to Wordsworth's poem. The concluding sentence, however, deserves quotation:

The Philosophy of Mr. Wordsworth's poetry is not a plan independent of though reconcilable with Christianity; to me it seems to be Christianity itself—the truths expressed or understood in the Gospel, illustrated by Imagination, the process by which the nature of man is refined and glorified, 'brought up into daylight', or made [noble?] by poetical symbols.

The critique illustrates, indeed, the merits and weaknesses of Sara Coleridge as a literary critic. She brought to her reading of Wordsworth a sympathetic and understanding mind, a sensitive imagination, and an acute perception of poetic truth, and these she put to work; but she allowed herself to digress, lost herself in a maze of secondary inquiries, and gave way to her ever-present preoccupation with religious questions. One must give her credit, however, for independent judgement. Devoted as she was to Wordsworth, she followed him, as she did her father, only when her intellect led in the same direction.

Sara Coleridge's review of Tennyson's *Princess* in the *Quarterly Review* for March 1848 opens with a long discussion on poetical temperament. Sara maintains that 'poetic genius is as truly a distinct gift as a mathematical, a pictorial, or a musical genius',[1] and goes on to insist that poetical power is 'stimulated by that condition of the body which belongs to

---

[1] *Quarterly Review*, lxxxii. 433.

youth when it is adult rather than adolescent, or what is called, in reference to corporeal advantages, the prime of life'.[1] This conclusion leads her to define 'what has been called "the school of Sensation rather than Reflection"',[2] to which the *Princess* supposedly belonged, and to show the connexions of the school with the poetry of Coleridge, Words-worth, and Shelley.

Sara in speaking of Tennyson comments on his popu-larity, which was far greater than Shelley's. She grants to Tennyson imagination and a command of diction, says he excels Shelley in liveliness and variety, but lags behind Shelley in 'force of imagination and clearness of expression, and . . . sustained dignity and refinement'.[3] She cites several examples to show that Tennyson was wanting 'in the *art* of numbers'. She uses *Locksley Hall* to show that Tennyson's excellence lies in presenting moods and sentiments rather than in describing trains of thought, and she deprecates the 'lavish gorgeousness' of the vision of the world in that poem.

Turning to the *Princess*, Sara classifies it as 'a fantastic metrical romance' and gives a brief résumé of the story. The moral of the tale, she says, 'is a truth which has been known and acted on ever since Adam received a helpmate, not to do his work, but other work he could not do; the single truth that woman, in soul as in body, is no duplicate of man, but the complement of his being; that her sphere of action is not commensurate or parallel with his, but lies within it, sending its soft influence throughout his wider range, so that the two have an undivided interest in the whole'.[4] After this remark Sara makes an analysis of the character of Princess Ida, the heroine of the tale; 'she is a modified, civilised Diana, who has not quite the heart to slay Actaeon outright, but hunts him a little way, and after he has undergone a proper quantity of mangling, takes him into favour, through pure compassion passing off (ut mos est) into love'.[5] Thus in succession Sara treats the various characters in the poem.

She remarks that 'the second title of this lively performance

---

[1] *Quarterly Review*, lxxxii. 433.   [2] Loc. cit. 435.   [3] Loc. cit. 436.
[4] Loc. cit. 442.   [5] Loc. cit. 443.

points out its principal defect; it is a *medley*, and, we must think, a somewhat incongruous one';[1] and she seriously questions whether the want of the supernatural 'in a tale so fanciful and impossible as "the Princess" ' is not a serious detriment. She proceeds, with copious extracts to prove her points, to discuss three minor defects in the poem: 'occasional absence of refinement, and failure of dignity and decorum'; an 'occasional want of clearness'; and an 'occasional want of truth in imagery and diction'.[2] To these she adds Tennyson's freedom with parts of speech, his profuseness (which she distinguishes from diffuseness), and his elaborate exaggeration. She concludes her review with the citation of passages distinguished for their beauty.

This review of *The Princess* is entirely in keeping with Sara's critical opinions. Despite her respect for Tennyson as a poet, she could not give him a place beside his immediate predecessors. Her review is somewhat rambling, but it appraises, none the less, the poem, without bitterness or sarcasm and with great perspicacity and poetic insight.

Sara's review of Dyce's edition of Beaumont and Fletcher in the *Quarterly Review* for September 1848 errs in being over-ambitious. In its original form it became almost a monograph; as eventually printed, it occupied nearly twenty-three pages of the *Quarterly*. She divides her remarks into five divisions. She begins by estimating Dyce's editorial labours, passes on to a consideration of the lives of Beaumont and Fletcher, gives a summary of her general opinions upon their dramas, examines briefly a number of the plays, and concludes with added praise of Dyce's textual emendations, restorations, and explanatory notes.[3] In her general criticism of the writings of Beaumont and Fletcher, she admits 'their high merits, which lovers of poetry appreciate, united with gross faults which every man of common sense can perceive',[4]

---

[1] Loc. cit. 445. [2] Loc. cit. 447–8.

[3] Throughout her review Sara alludes to George Darley's edition of Beaumont and Fletcher, which had appeared in 1840; in fact Darley's work as well as Dyce's is given at the head of her article.

[4] In a letter to a lady acquaintance Sara deals rather fully with the coarseness in Beaumont and Fletcher; she will 'by no means recommend to you such a study of B. and F. as would enable you to appreciate them fully, either as lyrical

and she is anxious to compare them with the works of Shake-speare and Ben Jonson.

That in a table of dramatic precedence they ought to rank above Ben Jonson we do not maintain: yet we can hardly admit that they ought to be placed altogether below him. . . . Admitting, as we freely do, that they were by no means as independent of . . . [Shakespeare] . . . as Jonson was, we must still maintain that they have a style of thought and conception—a peculiar ease and lightness—which distinguishes them from Shakspeare by a *positive* qualification; that they do not differ from him merely by wanting his elements of greatness. When they attempt the highest line of the drama, they fail from want of depth and intensity, as Jonson fails from want of emotion, tenderness, and grace.[1]

She finds them better in comedy or tragi-comedy than in tragedy, and she uses Schlegel for authority. She regrets particularly 'the unholy natures, the evil intermixtures in these otherwise delightful dramas', and longs for the day when there would be no more delight 'in the vivid representation of wicked affections, of envy, hatred, malice, revenge. . . . Poetry can never be more or less than the glorified shadow of our humanity: such as we are in the imaginations of the heart, such are the materials with which the poet has to deal.'[2]

Turning from these four topics let us examine her conclusions about her poetical contemporaries, the prose writers of her day, and early nineteenth-century fiction. Of the contemporary poets she preferred Joanna Baillie, Mrs. Browning, Tennyson, and R. C. Trench, though she gave only qualified approval to most of them. Tennyson's early work disappointed her, and *In Memoriam* seemed to her marked by quaintness and violence rather than force, and she considered Shelley's *Adonais* far superior. For personal reasons she said a good deal about the poetry of her friends, Henry Taylor,

poets or as comedians'. Her own circumstances, she says, have been peculiar. 'My male friends and guardians have held that works of genius, even if they contain much evil, may always be read without injury by pure-minded persons, —that where there is a rich play of fancy, and the work is read for the sake of its good not of its evil, the mere knowledge of the latter is no real and substantial corrupter of the mind.'

[1] *Quarterly Review*, lxxxiii. 386–7.   [2] Ibid. 387–8.

Moultrie, and de Vere. She thought her brother Hartley's poems of a high order of merit. His *Prometheus* delighted her; 'it is distinguished amid the poetry . . . [of the day] . . . by its manly simplicity, freedom from affectation—nothing twisted in it—nothing obscure—but the whole a sweet flow of pure, clear verse'. Concerning Hartley's poems she said, 'I cannot believe that they will ever perish, with the poems of the day— What *are* good of them are so good and perfect'. She liked Hartley's originality; all his verses she considered 'simple, genuine, and independent of fashion', and she went on to add that 'some of the poetry of the present day will look fifty years hence as Sir T. Lawrence's portraits with short waists and giraffe heads do now'.

Sara was unimpressed by Landor and she relegated to secondary importance such minor poets as Letitia Landon, Mrs. Hemans, and the spasmodic writers, but she recognized the power of Beddoes's *Death's Jest Book*. She probably underestimated her contemporaries and she apparently did not read the poetry of either Browning or Arnold. She pre-ferred the romantics, and she constantly found her contem-poraries inferior to them. 'Keats and Shelley owe more to their immediate predecessors than they owe to any poets before them—. . . because Coleridge and Wordsworth were the first poets of this aera.' She thought Shelley more pro-found and more truly imaginative than Keats. She insisted that Shelley was an irreligious writer only in extreme youth, though some of his religious ideas displeased her. Keats, on the contrary, had no religion; 'that very deficiency, . . . which prevented him from being a *very* good man, . . . must, I think, for ever prevent him from taking the highest rank as a poet'.[1] She noticed an effeminacy in Keats's poetry and wrote with great scorn of the representation of Adonis in *Endymion*. Byron, she said, was always manly, but his lack of intellectual power and his immoral tendencies made his work of secondary significance. Sara's criticism of the English romantics shows insight and intelligence, and on the whole she was right. She saw clearly, for example, that Thomas Campbell would live, not for his pretentious *Pleasures of Hope* or *Gertrude of Wyoming*,

[1] Edith Coleridge, op. cit. ii. 271.

but for some of his shorter poems. She erred, perhaps, in the high praise she bestowed upon the work of both Crabbe and Joanna Baillie.

Of the mass of miscellaneous prose produced during her day Sara read mostly that of a theological temper. Newman she recognized as the spiritual no less than the literary leader of the Oxford Movement, and though she seriously questioned his conclusions and the means of reaching them, she felt the charm and dignity of his prose style. Carlyle the author of *Sartor Resartus*, *The French Revolution*, *Chartism*, *Past and Present*, and *Heroes and Hero-worship* she deeply admired, but she felt the loss of power and the exaggerated mannerisms in Carlyle the author of *Latter Day Pamphlets*. His declamatory style and his grotesque Germanic humour did not offend her, for she felt the sincerity of his spiritual message; but she laid her finger on his faults—'repetition, and the saying in a round-about, queer way, as if it were a novel announcement, what everybody knows, without any suggestion of a remedy for the evils he so vividly describes'.[1] In her first burst of enthusiasm for Carlyle, she was ready to support him against all comers and she insisted that the general direction of his works was moral and spiritual. She defended his idea of hero-worship, even to the extent of accepting Mirabeau, Voltaire, and Cromwell as heroes in the Carlylesque sense. Whatever deficiencies and frailties they may have had, she believed that Carlyle presented them as men whose intellectual gifts were dedicated to the benefit of humanity and who were instruments in the hands of divine providence. She thought Carlyle excelled as a biographer, and she was profoundly moved by his conception of history. She believed that he fought an honest fight against sham, hypocrisy, and cant. Yet she shrewdly observed that he was more original in manner than in matter. She rated him much above Macaulay, 'the Utilitarian and anti-spiritualist'. She greatly underestimated Landor, allowing the narrowness of his critical power and the severity of his style to warp her judgement. She read the *Bridgewater Treatises* and *Modern Painters* (the latter of which she considered eloquent but erroneous

[1] Edith Coleridge, op. cit. ii. 295.

in its principles), but she hardly mentions John Stuart Mill or the political writers of the day. She complained, indeed, of the political flavour of Harriet Martineau's tales; 'I wish Miss Martineau', she said, 'would let alone Political Economy and try to rival Miss Edgeworth, instead of stretching her genius on the rack of that difficult science'. She read several of the historians, thinking highly of Thomas Arnold and Henry Hallam. She enjoyed biography, especially when the subject was some one she had known. 'I cannot tell you in one short day, or the longest summer day', she wrote of Stanley's *Life of Arnold*, 'what I think and feel about . . . [it] . . . how I rejoice over it, how I glory in it, what good I augur from it.' Lockhart's *Scott* held a high place in her estimation, but she had no patience with those biographers who presented the most intimate details in the lives of Keats and Shelley.

Of the prose writers of the romantic era Sara had but little to say. She perceived the excellence of De Quincey's prose style. 'Hazlitt', she once remarked, 'is the only man that ever wrote like . . . [my father] . . . on some subjects', but she did not rank him highly. Concerning Leigh Hunt, who had 'vilified people of my Kith and Kin in a manner which I don't approve—any more than the Frenchmen did Wellington's conduct at Waterloo', she once asked, 'Why do I give a corner in my memory to such fungus-fibs, who have lived their little noisome hour and perished, or would have done so, were they not revived?' Charles Lamb held a high place in her estimation. She delighted in the *Essays of Elia* and was vexed and surprised to learn from Moxon in 1850 that Lamb's essays were no longer read; she agreed with Moxon that 'they must come into requisition again, . . . unless the world loses its sense of exquisite humour and pathos and good sense combined'. She believed that her father had contributed more than any one else to the thought of his day, and her prodigious labour in editing his work tended somewhat to restrict her reading of prose. She seems to have had less appreciation of prose than of poetry.

Throughout her life Sara read fiction, though she agreed with John Taylor Coleridge that 'novels take up far too much time in proportion to any good one gets from them to be satisfactory reading, except a few of the very best sort'. Beyond asking for a unified and convincing plot, clear and plausible characterization, and a freedom from vulgarity or subversive influence, she developed no critical theory of fiction, but most of the novels she discussed at length are still read to-day. Jane Austen was her favourite novelist— 'Hers is almost the only literary line in which women are not only unsurpassed by men, but in which they have done that which woman alone can do to perfection. Miss Austen's peculiarly feminine genius gives an especial charm and value to her writings'. Maria Edgeworth occasionally excelled in sublime passages, Sara wrote, 'but those Shakspearean tragic passages in her works are separated by dreary intervals sadly deficient in common novel interest'. Mrs. Trollope, on the other hand, 'deserves to lose her place in society almost for her novel falsities and impertinences . . . oh she is a "*coarse un*!!" as one of our Keswick cooks said of the poor old cat Rumpelstilzchen'. *Jane Eyre* Sara thought written by a man, and she was undisturbed by the ruggedness of *Shirley*. Lady Fullerton's once popular *Grantley Manor* disappointed her; she found the story dull and languid until the middle of the third volume, and 'the heroism and oft-repeated agonies . . . of the Romish heroine were . . . more wearying than affecting'.[1] T. H. Lister's *Granby* pleased her better and she was delighted with the ease of its prose style. Susan Ferrier and Mrs. Anne Marsh both enjoyed Sara's approval; the latter's *Admiral's Daughter* 'is one of the best Tales and the most deeply pathetic of the present day'. Sara was entranced by *Vanity Fair*. 'Thackeray', she wrote,

seems to me as clever almost in his way as Dickens, certainly as the author of *Jane Eyre*. . . . There are more fine *broad* effects in *Jane Eyre*, but for fine touches and conscious insight into life and human nature Thackeray stands as high as the other. Amelia in real life would be a bore and inspire contempt, but she makes capital situations and contrasts well with Becky.

Dickens's sense of humour and profound humanity won favour with Sara, and she was especially fond of *Pickwick*

[1] Edith Coleridge, op. cit. ii. 137.

Papers. She looked for truth in fiction and until late in life seems to have depreciated romantic novels. Not long before she died she turned back to Scott. Probably her increased infirmity and the proximity of her death lessened her hold on the present and led her to indulge in the rich romance of the Waverley Novels. Even then, however, she noted a lack of verisimilitude in characterization; 'Scott too often makes his heroines the mere author in petticoats.'

In her comments on the novels of her own day Sara seems to have had no idea of the technical development of fiction, nor did she appreciate the increasing use of the novel for sociological purposes. In general she thought such reading mere diversion. Certain novels profoundly affected her, it is true, but she preferred to think of fiction as a representation of life rather than as a criticism of life. In only one case, in her remarks upon Kingsley's *Alton Locke*, does she touch on the relationship of fiction and social conditions:

Alton Locke is a remarkable specimen of boldness and talent. It is truly poetic and its poetry of conception is of a high order. It is one of the productions which describe and produce the tremendous social change which Southey *saw* impending, and which we, who are in it, do not choose to see.

Enough evidence has been adduced to show that Sara Coleridge was not an impressionistic critic or an undisciplined thinker. Her limitations are pretty clear. She was so thoroughly a devotee of the romantics that she sometimes underestimated the poetry of her contemporaries. Her view of life was partly moulded by Victorian morality, and a feminine bias often interferes with her judgement. More than all this, her critical comments are too casual to be fitted into a system. Reading and criticizing the literary productions of her day was her diversion. We must not fail, however, to do justice to her. There is in her criticism an ever-prevalent right-mindedness, and with few exceptions her conclusions about her contemporaries agree remarkably well with present-day estimates. Her fault was understatement, not exaggeration. If she failed to recognize Browning, Tennyson, and Landor as we do to-day, at least she did not set up Letitia Landon, Hannah More, and Mrs. Hemans as leading figures.

Blue-stocking

Was it generally recognized that Mrs. Browning's poetry could hardly stand the test of time? What devotees of Wordsworth before Matthew Arnold's famous essay selected the accepted canon of Wordsworth's poetry from the mass of unsorted poems? Is it not remarkable that Sara Coleridge, tutored and, in large measure, reared by Robert Southey, had sufficient perspicacity to discern the mediocrity of his poetry? Had she been less intelligent and less independent in her critical judgements, she might have become merely an imitator of her father's and Wordsworth's principles and opinions. Hers was, indeed, a rare environment. The daughter of a poet, as a child nurtured and moulded by poets, and during her maturity accepted in the best literary circles of her day, Sara Coleridge enjoyed intellectual advantages seldom extended to any one; but she was an active participator in the affairs about her, not a passive spectator on the sidelines. Much as she reverenced her father and Wordsworth, much as she considered them the *ne plus ultra* among their contemporaries, she never worshipped them in slavish idolatry, never surrendered her own critical convictions to theirs. This sturdy self-reliance, combined with an inborn and refined sense of literary values, explains, perhaps, why she so often freed herself from the limitations and prejudices of her generation and why her critical estimates have so well stood the test of time.

X

LAST YEARS

HENRY NELSON COLERIDGE'S death in January 1843 cast Sara upon her own resources, and her unceasing intellectual application was in great measure an escape from desolation and loneliness. Edith, in speaking of her mother, remarks that Sara never really recovered from the shock of her husband's death; but she did not yield entirely to her grief. She found comfort 'in thinking that the anguish I have gone through . . . is probably the heaviest part of my earthly portion'.[1] All of her letters written at this time show strength, not weakness. 'I cannot afford to give way to grief,' she wrote to John,

as I should certainly have done on a lesser occasion. I have struggled and am still struggling, as for life. I have felt that if I did not convert all these recollections into something like happiness, they must enter like iron into my soul, and bring me to the grave, or worse, must make me my own living tomb. The struggle is its own reward, for it calls forth new energies, a new life in the mind. Nothing is hopeless except the stagnation of the spirit, when it lies passively a prey to vulture grief.

With such clear thinking as this, Sara was certain to overcome her suffering. Gradually she found repose of spirit, and as her daughter says, she was supported 'by that truly Christian resignation (not a passive but an active virtue) which led her to exert herself for the sake of others, and resist the natural tendency to brood over thoughts of grief'. But Henry remained present to her mind; every joy, every sorrow, she somehow shared with him; and ever afterward when she mentioned his name, she always spoke of him as 'my beloved Henry'.

Sara often spoke of her husband to Edith and Herbert— 'almost as if he were on a journey, or absent in another country'. As she became more reconciled to his death, she entered whole-heartedly into the plans and activities of her

[1] Edith Coleridge, op. cit. i. 268.

children. But there were times, too, when she mourned alone and regretted bitterly that Henry could not be present to rejoice in some special honour Herbert had won, or over Edith's progress in painting.

Sara regretted that her home in Chester Place was a house of mourning and she made every effort to provide a cheerful atmosphere for her children. She treasured 'every scrap of happiness' from the past and devoted herself to the well-being of those around her. During the summer of 1843 she took Herbert and Edith to Margate and Tunbridge Wells, that they might escape from the mournfulness of Chester Place. Then in October she visited Edward Coleridge at Eton. Edward wished her to have her portrait painted, before she advanced 'still further into the vale of a certain age', and accordingly George Richmond was commissioned to do the work. Richmond's portrait presents a beautiful woman, pensive rather than sad. The features are classic and regular; the eyes large and deep blue. The hair is still beautiful, and the complexion has not lost its dazzling fairness. There are no lines of age, nor evidences of sickness, save an almost ethereal expression. Richmond may have idealized his subject; but if he saw traces of age and pain in Sara's appearance, he subordinated them to the expression of her inward being. Years later, when Sara had her portrait painted by Laurence, she contrasted his work with Richmond's. Richmond she thought a more genial, mild, and popular man; Laurence had 'a severer cast of mind'.

When he is successful at all, his success is of a high order. He paints the mind. So indeed does Richmond, but Laurence sees the mind, I think, in a sterner way.

In her widowhood Sara found comfort in her many friendships. She did not mind being alone during the day, but in the evening, as she wrote:

I seem to crave a brightly-lighted room, and lively faces and animated conversation, both male and female. I crave it far more than I used to do, when I had such rich and perfect domestic enjoyment. Our evenings have a darksomeness about them. . . . I cannot now bear to live a quiet life—I want either society or brisk intellectual occupation to keep me from brooding.

Sara Coleridge in widowhood
From the portrait by George Richmond

She went out a good deal, and occasionally accepted invitations to spend a few weeks with friends living near London. We have already seen something of her relationship to the better known of her contemporaries and how easily she moved in intellectual circles. There were also more intimate friends —women with whom Sara exchanged frequent letters. But probably her most significant friendship during her widowhood was with Aubrey de Vere, an attractive Irish poet, twelve years her junior. Between Sara and de Vere there existed sympathetic understanding, mutual respect, and parallel intellectual interests. Each of them was absorbed with religious questions, and though eventually they travelled different roads, de Vere turning to the Roman Catholic communion, they talked and wrote constantly on theological questions. They shared, too, a love of poetry. De Vere's creative vein was deeper than hers. He cannot take his place among his major contemporaries, perhaps, but in his own day he was rather highly regarded as a poet. For Sara's taste and judgement he had the highest regard, and she dealt frankly with him. His friendship kindled to some extent her own creative ability, and among her papers is a notebook which begins:

My conversations with Mr. de Vere in the years 1843, 4, 5; our discussions of Wordsworth especially, re-excited my little, weak poetic faculty. The poems which were produced under this influence, I shall mark thus—*for A de Vere*—as they were sent to him in letters during our early correspondence.

De Vere's high spirits and healthy optimism were a constant inspiration to Sara and he kept her from dwelling morbidly on the past. His refreshing enthusiasm for Wordsworth and the romantics and his hearty partisanship of Tennyson stimulated her critical powers. She thought his praise of Shelley and Keats excessive, and her own comments upon them were in great measure due to attempts to answer him. Her efforts to rate Wordsworth's poems and her critiques of *Laodamia* and *The Triad* were contained in letters to de Vere. Thus he helped her to avoid the melancholy effect of undue introspection, a tendency which might have undermined her peace of mind, as it undoubtedly did Hartley's. Sara was herself conscious of the beneficial effects of de Vere's friendship; 'I have found', she wrote in 1846,

[de Vere's] conversation delightful. He lives as in a region of poetic thought, 'an unsubstantial faery place', outside the workyday world that to my weary, heavy spirit communion with him has ever been most soothing and refreshing and the more so as his poetry . . . does not prevent him from considering the realities of the life to come.

For Sara, however, de Vere's refusal to take life solemnly was not wholly satisfactory. She would not throw off the burden so easily, and certainly her store of grief and suffering had been greater than this. His superior intellectual gifts, she felt, should be dedicated to some high purpose, not wasted in play. 'As regards what he is to himself', she said in attempting to estimate him:

I cannot help agreeing with Mr. H. Taylor that he seems much too inclined to look on 'life's business as a summer mood', without or with very slight literary ambitions. . . . Perhaps a pair of bright eyes would do more to persuade him into a profession—than the highest thoughts.

Warm as this friendship for de Vere was, it never developed into love. Sara was too conscious of her own declining beauty to supply 'a pair of bright eyes'; she saw too clearly 'the shades of the prison house' to think of a new companionship; and more than all this, the divergency of their religious views gradually widened the gap between them. One poem of Sara's, however, is so filled with feelings of what might have been that it may be included here:

DREAM-LOVE

The union of thy heart and mine,
Ah yes! I know 'tis all a dream:
For I am dark, in life's decline—
Round thee the noon-day splendours beam:
But let this fair tho' flickering gleam
Of fancied love one moment shine;
Thou mayst afford at least to seem
For one brief moment to be mine.

Haste not at once to break the spell—
Before thee is the long long day
With gayer hearts than mine to dwell,
In laughing meads far off to stray:
One little hour beside me stay,
And let the conscious dream go on;
E'en now the tears are on their way
To flood my cheeks when thou art gone.

More brightness than is wholly thine
Will vanish with thy last adieu,
For whilst I dream that thou art mine
It seems my youth is with me too;
My glittering youth thy looks renew,
That turn'd on me so brightly beam,
As if from mine fresh light they drew—
Of light and love is all my dream.

Can dream-light to the soul be dear?
Ah! who would weep 'mid light of day,
To see the meteors disappear,
'The cold phosphoric fires decay'?
But when my dream-light fades away
What darkness will my soul invade?—
For sunshine or the moon's mild ray
One mass of cheerless, starless shade.

Fade phantom dream-light, full of strife,
Oh fade before that serious mien,
Which, kind and warm as day and life,
Is e'en as painless death serene.
The storm-clouds 'mid the radiance keen
Of Heav'n's deep vault how lost are they!—
So might I 'mid the azure sheen
Of that pure spirit melt away!

At first Sara and de Vere's religious differences seemed of
slight importance. Almost humorously she wrote in 1845 to
a friend about their conflicting notions of heaven.

Yesterday I told him that the views which he was setting forth,
in regard to the future world, the glorified body, and the new
heavens and earth, were . . . [like yours]. . . . *I* am much more *dry*,
alas! on these subjects. . . . *We* somehow fancy that we are to have
a quintessence of all that is exalted, and glowing, and beautiful,

in your new-world creed hereafter, only not in the same way. Mr. de Vere cannot bear to part with our human body altogether, nor with this beautiful earth with its glorious canopy. He wants to keep these things, but to have them unimaginably raised, and purified, and glorified! *I* think that *they* must go, but that all the loveliness, and majesty, and exquisiteness, are to be unimaginably extracted and enshrined in a new, unimaginable form, in another, and to us now, inconceivable state of existence. He said . . . 'But I want *this earth* to have a fair trial, to have it show what it can be at the best, in the highest perfection of which it is capable, which never has been yet manifested.'[1]

Beneath the surface, however, lay an insurmountable difference in opinion. Sara asked no beauty in her religion. She resented, for instance, the increase in church decoration. The poetical nature of Aubrey de Vere, however, yielded to the richness of the service. Intellectually, too, he felt drawn to Roman Catholicism. He disagreed with Sara's Protestant view of baptism and regeneration. But it was not until November 1851 that he finally joined the Church of Rome. Sara had long since recognized the inevitability of the step and graciously accepted it, but she rejected his attempts to convert her.

During the years of Sara's widowhood de Vere was deeply concerned with the destinies of his native Ireland. He supplied Sara with considerable information about actual conditions in Ireland, and it was in part due to conversations with him that she wrote in such detail of that country in her introduction to *Essays on His Own Times*.

De Vere's friendship for Hartley Coleridge also drew Sara to him. He held Hartley almost in reverence and always spoke of him as scarcely of this world. 'He might', de Vere once wrote, 'perhaps, have been more easily changed into an angel than into a simply strong man.'[2] After Hartley's death, it was de Vere who reviewed the *Poems* so sympathetically in the *Edinburgh Review*.

In the latter part of March 1843 Sara received news from the north of the death of Robert Southey. Unlike her husband's death, Southey's was 'a blessed change for him who

[1] Edith Coleridge, op. cit. i. 338–9.
[2] Aubrey de Vere, *Recollections*, 1897, 134.

is gone, and for survivors . . . what a relief'. She had never ceased to love and reverence her uncle, but his diseased mind during his last years lessened her grief over his passing. For the death of an older person, too, she was more prepared than for the untimely loss of her beloved husband. But she never forgot Robert Southey, who, during the unhappy years of her engagement, had so softened the trials of her youth. As she grew older, she realized, it is true, that Southey's literary powers were of a second-rate order; but to the end of her days she loved the humane and kindly protector of her girlhood.[1]

Regretfully she saw that even the death of Southey could not reconcile the estranged members of the Southey family. The seeds of dissension had been sown too deeply for that. She learned that at the funeral her cousins did not speak to one another, but stood apart in two groups, cherishing the affronts and hatreds of the last few years. Sara was powerless to interfere and could only deplore such unseemly behaviour. In her own immediate family, at least, there was always a spirit of harmony and co-operation.

Henry's death required of Sara not only the task of struggling alone with the editing of Coleridge's work but it also placed upon her the full responsibility for her two children. Herbert, under his uncle's tutelage at Eton, needed both affection and discipline; Edith, though still a child, needed training and companionship. At first, indeed, the children buoyed her spirits—'One cannot brood with children to care for'—but she had no knowledge of business affairs. Henry had given her a sheltered existence, and she herself admitted that she had never known the state of their finances, though she said she urged her husband to get out of debt as soon as possible. The utter dependency of her years at Greta Hall was never forgotten; it made her unduly cautious about expenses after her husband's death. John Taylor Coleridge

[1] In 1847 Sara's attitude towards her uncle was somewhat modified by her reading of his manuscript autobiography. 'There are some things in it', she wrote to Miss Fenwick, 'which I read with regret—some flings. . . . But alas! in my Uncle's later writings there were too many of these. It is a sore subject and lest in defence of the disparaged I should bring forward what might impeach the disparager's judgment and testimony against S. T. C.—I say no more.'

took a paternal interest in Sara's affairs and managed for her, but within two months after Henry's death she asked for a full statement of her finances, for she was determined to know what her annual income was and to live within it. Before his death Henry had loaned his brothers-in-law, Judge Patteson and Derwent Coleridge, rather large sums of money, but they seem to have looked lightly at their indebtedness, and Sara had to manage without repayment or even interest. She thought John Taylor Coleridge decidedly remiss in urging members of the family to repay her, and when she spoke to him of her financial worries, he jestingly told her not to fret. Even if you live a little beyond your income, he argued, you can borrow or use a portion of your capital. Sara wrote rather pitifully to Mary, her sister-in-law, that such an attitude was not very fair to a widow left alone in the world. Likewise there was no justification for William Hart Coleridge's conduct in paying in 'dribs and drabs' a bequest of £600 left to Sara by George May Coleridge, especially when she was in such desperate need.

At first Sara expected to have £650 per annum, but the failure of her debtors even to pay interest, as well as losses in railway investments, reduced her income considerably and she had to practise the severest economy. Herbert's education proved increasingly expensive. During the years at Eton Edward Coleridge generously paid his nephew's board and tuition, but Sara insisted on paying all miscellaneous expenses. When Herbert went up to Oxford, his expenses increased. Educating a son at the University, providing private instruction for Edith, and maintaining a home at a decent cultural level taxed, indeed, Sara's slender resources. She seriously considered moving from Chester Place to cheaper quarters, but she could not bear to cause discomfort to her aged mother or to deprive Edith of the wide circle of young friends living near by. She learned to manage on a meagre income and she managed well, but certainly her relatives took advantage of her and she found it necessary to concern herself constantly with expenses. Even during her fatal illness lack of money continued to haunt her.

Sara seldom bought any clothes for herself and she was

forced to have her old dresses altered for Edith, now growing
to womanhood. She thought Edith beautiful in one of these
gowns; 'it looked very handsome worn over a satin slip, one
of the relics of my smart married days'. Only a few months
before she died, she sent out her 'blue brocaded silk' to be
made up for Edith; it was, she said, 'my last piece of wife
finery, chosen by dear Henry'. She contrasted her widowhood
and its enforced shabbiness in dress, with her married life:

I sometimes smile to think what a peacock I should have gone
for the rest of my days had I kept my beloved. For he was one
who never thought that a woman could be well enough drest—
and would have gone on dressing me more and more the richer
he had grown. Never shall I forget his bursting into tears about
my dress—in his last illness—thinking that I should be too ill
drest if he did not regain health and power of working. But no
more of that theme of tears!

An additional source of financial loss came from the
publishers of Coleridge's works. After Henry's death Sara
had to reopen the entire publishing arrangement with Pickering. She knew only too well the circumstances, for she recalled her 'dear husband on his sick bed disturbed by this
man's grasping, narrow, unhandsome ways. How painfully
he dictated.' Henry had tried in vain to modify the original
agreement and obtain for the estate two-thirds rather than
one-half of the net profits. Sara was equally unsuccessful but
she did succeed in getting Pickering to cancel his five per cent.
commission on all copies sold. When she made the new
arrangement she also demanded half-yearly settlements from
him. The new terms were no more satisfactory than the old
ones. Pickering fell hopelessly behind in his payments, once
being as much as a year and a half in arrears, and as time
went on there was every reason to believe that he over-
charged for printing costs, thus making his own profits two-
thirds. Protests brought from him merely 'obstinate, sullen
silence', and Sara became convinced that 'great and unusual
dishonesty was practised' towards Coleridge's family. Derwent at length determined to interfere, Sara being too ill to
undertake the matter, and finally in 1851 Moxon purchased
the entire stock of Coleridge's works for £831, Pickering's

half-share in the stock. Thus after '23 years' connexion' the Coleridge family were released from the clutches of one whom Coleridge had humorously dubbed 'Pickle herring'.

Nor was Murray much better. 'Pickering', Sara wrote to Derwent's wife,

keeps us an entire year out of our money—and as for Murray, . . . I can get no account from him at all. I have asked him but once, but he takes his ease about the matter.

In 1850 she tried to get Murray to allow her to reissue the *Table Talk* under another publisher, but he, having bought the copyright for that work, would not agree.

Her children were, however, all she could ask. Her chubby little Edith bubbled over with enthusiasm and affection, making friends easily. 'Indeed,' Sara writes to Hartley,

she is altogether far better and far worse, and a different creature from me . . . I had the discipline of circumstances in my youth, . . . from which she has been quite exempt: no child can have grown up more at ease, with less pressure from *anxiety* of any kind. A keen sense of the infelicity which certain anxieties and constraints caused me in my childhood and girlhood, has made me careful to guard her from the like. . . . Though these fretting trials *may* be turned to good account, may strengthen the mind, and do certainly purchase considerateness and reflective habits, their direct tendency is to injure: all pain is injurious unless made otherwise by an effort of the will. . . . Edith is much liked. She is not nearly as timid and fearful of giving offence as I have ever been.

Edith was less studious than Herbert, but she was by no means lacking in intellectual curiosity. She did not possess, it is true, her brother's brilliant gifts. Sara held her to daily lessons. Edith once begged to postpone the study hour; Sara agreed, 'but', she writes,

I bargained that she should come back in a reasonable time and read a little Greek Testament. An ode of Horace she read with me this morning. She can translate Horace and Virgil pretty well and Homer a little. She is intelligent . . . but she is not studious, as I had begun to be at her age.

Sara's persistence was successful, for Edith was to become a genuinely learned woman.

Both for Sara's sake and her daughter's, John Taylor

Edith Coleridge

From the portrait by George Richmond

Coleridge suggested that Edith should be her mother's constant companion. Sara was wiser. 'As to having her *always*
with me,' she wrote,

I think this can never be and I doubt whether it ought to be.
All my life I have been accustomed to spend much of my time
alone—this loneliness I sought as by instinct; it was so with me
at Greta Hall, it was so at Hampstead, and it has been so since
I have lived here [at Regent's Park]. . . . If this was so in my
earlier life, how can it cease now [1846] when I am weaker than
ever? . . . Hitherto I always thought it desirable that Edith should
be part of her time at least in the company of girls. . . . It is certainly right that parents should form as much as possible a friendship with their children and seek mental association with them,
but it seems to me that their desire of this end and endeavour
after it should not be without its limits.

As Edith grew into a 'rosebud of seventeen' she became
her mother's confidante, and between them developed an
almost sisterly devotion. They travelled to the sea together
during the summers and they both enjoyed parties, balls, and
art galleries in London. Sara rejoiced 'in Edith's growing
seriousness':

it is so quiet, gradual, steady, and solid; not superficial but a habit
of mind interwoven with its main tissue. She is a most solid
reader.

They enjoyed the same circle of acquaintances, though
Herbert, handsome and gay, thought their friends 'seedy
and dull' and 'poked fun at the Barrett-Brownings'.

Sara read a good many novels with Edith and talked to
her on intellectual subjects. With the true instinct of a
mother, however, she was pathetically anxious for Edith to
be popular, and during the last years of her life, when she was
almost too ill to be away from home, she occasionally attended
social functions for Edith's sake. She once noted in her
journal: 'Edith danced as much as I could wish and even
had to refuse.'

Herbert 'in his tail coat begins to look like a slender young
man instead of a great boy', and Sara was especially pleased
that everyone 'who knows him best and with whom he has
most opened himself out has especially noticed to me his

affectionateness'. She thought his fondness for her as great as she had ever noted in a boy towards his mother. She was proud, too, of Herbert's handsome appearance and thought he looked like Byron. 'He reminds me a little at times at home,' she wrote,

when he wears his throat half open with a black tie carelessly put round his neck, of the youthful portraits of Lord Byron. . . . It is when Herbert throws up his face in a particular way that he looks so like Phillips' portrait of Lord Byron.

With his natural brilliance, Herbert not only swept Eton of every prize but also garnered every honour at Balliol College, Oxford, ultimately winning double first-class honours in 1852,[1] the very year of Sara's death. She proudly recorded in her journal in 1848:

Herby declared Newcastle Scholar, Saturday, April 8, 1848. Spring before at 16½ years he was Newcastle Medallist. In autumn of that year, 1847, got Prince Albert prize for Italian, and 2nd Balliol Scholarship. In same year he gained the 1st prize for best English Essay, a Life of Julius Caesar, which Dr. Hawtrey declared of unusual merit.

The Master of Balliol College praised him unstintingly and even *complimented* him on not being like his family'; three of his cousins, Derwent Junior, Edward's son, and Frank's son, all having been recently expelled from Oxford. 'So is our name fallen at Oxford!' Herbert limited his expenses, supplemented them by private tutoring, and only occasionally indulged in his special hobby, book-buying. He soon acquired a library of five hundred volumes, of which he was very proud. 'I have great reason', Sara wrote to Miss Trevenen, to be satisfied with his Balliol course so far. He has spent no money which he could avoid spending, has given clear, regular accounts of all his expenses, has written constantly and pleasantly, has been most commended by the Dons of the College, and seems to enjoy the Oxford life exceedingly.

She confessed, however, that he 'sometimes indulged in more Scandinavian literature than was absolutely necessary to

[1] 'He never actually graduated . . . because he could not conveniently afford it. He had inherited a small independent fortune, [on his mother's death] which, by the rules . . . would have raised the fees on his Bachelor's degree up to something near 100£.' Note by John Duke Coleridge.

Herbert Coleridge
From the portrait by George Richmond

comfortable existence'. Occasionally, too, he went 'a few times oftener to the Play and the Opera and . . . drank up with assistance of college friends a present of ale rather sooner' than she approved.

Herbert had the utmost confidence in his mother's learning and frequently consulted her about his studies. She admitted that she spent much time and effort in answering his inquiries, but she must have known that few mothers were capable of so assisting a son in college.

In many ways Mrs. Coleridge was an even greater responsibility to Sara than Edith and Herbert. Old age had crept up gradually on Mrs. Coleridge, but she remained fairly active until her death. She still retained a deep-seated, nervous fretfulness. Sara once observed that her mother's feelings are all good and simple-hearted, but from want of a sufficiently powerful intellectual or spiritual counterpoise, there is a 'disproportion in her soul,' 'a strife,' and little matters have acquired a morbid monstrosity in her imagination.

Mrs. Coleridge had, it is true, much to distress her, but she seemed destined to misunderstand, first Coleridge, and then Hartley. Maternal instinct explains, perhaps, her solicitude for Hartley, but it hardly justifies the kind of letters she wrote. She never seems to have realized that he had grown to man's estate—indeed, she never was able to understand her eldest born. Her letters are a strange mixture of genuine affection and ranting condemnation. One moment she makes inquiry about the state of his 'shirts, drawers, Trowzers, and coats'; the next she implores him to remember his name and station and to keep from alcoholic indulgence. She promises to pay his board for the next quarter, but complains about his disregard for her in an ecstasy of self-pity. Poor Hartley bore with her as best he could. She should be pitied rather than blamed; a good, honest, practical, and intelligent woman, she might have lived contentedly with a successful family; as it happened, she had the misfortune to marry a man of rare genius and to be the mother of 'the oddest of all God's creatures . . . [who] . . . becomes quainter and quainter every day'.[1]

[1] J. W. Warter, *Selections from the Letters of Robert Southey*, 1856, i. 311.

For one as sensitive as Sara Coleridge, her mother must have been a trial; and yet there remains no evidence of strained relations between them. Sara occasionally called her mother 'Frettikins', and she sometimes wished that 'your nerves were more tranquil and that you could care little about my *external* affairs'; after all, Sara said, the 'only things to grieve about for me are my widowhood and my weak health'. They were separated for more than a few weeks on only two occasions—when Sara paid her second visit to London in 1826, and during her first year of married life. She seems always to have soothed and comforted her mother. During their days of dependency at Greta Hall her calm and exemplary conduct did much to reconcile Mrs. Coleridge to their lot. With her engagement and marriage she unconsciously reunited her parents. No matter how much she suffered from her own ill health and disordered nerves or how trying Mrs. Coleridge's fits of despondency, Sara never scolded or upbraided her but always strove to view everything in a hopeful and pleasing light. Whatever her own feelings may have been, she minimized Hartley's waywardness and tactfully tried to persuade her mother to be less fretful about his shortcomings. Mrs. Coleridge, for her part, was a source of inestimable comfort to Sara. She helped to instruct the children and run the household, assuming full charge when Sara was ill. Her good sense and courage in the face of disaster helped Sara through the misery of Henry's illness and death. She was not, as Coleridge's defenders have frequently presented her, hopelessly ignorant and unintelligent, one whose sole interest lay in a secure existence. All five of the Fricker sisters, as a matter of fact, were self-respecting women. Edith, who married Southey, was until her mental affliction an ideal wife and mother; Mary, early left a widow on her husband's (Robert Lovell's) death, made every effort to be self-supporting; Eliza and Martha, both of whom were unmarried, eked out a slender livelihood and never became dependent upon their relatives, Martha leaving an estate of £500; and Mrs. Coleridge certainly possessed a sturdy self-reliance. The vicissitudes of fortune emphasized her weaknesses, but she was 'honest, simple, truthful, sincere,

just [and] generous in according praise where it was due'.
Sara confided to her journal:

> That excellent woman Mrs. Wordsworth was in one respect,
> far below my dear less talked of for excellence, Mother—she was
> not so honest. She does much to *appear* in the eyes of men to be
> good and wise and well regulated. Yes, she has a higher name
> but who except her spouse—will weep for her as a few wept for
> my poor mother when she died.

Thus for Sara, and for those who knew and loved her,
Mrs. Coleridge's death on September 24, 1845, came as a
distinct shock. Sara was visiting the Edward Coleridges at
Eton when it occurred. Only the day before Mrs. Coleridge
had written cheerfully, and though she had confided to the
nurse her premonition of death, no one could have anticipated her decease. She died suddenly of a heart attack, with
no interval of consciousness. Derwent, who was immediately
apprised of the news, rushed to Eton, to bear in person his
sad tidings. Sara did not collapse. She gave way to hysterical
weeping, it is true, but within a few hours was ready to return
to London. The circumstances of her mother's death were
particularly tragic to Sara:

> How strange it was that I should be absent from her at the last
> —after living all my life with her. . . . I left home but two weeks
> this year—and in one of those two weeks I lost her.

As Sara and Derwent drew up plans for the funeral, it
never occurred to them that Hartley might attend. When
Sara discovered that Hartley wished to come she was greatly
agitated. She feared that under the stress of emotion he would
indulge in strong drink, and she remembered with sadness
the Wordsworths' injunction '*never to induce* him to come to
London'. But she found it painful not to have him come.
She was to suffer still more on learning that Hartley received
the sad tidings at a time when Rydal Mount was temporarily
deserted and he could find immediately no one who had
known his mother. When all was over, and Mrs. Coleridge
had been laid to rest beside the remains of her husband in
the family vault at Highgate, Sara wrote at length to Hartley.
A few passages of her letter will show how deeply she felt the

loss of her mother; the letter was written in answer to Hartley's beautiful epistle of October 11, 1845.[1]

Dear Hartley, I always knew that you in some respects must suffer more from dearest mother's death than any of us. You are *alone*, and your long separation from her must make it very sad for you thus to be separated from her for ever, without seeing her once again. But upon the whole neither you nor D[erwent] can feel her loss hourly, I may almost say momently, as I do. I think the shock from the breaking up of old habit greater in this case, than when I lost my beloved husband. He contributed more to my enjoyments, my positive conscious happiness, but she was more bound up with my whole life, and with this house she was far more associated in my mind than he was. Then her death was to me perfectly sudden. Infirm and delicate as she was, I had woven gradually and as it were insensibly a chain, a network of reasons, for thinking that she was to live to a great old age. . . . I wish, however, to assure you, dear Hartley, that our beloved mother, though anxious every now and then, as you know, about what concerned you, and always longing for you to be *more in print*, had, in the main, very happy feelings about you—more so— I think, this last summer than ever. . . .

My dear mother's death seems to have thrown down another great barrier between me and the grave. My children cannot well spare me yet, but I feel a satisfaction in thinking that I am less strongly tied to earth than I was. . . . In her I have lost the one being who had common remembrances with myself of all my past life.

During her widowhood Sara kept what she called a death book, in which she recorded all that she could gather of the last days and funerals of those whom she loved. Like Christina Rossetti, Sara Coleridge had a somewhat morbid interest in death, an interest which a long series of bereavements tended to intensify. Already in 1845 she had lost three babies, father and mother, a beloved husband, and her Uncle Southey; during the few years she was to survive she had many other deaths to record. When she had got over the shock of her mother's death, she plied the faithful nurse for every detail of Mrs. Coleridge's last days, and in the death book the melancholy story is duly recorded.

[1] G. E. and E. L. Griggs, op. cit. 283–6.

Not long afterwards ominous tidings arrived from the north that Dora Wordsworth Quillinan was wasting away, a victim of the ravages of tuberculosis. Sara had always loved Wordsworth's vivacious daughter, although she confessed that in girlhood Dora preferred Edith Southey to herself; but during the long years of Hartley's unhappy exile in the Lake Country Sara was pleased by Dora's ever-present sympathy for poor Hartley. Dora, more than anyone at Rydal Mount, seems to have understood him. She loved him with that simple directness of her nature, and she was always ready to say a kind word in his favour. Sara, grateful for any generous judgements of her brother, drew closer to Dora than she had been in childhood.

In March 1847 Sara went down to Bath, to spend three weeks with the Wordsworths, who had left the north with the assurance that Dora was in no immediate danger. Sara found her old friends much altered and in great anxiety about their daughter. They were 'parentally affectionate' to Sara. She noted that

Wordsworth talks a good deal in the course of the day, in a slow and interrupted manner, but he never now talks continuously— never with the force and fire and freshness of his discourse in former days. . . . But he has much bodily vigour left and can walk above 8 miles without fatigue, though very apt to be bewildered and lose his way. . . . Dear Mrs. Wordsworth is wonderfully active, but looks frail and speaks with a faint voice.

In April, however, the Wordsworths were recalled to the north, and it became apparent that Dora could not recover. On May 25 Mrs. Wordsworth wrote that Dora had been told of the seriousness of her illness. Sara's letters to the Wordsworths and to Quillinan were read to Dora, and, as Mrs. Wordsworth wrote, 'her overflowing heart is in full sympathy with all the expressions of love and consolation which her many friends [have shown] to her, and yet more *towards* us all'.[1] Mrs. Wordsworth went on to tell Sara that she was a babe in the house when Dora was born. 'Poor afflicted Father's love is ever with you,'[2] she concluded. A few days

[1] E. de Selincourt, *The Letters of William and Dorothy Wordsworth. The Later Years*, 1939, iii. 1309.   [2] From an unpublished postscript to this letter.

later Sara replied. Her letter must have afforded great comfort to the sufferers at Rydal Mount.

I must repeat to you . . . what love and esteem I have felt for her and this increasingly as she and I increased in years. . . . Her fortitude and firmness are a lesson to us all. I am anxious that you should know from myself, that I am deriving, as I humbly but earnestly hope, real and lasting benefit from this blessed example of dying set me by my early friend—the earliest that I could call a companion friend save one, who will, I trust, be touched and affected for good also, when she hears of these things. As for dear Mr. Wordsworth I will not attempt to describe what I feel for him, or how I keep recalling his sayings (for no sayings of man heard with the ear, ever sank into my mind as his have done) about his beloved child Dora from time to time. I pray that both he and you, dear Mrs. Wordsworth, may be sustained more and more, and only the more prepared for the *city above* by this sorrowful trial.

On July 9, 1847, Dora Quillinan died. Not long before her decease she transmitted to Sara the manuscript of a sonnet which Coleridge had written for Sarah Hutchinson and given to her many years earlier. 'Dearest Sara,' Dora wrote on May 22,

This original M.S. of your Father's was transcribed for Aunt Sarah—my Mother gave it to me on my Aunt's death: and I give it to you knowing how precious it must be to you for all their sakes, and being sure it will be prized for mine also as a memorial of a lifelong friendship, and of my undying love.

The poem, which was not published until 1893, is the poetical counterpart of the heart-felt sentiments Coleridge confided to his journals.

> Are there two things, of all which men possess,
> That are so like each other and so near,
> As mutual Love seems like to Happiness?
> Dear Asra,[1] woman beyond utterance dear!
> This Love which ever welling at my heart,
> Now in its living fount doth heave and fall,
> Now overflowing pours thro' every part
> Of all my frame, and fills and changes all,

[1] Coleridge's anagram for Sara.

> Like vernal waters springing up thro' snow,
> This Love that seeming great beyond the power
> Of growth, yet seemeth ever more to grow,
> Could I transmute the whole to one rich Dower
> Of Happy Life, and give it all to Thee,
> Thy lot, methinks, were Heaven, thy Age, Eternity!

Sara received the gift graciously, glad, indeed, to have been in poor Dora's dying thoughts. She felt the

satisfaction of having this testimony that the dear departed Saint thought of me, and with earnest affection, in her last illness, when she was raised so far above this earth in her frame of mind.

Four years later, on August 18, 1851, Mary Wordsworth sent Edith 'a much-prized relic of your Grandfather, a Watch that was given by him to my beloved Sister Sarah; as you will see by the date, 44 years ago'. Mrs. Wordsworth went on to say:

Before your dear Mother was Mistress of a watch, my Sister used to say that she would leave it to her; and remembering this, since it came into my possession I have designed it for you. You will not value it the less I hope, for its having been worn 15 years by my side, as a treasured Memorial, whence, it was only removed, alas! to give place to a more sacred Trust.

The sending and acceptance of the manuscript poem and the watch show how reconciled the surviving Wordsworths and Coleridges had become to Coleridge's love for Sarah Hutchinson. That love was once at the core of the Wordsworth-Coleridge quarrel; now, with the principal actors gone to their reward, time had healed the wounds, and all could recognize the tragic implications of the affair.

During her widowhood Sara read over everything of Coleridge's which came her way and she must have examined with great interest his many diaries. As she read the strange and tragic story in Coleridge's own chaotic telling, she could forgive him everything. In the earlier note-books she found a man brilliant, hopeful, and happy; in 1799 there is an ominous entry, reporting the first meeting with Sarah Hutchinson; thenceforth for many years there are references to her, now burning with passion, now overflowing with the agony of frustration. In that record, too, Sara could find signs of domestic disharmony, the effects of which she had felt so keenly as a child. Then in the entries for the years 1810 to 1812 she traced the quarrel with Wordsworth and the woeful plight of Coleridge, now cast adrift on his own resources. Coleridge's belief that both Sarah Hutchinson and Wordsworth proved unworthy of his devotion Sara found recorded in his unpublished note-books. She read the agonizing entry, made not long after the quarrel: 'O when I reflect what most stings, or most weighs on my heart, and trace it to its remote causes, still I too must exclaim, "*God is just!*" I dare not therefore be angry.' The examination of Coleridge's diaries, even more than the reading and editing of his published works, brought Sara Coleridge to an under-standing and sympathy which made her pity rather than condemn her father.

In April 1848 the struggles of the Chartists came to a crisis, and the government of England prepared for what promised to be a revolution. Sara was not unsympathetic with the poor, but she was convinced that the Chartist leaders were misguided and in many cases vicious. She insisted that what the poor really wanted was to be better off—'they care not for more representation except as that may favour their pockets'.[1] She saw clearly that there was no advantage in extending the franchise until men were better educated. Believing that the lower classes would join forces with the middle and upper classes should actual violence occur, she was undisturbed by reports of a revolu-tion, but the solicitude of her servants and finally a rumour that the Coldstream Guards might espouse the Chartist cause, persuaded her to leave Chester Place and seek safety with Edward Coleridge at Eton. The Chartist uprising came to naught, for Wellington had carefully prepared for any attempt to overturn the government. Sara returned to London, agreeing with a writer in *The Times*, who spoke of the 'sublime spectacle' of England in an emergency. Sara agreed wholly with Wellington's methods. 'The arrange-

[1] Edith Coleridge, op. cit. ii. 164.

ments of the Duke for the preservation of the metropolis', she wrote to de Vere,

were worthy of the hero of Waterloo, and how merciful thus to preclude, by the formidable and complete nature of the preparations, any attempt on the part of the misguided Chartists. Even if their demands were in themselves reasonable, or such changes as they propose could benefit the people at large, the *manner* of making them is contrary to all government whatsoever, and if yielded to must lead to pure anarchy alternating with despotism.[1]

From the time of her mother's death in 1845 Sara Coleridge assumed special responsibility for her brother Hartley. She saw in him much to admire—an excellent mind and even genius, a lovable personality, a genuine honesty; but she saw all these thwarted by his restless nature and incurable addiction to drink. 'How unaltered he is', she wrote in 1847, 'in his goodness and strength and in his weakness! Pure as snow in great part of his mind—but with the one dark spot just where it was—a little softened by time, but unremoved.' She accepted him for what he was, a wayward child of benevolent intentions, and she strove, not to amend or correct him, but to provide whatever comforts and protection he needed. In his will Coleridge had made special arrangements for Hartley, providing that the executors should manage his funds but in no way interfere with his personal freedom. During her lifetime Mrs. Coleridge received the whole income from the estate, but she continued to pay Hartley's bills and tried to make him comfortable. After her mother's death Sara took charge of Hartley's financial affairs. His annual income amounted to about £80, in addition to small sums he earned by his pen. This was not enough to keep him, and Sara, though she stinted herself, gladly supplied the deficiency. She kept his money in a separate drawer, as her mother had done, that it might always be ready for him when needed. Her only restriction was her refusal to send directly to him the money for board and lodging.

Between brother and sister there existed a profound affection. Separated as they were during their adult lives, there

[1] Ibid. ii. 164.

was on one side an almost dog-like devotion and respect, and on the other a warm and understanding solicitude. Hartley understood himself well enough; he knew why he was not allowed to be at his mother's funeral, why exile in the Lake Country was imposed upon him; all the keener, then, was his remorse at being unable to assist Sara in her hours of trial—when Henry lay dying, when she was seriously ill, or when their mother passed away. Always ready to disparage his own literary compositions, he wrote his poetry, criticism, and essays only when the mood was upon him. Reckless in making promises, he seldom fulfilled them; and as he watched his sister slowly putting Coleridge's house in order, by dint of persistent and unremitting application, he was moved, not to a burst of activity, but to a further conviction of his own incompetence.

Sara longed for a visit with her brother, but she dared not invite him to London and even the idea of the long journey northward distressed her. Gradually she accepted the fact that she must rest content with her girlish memories of a brilliant, lovable, child-like youth, and that Hartley's occasional letters were the only communion she could have with him.

When in the closing days of 1848 news of Hartley's serious illness arrived, and Derwent rushed to his brother's bedside, the tragic significance of their long separation flooded Sara's being. On Christmas Day she received a letter from Mrs. Wordsworth, sent not to alarm but to explain why Hartley had not written. A heavy cold, 'attributable to his imprudently having been late out twice within the last 3 weeks—leaving his friends' several houses when they ought either to have detained him all night, or seen him home', had stricken him with pneumonia. On his arrival Derwent found Hartley somewhat better, under the care of three physicians, but his constitution proved unequal to the disease. His last days were deeply affecting. Most of the time he was concerned over religious matters, and when he died he had twice received the sacrament from his brother. Once, after he had been revived by a dose of brandy, he declared in his old inimitable manner:

Now I see more clearly than ever that the regeneration of Ireland must be founded on tee-totalism.

During his illness the Wordsworths called regularly. Derwent described one occasion when

> Mr. Wordsworth read prayers himself from the Prayerbook, as I have never heard them read before nor (I confidently expect) ever shall again. His voice, when he prays, especially for her who has long been prevented by infirmity from joining in our prayers and again when he alluded to those who have already departed this life was most touching, yet the emphasis was not obtrusive. I have no terms to express the solemnity of the manner, the rich tone, and rhythmical movement of the voice and the moving propriety of the intonation. The old man knelt before the window and read without spectacles. He seems composed but is very serious. Mrs. Wordsworth is altogether *herself*. The household bears a simple patriarchal character.

Hartley succumbed on January 6, 1849. When all was over, Wordsworth accompanied Derwent to the Grasmere churchyard. Selecting a spot next to the place where Dora had only recently been laid, he said in a broken voice, 'Keep the ground for us—we are old people, and it cannot be for long. . . . Let him lie as near us as possible. . . . It would have been his wish.' Just before the funeral the Wordsworths called at Nab Cottage, for one last glimpse of their beloved friend. Mrs. Wordsworth decked the body with flowers and kissed the cold face three times, but Wordsworth was too moved to enter the room.

Sara read Derwent's letters with tears and comfort. The attention of the Wordsworths, the general mourning of the whole country-side, and the complete forgetfulness of any waywardness on Hartley's part soothed and quieted her. But she had never expected to survive him. 'I always thought he would live to old age', she wrote, 'and that, perhaps, in our latest years, we might cherish each other. . . . There were three who loved me best in this wide world, to whom I was most dear, most important. Now all three are gone, and I feel, even from earthly feeling, as if that other world were more my home than this.'[1]

Poor Sara had added another name to her death book.

---

[1] Edith Coleridge, op. cit. ii. 209.

Sara and Derwent determined to do what Hartley had not done himself—prepare for publication selections from his miscellaneous writings, both published and unpublished. Sara was too preoccupied with *Essays on His Own Times* to undertake the task, but Derwent set out to do so. They both felt that a memoir ought to be prepared, that the full truth about their brother should be known. To John Taylor Coleridge Sara expressed her opinions in the matter. John had apparently feared that Derwent intended to suppress 'a full and frank statement' of the 'one bane to his peace and well being'. Sara insisted, as she had done in the case of her father, that a complete statement of Hartley's aberrations would be the best vindication of them. 'Some persons', she said,

may think that this unhappy point of Hartley's conduct renders it undesirable for a brother to publish a Memoir of him at all—and one friend has even written to Derwent and Mary to that effect. I certainly think it will render the task painful and difficult but I do not agree that therefore Derwent ought to abandon it altogether. It is not to be expected in these days, that what is to be lamented in Hartley's life and character can be 'veiled in silence;' . . . at least, if his prose and verse live, his personal history will live also, and the story can be in all respects better told by one deeply interested than by any one else, from longer and more general knowledge of the facts and all attendant circumstances of what Hartley was as child, boy, and man.

Wordsworth, on the contrary, 'seems to object to *any high eulogy*' of Hartley. Sara rose vigorously to her brother's defence:

Now to abstain from speaking in warm terms of what was excellent and amiable in our brother's mind and disposition, would be to render the account a gloomy record indeed. Truth, in my opinion, warrants praise enough to make the portrait on the whole by no means a painful one; for Hartley's virtues, those for which numbers of witnesses have given him credit, . . . were as high and uncommon as his infirmities were strange and deplorable. It should be remembered, too, I think, that the Memoir is not written principally for Ambleside and Grasmere—though nothing which can *justly* offend his friends there ought to be admitted; but for all persons now and hereafter who take an interest in the products of his genius.

With far greater animus than was usual for her, Sara burst out in a letter to Derwent, referring to Wordsworth's early experiences in France:

There are some who bear a high name for respectability of conduct, whose history it would be almost as difficult to write quite *truthfully* as Hartley's—whose history *never will be written truthfully* by any relation, wife, or friend. But this is *between ourselves*.

While Sara did not actually prepare a memoir herself, she outlined the plan very carefully. 'The success of such a memoir', she wrote, 'must more especially depend on the skill and power of the writer.' With 'very scanty material of an outward kind, very few and hardly any cheerful events and . . . a scanty literary correspondence', the task would be difficult. Still she felt that

if a lifesome portrait could be given of Hartley's moral and intellectual character, with an animated record of his conversation— this, interwoven with some of his letters and connected into a whole by a sketch of his life's career, would be an interesting preface to his poems and biographical sketches.

Derwent proceeded with the memoir in conformity with Sara's wishes, and though he did not always handle the narrative as she would have desired, nevertheless he did prepare a truthful and sympathetic account of his brother. Published as a preface to two volumes of Hartley's poems, the *Memoir* met with a favourable reception. Some of the reviewers, it is true, took occasion to use Hartley's life as a moral lesson, much to Sara's indignation; but no one saw fit to object to Derwent's handling of the story or to speak of Hartley in any other terms than those of sympathy.

Not all of Hartley's unpublished writings had come into Derwent's hands, and he and Sara were greatly enraged over a threat by one of Hartley's associates in the Lake Country, Joseph Burns, to issue a separate edition of the poetry and thus to 'forestall Mr. Derwent Coleridge's publication'. Burns had in his possession a considerable number of

Hartley's manuscripts, given him, he said, 'in return for hospitality', and he proposed to publish the poems, along with a memoir of his own. Among them, Sara learned, was a parody of Wordsworth's *Peter Bell*, as well as a group of 'alehouse' poems. While Sara agreed that such poems, if they could be got from Burns, should be consigned to the fire,[1] she did not whole-heartedly condemn them:

> I confess I should like to see Hartley's alehouse improvisations and rustic-feast effusions—just to see them before they are committed to the flames. They may perhaps contain much life and spirit, and appear less intolerable to some than to others—especially of Quaker bringing up. However it is most desirable to prevent their publication—by any low and injudicious person and any quiz of W.W. must *by all means* be kept as quiet as possible.

Eventually, after a distressing correspondence on the part of Sara and Derwent, Burns was persuaded that he had no legal right to issue Hartley's poems, and his memoir and manuscripts were transmitted to Sara in return for 20 guineas. Neither the memoir (which is, to be sure, naïve and ingenuous) nor the poems were as shocking as Sara and Derwent feared they might be.

Wordsworth had said to the sexton when choosing Hartley's grave, 'it cannot be for long'; and fifteen months later on April 23, 1850, he joined his beloved Dora. Sara was relieved that the poet did not suffer a lingering illness, but she felt 'stunned to think that my dear old friend is no more in this world. It seems as if the present life were passing away, and leaving me for awhile behind.' Still she gloried in the fame Wordsworth had attained:

> His work was done, and gloriously done, . . . and will survive, I think, as long as those hills amid which he lived and thought, at least, if this continues to be a land of cultivated intellects, of poets and students of poetry.[2]

Wordsworth's death, along with that of Edward Quillinan in the next year, were duly recorded in Sara's death journal.

---

[1] Apparently the plan to consign Burns's memoir and the alehouse poems to the flames was abandoned, for much of the material is still extant. A forthcoming edition of Hartley Coleridge's unpublished poems will include much of this material.   [2] Edith Coleridge, op. cit. ii. 314–15.

Certainly her last years were filled with a sorrowful succession of deaths.

That Derwent was able to write so sympathetic and understanding an account of his brother's life was perhaps due in part to the great affliction in his own household. In contrast to the brilliant record made by Herbert at both Eton and Oxford, Derwent's eldest born, two years his senior, lacked stability and self-control, and occasionally abandoned himself entirely to dissolute living. At such times he seems to have forgotten completely his station in life and his responsibility to his family. The desolation caused by Derwent Junior's conduct afflicted Sara almost as if she had been his mother. She had tutored him along with Herbert in Homer and Aeschylus and had taken great pride in his comely appearance and kindly disposition. 'I must write . . . to you about this deep sorrow that is become the portion of us all', she wrote to his parents:

It is a personal grief to me. . . . How often have I in my day dreamings, fancied that if I were childless, he might have been a son to me! . . . The disappointment is bitter . . . and I feel greatly dispirited——

Derwent Junior having been expelled from Oxford, his father determined to make one last effort to redeem him, and accordingly he was enrolled at Jesus College, Cambridge, in the autumn of 1850. Within a month he had returned to his old habits of dissipation and reckless spending. This was the complete destruction, as Sara remarked, 'of all our Cambridge hopes', and it was decided that he should be exiled to Australia where he would be forced to earn his livelihood by manual labour. Fearing that 'Mary's heart might fail' at this plan and grieving over her brother's anxiety and disappointment, not to mention the 'cruelty to their younger children', Sara went to St. Mark's resolved to urge immediate execution of the emigration scheme. Finding them resigned, she could but feel regret 'for the poor wanderer himself'. She hardly dared hope for his amendment. She said that his instability was a sort of insanity, for he made no effort to conceal his wrongdoings but completely abandoned himself when the mood was upon him. The long ocean

R 2

voyage and the necessity of earning his living in Australia might bring out a sense of moral responsibility, she argued, but she saw him depart with sorrow in her heart.

Derwent Junior's farewell letter, written aboard ship in late November 1850, shows that he was not wholly degenerate. 'My dearest Mother,' he wrote,

I cannot set forth upon my perhaps life-long pilgrimage, without leaving behind me a few farewell words. I say a *few*, because as regards the *past*, the less said the better, and for the future, I or any one, can as yet say nothing. . . . I may even now, at the eleventh hour, become by degrees as great a comfort, as I have till now been a burden and distress—and already look forward to a time when I may be worthy once again to look you and all my friends fairly in the face. In a word that I may become an honest upright man. Teach the dear children still to love their exiled Brother. He will often, often think of them . . . and may [you] one day find joy from your dearly attached Son.

Throughout the agony of Derwent Junior's downward course, Sara offered comfort to her brother and sister-in-law. While she could, she bade them hope; when the young man proved irredeemable, she counselled resignation and courage. Derwent, she insisted, must be strong and face his sorrow, even as Coleridge, a generation before, had accepted the tragic facts of Hartley's failure.

In the summer of 1850 Sara sent Edith to the Lake Country. She would have liked to accompany her but was not well enough to do so. The thought of her daughter visiting the scenes of her own youth led Sara to speak in glowing terms of the north. 'Keswick', she wrote to Miss Trevenen,

is the place where I long to be and which to my imagination is a sort of terrestial Paradise. If there were to be a Millennium, I should always fancy Keswick Vale, purified and glorified, to be the scene of it for me. . . . I love the spring in my own native vale, and perhaps that season and the winter are most connected with my remembrances of *childhood*. It is autumn, however, with its rich yellowing foliage and its mellow atmosphere that connects itself most with my remembrances of youth, the pleasures of out-of-door social entertainments of my girlish days.

In the closing months of 1850 Sara was to face her first real disappointment in Herbert. He had become engaged in secret to Ellen Phillips, the daughter of a solicitor then living in Penn, Staffordshire. When Sara learned the grievous news from Herbert she was most indignant. She thought of many plausible objections—'Herbert's youth, non-settlement in any profession, unformed judgment, my unacquaintance with the family except at second hand, . . . a pretty portion-less maid, without relations that might be of service and credit to himself'. Edith, however, was conciliatory and soothed her troubled mother. 'You know, mamma,' Sara reported her as saying, 'he never would like the sort of girl that we should prefer and wish him to have for a wife. The friends and acquaintances that suit our tastes are too grave for his. The match is respectable though not what we should have chosen.' At first Sara merely resigned herself to the inevitable, but her love for Herbert and her waning health gradually won her over to his side:

I now begin to look at the brighter side and hope that all will turn out well. I have long foreseen that he would never be easy till he had secured a wife—and that he never would choose the exact sort of young lady, or exact sort of marriage connection, which would most please me. . . . I saw he would choose a good deal by the eye. Indeed his dear Father before him had much the same taste. He oft told me that my looks *first fixed* him, and that all our *mind-congeniality* was a blessing found out after his desire of our union and resolve to effect it . . . had been formed un-alterably.

Sara was comforted by the report of one of her friends that the Phillips family were highly respected in the county in which they resided and that they enjoyed ample means. Herbert, now entered at Lincoln's Inn, thought, too, that Mr. Phillips would put him forward in his profession. Thus, at last, Sara was able to write in December 1851:

There has been some little 'roughness' at the onset of the course of their true love, but I trust all that is now passed over, and that his attachment to his fair Ellen will prove a source of as much happiness to us hereafter, as it is to himself at present. She is a very sweet little person, as gentle and amiable as she is pretty looking, a beautiful musician, and I have no doubt well informed and sensible—in short, just the person to suit Herbert, and make him happy.

XI

THE END OF THE STORY

AS Sara lived over again the scenes of her childhood through Edith's joyous letters from the Lake Country, she was rudely awakened from her reveries by a sudden and unanticipated blow. She discovered a lump in her breast, and as it did not recede she called in her medical attendant, Mr. Newton, who advised a consultation with Sir B. Brodie. Plasters were applied without avail, and Green, who had been asked to break the news to Sara, warned her on September 25, 1850, that the tumour at her right breast 'might remain in an inert state for many years and not shorten her life, but *might become cancerous*'. Sara heard this news with heart-sinking despair. 'Alas!' she confided to her journal, 'I live in constant fear—like the Ancient Mariner with the Albatross hung about his neck, I have a weight always upon me.' At first Sara was hysterical but she soon regained her composure and determined that Herbert in Devonshire and Edith in the Lake Country should finish their holidays in ignorance of her almost certain fate.

The story of the closing months of her life, as recorded in her journals, is at times almost too painful to read. It reveals the struggle of a brave and courageous woman who did not wish to die. Deep as was her religious faith she grasped at every ray of hope, only to be disappointed. She took constantly increasing doses of opium, and turned to mesmerism, learning of its 'miracles' from Mr. Newton, although Brodie scorned such 'quackery and nonsense'. At last her greatest hope was dashed when she found that her surgeon thought an operation inadvisable. 'My best chance consists in keeping the disease! Oh woe is me—A cloud is come upon my life never to pass away. Alas! Never have I been so sad as this evening. My dear, dear children.'

As Sara felt herself gradually sinking lower and lower she pathetically wished that she might have been spared ten years more with her children. At times even her religious faith seemed to waver as she faced the reality of death, and in anguish she called out to the spirits of her departed loved ones:

My Father—musing, speculative, imaginative. Father—where now is your spirit? Hartley, more beloved, though less an object of admiring wonder, where is thy dear spirit? My mother, ever most near and dear, guardian of my weakly childhood and tender mournful girlhood, where art thou? My honoured Uncle Southey, Wordsworth, admired and affectionately regarded, Dora and Edward Quillinan, am I going to you? Henry, my dearest, fond, admiring husband, whom I could please ten times more I fancy than ever before could we meet—both meet again in health and strength—shall I indeed behold thee again?

Dreaming over her children, she half wished that they could follow Charles and Mary Lamb in 'double celibacy', but as Herbert's plans for marriage progressed, she acquiesced in Edith's firm determination not to be separated from Herbert even following his marriage, and it was especially comforting to Sara to note the deep affection between her children. With motherly instinct she wished 'that Edith were the engaged one instead of Herbert!' But Sara had now come to realize more deeply than ever before 'how vain to try to shape the future'.

With a heavy heart she set about preparing her will. Wishing to provide equally for Herbert and Edith, and particularly to prevent Edith from disposing of her inheritance through excessive generosity, she consulted John about legal questions. She struggled, too, to arrange her financial affairs in good order.

Nor was she content merely to set her own house in order, for she still retained a deep and abiding interest in editing Coleridge's works. Too weak to undertake an edition of the *Poems* without assistance, she collaborated with Derwent in editing the volume which appeared in 1852, not many weeks after her death. Even as she lay dying she worked industriously on the poems, and when she could no longer hold the pen, she dictated to Edith. Derwent graciously acknowledged that the publication of the volume was due almost exclusively to her efforts and he added an Advertisement (dated May 1852) in expression of his appreciation of her labours:

This volume was prepared for the press by my lamented sister, Mrs. H. N. Coleridge. . . . At her earnest request, my name appears with hers on the title-page, but the assistance rendered by me has been, in fact, little more than mechanical. The preface, and the greater part of the notes, are her composition:—the selection and arrangement have been determined almost exclusively by her critical judgement, or from records in her possession.

This was not all. She continued to gather biographical information about Coleridge and she made elaborate plans for further editions of his works. She intended, for instance, that the *Lay Sermons* and the *Church and State* should appear separately, not in one volume as Henry had issued them. She explained fully to Derwent, too, plans for editing the theological works. Derwent actually 'pressed her for assistance'. She writes in 1851 that,

My brother wishes to have some of the Esteesian remains prepared for new editions, and this cannot be done without work on my part, as I have been so long the housekeeper of the S. T. C. literary house.

Derwent followed her advice, and his editions of the *Lay Sermons* and the *Church and State*, published as separate volumes in 1852, and of the theological works in 1853 bear witness not only to his own efforts but to Sara's foresight as well. Of less importance, though almost as laborious, was her proof-reading of Derwent's editions of Hartley's works issued at this time.

At Christmas in 1851, once more came the haunting sound of the waits to fill Sara with poignant memories of that scene nine years before when her beloved Henry lay on his death-bed. She felt that she was more resigned than he, life having given her more experience. She recalled James Coleridge's question, 'Are you resigned?' and Henry's mournful reply, 'What can a man be else?' Even now she could say, 'Alas! the tears in which that speech was drowned shewed that this was but unstruggling sorrow.' In honesty, however, she analysed her feelings about her approaching death:

If resignation consist in a willingness to depart—I cannot boast of that heavenly grace—for I still cling fondly to this earth with so much that it contains, which is beautiful in my eyes, interesting to the mind, and dear, most dear to the heart. But I trust I can say feelingly, 'God's will be done,' although that will inflicts a bitter cross on my poor, weak human nature. I can acknowledge that all He does is right and must be for the best.

Everything that could minister to her suffering body and spirit was provided. Edith and Herbert, devoted attendants at her bedside, were all that she could wish in a daughter and son. Mary and Derwent were constantly at hand, the latter to administer the sacrament. Friends from far and near poured out their affection and sympathy. Miss Fenwick, whom Sara called her 'Good Angel', presented her with £100 that nothing might be lacking to make her last days as free from pecuniary anxiety as possible. But cancer is inexorable, and on May 3, 1852, death claimed her as his own. She was laid to rest beside her parents and her beloved husband at Highgate. Hers had been a life of great happiness, as well as of sorrow and bereavement, but she closed her eyes in peace and in harmony with all. Her death book was now complete.

APPENDIX

BIBLIOGRAPHY

A. Principal References

Allsop, Thomas. *Letters, Conversations and Recollections of S. T. Coleridge*. London, 1858.

Blunden, E., and Griggs, E. L., Editors. *Coleridge: Studies by Several Hands.* . . . London, 1934.

Broughton, L. N. *Sara Coleridge and Henry Reed*. Ithaca, New York, 1937.

Campbell, J. D. *Samuel Taylor Coleridge. A Narrative.* . . . London, 1894.

Chambers, Sir E. K. *Samuel Taylor Coleridge.* . . . Oxford, 1938.

Coleridge, Lord. *The Story of a Devonshire House*. London, 1905.

Coleridge, Edith. *Memoir and Letters of Sara Coleridge*. 2 vols., London, 1873.

Coleridge, E. H. Editor. *Letters of Samuel Taylor Coleridge*. 2 vols., London, 1895.

Coleridge, Hartley. *Complete Poetical Works*. (Muses Library.) London, 1908.

Coleridge, S. T. *Aids to Reflection*, ed. by H. N. Coleridge. 2 vols., London, 1843.

—— *Biographia Literaria*, ed. by J. Shawcross. 2 vols., Oxford, 1907.

—— *Specimens of the Table Talk of the Late S. T. Coleridge*. 2 vols., London, 1835.

De Quincey, Thomas. *The Collected Writings of* . . ., ed. by D. Masson. 14 vols., Edinburgh, 1889.

De Selincourt, Ernest, Editor. *Early Letters of William and Dorothy Wordsworth*. Oxford, 1935.

—— *The Letters of William and Dorothy Wordsworth. The Middle Years*. 2 vols., Oxford, 1937.

—— *The Letters of William and Dorothy Wordsworth. The Later Years*. 3 vols., Oxford, 1939.

De Vere, Aubrey. *Recollections*. London, 1897.

Flagg, J. B. *The Life and Letters of Washington Allston*. London, 1893.

Griggs, E. L., Editor. *Unpublished Letters of Samuel Taylor Coleridge.* . . . 2 vols., London, 1932.

GRIGGS, E. L., Editor. *Wordsworth and Coleridge.* . . . Princeton, New Jersey, 1939.

GRIGGS, G. E., and E. L., Editors. *Letters of Hartley Coleridge.* London, 1936.

KNIGHT, WILLIAM, Editor. *Journals of Dorothy Wordsworth.* 2 vols., London, 1897.

LUCAS, E. V., Editor. *The Letters of Charles and Mary Lamb.* 3 vols., London, 1935.

MORLEY, EDITH J., Editor. *The Correspondence of Henry Crabb Robinson with the Wordsworth Circle.* 2 vols., Oxford, 1927.

POTTER, STEPHEN, Editor. *Minnow among Tritons.* . . . London, 1934.

RAYSOR, T. M., Editor. *Coleridge's Miscellaneous Criticism.* London, 1936.

—— *Coleridge's Shakespearean Criticism.* 2 vols., London, 1930.

SCOTT, Sir WALTER. *Familiar Letters of* . . . 2 vols., London, 1894.

SOUTHEY, C. C. *The Life and Correspondence of Robert Southey.* 6 vols., London, 1849–1850.

TOWLE, ELEANOR A. *A Poet's Children.* . . . London, 1912.

WARD, WILFRID. *Aubrey de Vere, a Memoir.* London, 1904.

WARTER, J. W., Editor. *Selections from the Letters of Robert Southey.* 4 vols., London, 1856.

WATSON, SETH B., Editor. *Hints towards the Formation of a More Comprehensive Theory of Life.* London, 1848.

WISE, T. J. *A Bibliography* . . . *of Samuel Taylor Coleridge.* London, 1913.

B. WORKS BY SARA COLERIDGE

Phantasmion. London, 1837.

Pretty Lessons in Verse for Good Children. London, 1834.

C. WORKS EDITED BY SARA COLERIDGE

Biographia Literaria . . . *by Samuel Taylor Coleridge.* 2 vols., London, 1847.

Notes and Lectures upon Shakespeare . . . *of S. T. Coleridge.* 2 vols., London, 1849.

Essays on His Own Times . . . *by Samuel Taylor Coleridge.* 3 vols., London, 1850.

The Poems of Samuel Taylor Coleridge (in collaboration with Derwent Coleridge). London, 1852.

D. Works translated by Sara Coleridge

An Account of the Abipones, an Equestrian People of Paraguay, from the Latin of Martin Dobrizhoffer. 3 vols., London, 1822.

The Right Joyous and Pleasant History of the Facts, Tests, and Prowesses of the Chevalier Bayard, the Good Knight without Fear and without Reproach: by the Loyall Servant. 2 vols., London, 1825.

E. Magazines

Edinburgh Review, vol. xxvii (Sept. 1816). 'Review of Coleridge's *Christabel* . . .'

Fraser's Magazine, vol. xi (Jan. 1835). 'Coleridgeiana.'

Gentleman's Magazine, vol. ix (June 1838). 'The Newspaper Writings of the Poet Coleridge.'

Quarterly Review, vol. lii (Aug. 1834). 'Review of *The Poetical Works of Coleridge.*' [By H. N. Coleridge.]

—— vol. lxxxii (Mar. 1848). 'Review of Tennyson's *The Princess, a Medley.*' [By Sara Coleridge.]

—— vol. lxxxiii (Sept. 1848). 'Review of Alexander Dyce's *The Works of Beaumont and Fletcher* . . . and George Darley's *The Works of Beaumont and Fletcher.*' [By Sara Coleridge.]

Tait's Magazine (Sept., Oct., and Nov. 1834 and Jan. 1835). 'Samuel Taylor Coleridge: By the English Opium Eater.'

Publications of the Modern Language Association of America, vol. xxxviii (June 1923). Walter Graham, 'Contemporary Critics of Coleridge, the Poet.'

—— vol. xlvi (Dec. 1931). E. L. Griggs, 'Hartley Coleridge on His Father.'

INDEX

Aeschylus, 196.

Allen, Geo., 185.

Allsop, Thos., 47 n., 111, 112.

Allston, Washington, 153, 183.

Amulet, The, 159.

Annual Anthology, The, 159.

Arnold, Matthew, 202, 211, 216.

Arnold, Thomas, 78, 148, 213.

Athenaeum, The, 101.

Austen, Jane, 198, 214.

Bacon, Francis, 177, 178.

Baillie, Joanna, 78, 119, 179, 210, 212.

Bancroft, Mr., 189.

Barker, Miss, 10, 31.

Bartram, William, 55.

Beaumont and Fletcher, 197, 203, 209–10.

Beaumont, Sir George and Lady, 16, 41, 56, 61, 66, 68, 69.

Beddoes, Thomas, 211.

Bell, Dr. Andrew, 9, 158.

Biographia Borealis, 36.

Blackwood's Magazine, 101, 107, 108, 145, 148 n.

Bowles, Caroline, 125.

Bridgewater Treatises, 78, 193, 212.

British Magazine, 109, 146 n., 147.

Brontë, Charlotte, 214.

Browning, Elizabeth Barrett, 78, 172, 173 and n., 174, 175, 176, 199, 201–2, 210, 216, 227.

Browning, Robert, 4, 72, 167, 172, 175–7, 211, 215, 227.

Bruce, James, 55.

Brun, Frederica, 104, 109.

Bryant, Jacob, 55.

Burns, Joseph, 241, 242 and n.

Byron, Lord, 95, 179, 196, 202, 211, 228.

Calvert, Mary, 28.

Cambridge Intelligencer, 159.

Campbell, J. Dykes, 7.

Campbell, Thomas, 211.

Carlyle, Thomas, 78, 91, 167, 169–72 and n., 189, 212. *Life of J. Sterling,* of, 171.

Cervantes, 57.

Chalmers, Thomas, 193.

Chambers, Sir E. K., 48 n.

Chartist rising, 167, 169, 236–7.

Christian Miscellany, 149.

Clarkson, Thomas, 9, 45. 170 and n.

Claude Lorrain, 195.

Coleridge, Berkeley, 2, 3.

Coleridge, Bertha Fanny, 121.

Coleridge, Christabel Rose, 122.

Coleridge, Derwent, 1, 4, 7, 9, 10, 12, 15, 17, 22, 24, 25, 27, 28, 33, 34, 36–7, 41, 45, 46, 54, 55, 57, 60, 61, 63, 64, 65, 66, 69, 72, 73, 74, 93, 94, 111, 117, 121–23 and n., 129, 131, 142, 144 and n., 155, 156, 164, 165, 166, 177, 183, 185, 187, 224, 225, 231, 232, 238, 239, 240, 241, 242, 243, 244, 247, 248, 249.

Coleridge, Derwent, Jr., 228, 243, 244.

Coleridge, Edith, 67 n., 74, 75, 78, 79, 81, 90, 127, 128, 137, 175, 176, 189, 190, 217, 218, 223, 224, 225, 226, 227, 229, 235, 244, 245, 246, 247, 249.

Coleridge, Edward, 126, 138, 218, 224, 228, 231, 236.

Coleridge (Patteson), Fanny, 43, 44, 45, 138.

Coleridge, Florence and Berkeley, 76.

Coleridge, Frank, 228.

Coleridge, George, 17, 49.

Coleridge, George May, 224.

Coleridge, The Rev. G. H. B., 67 n.

Coleridge, Hartley, 1, 2, 4, 6, 7, 9, 10, 12, 15, 17, 18, 22, 24, 25, 27, 32–8, 39, 41, 45, 46, 47 and n., 48, 49, 51, 63, 66, 68–71, 72, 74, 76, 86, 90, 93–4, 100, 108, 111, 119, 121, 122, 125, 129, 131, 133, 138, 140–1 and n., 142, 143, 144, 155–6, 184, 185–6, 187, 190, 193, 196, 205, 211, 219, 222, 226, 229, 230, 231–2, 233, 237–42 and n., 244, 247, 248.

Coleridge, Henry Nelson, 46, 55, 70, 73; 74, 75, 78, 79, 86, 88, 89 n., 93, 105, 121, 122, 123, 124, 128, 129, 131, 144–5, 147, 161, 165, 167, 171, 184, 193–4, 217, 218, 222, 223, 224, 225, 230, 231, 232, 238, 247, 248, 249.
    Engaged to Sara, 42–4, 46, 47–54.
    Described, 44–5.
    Plans *Table Talk,* 61–2.
    Marriage of, 62–4, 67.
    Settles in London, 65–6.
    Relationship of, with Coleridge, 67–8, 89–90.
    Settles at Hampstead, 71.

Index

255

Index

COLERIDGE, SARA (*contd.*)

poem for, 13; frailness of, 16; described by Dorothy Wordsworth, 16–17; journey to Bristol, 17–18; visits Wordsworths with her father, 19–21; describes herself as a child, 21–2; described by Coleridge, 24–5; remembrances of Allan Bank, 25–6; devotion to the Wordsworths, 26; life at Greta Hall, 26–8; early companions of, 28–9; loss of her cousin, 29; studies of, 29–30; beauty of, 30; education of, 31–2; Collins's portrait of, 32; affection for brothers, 33; pride in Hartley, 34; suffering over Hartley, 35–6; worry over Derwent, 36; visits Liverpool, 37; visits London, 38–45; descriptions of, 39–40, 43; becomes engaged to her cousin, Henry Nelson Coleridge, 42–5; visits Ottery, Bristol, and Cambridge, 45; returns to Keswick, 46; life at Greta Hall described, 47; love for Henry, 47–8; objections to engagement of, 48–53; sufferings of, 53–4; turns to translation, 54–7; influences on thought of, 57–8; described by Wordsworth, 58–9; reading and intellectual development of, 59–60; second visit to London, 60–2; marriage of, 62–4; settles in London, 65; delights her father, 66–7; effect of Hartley's wanderings on, 68–70; removal to Hampstead, 71; congeniality of her marriage, 71–2; Mrs. Coleridge joins, 72; births of Herbert and Edith, 72–5; illness of, 75–6; birth and death of her twins, 76; reading of, 77–8; as a mother, 78–81; differs with mother about discipline, 80–1; educational ideas of, 81–3; writes poems for Herbert, 83–6; publishes *Pretty Verses*, 86–7; last visits with Coleridge, 88, 90; death of Coleridge, 92; writes to Hartley after Coleridge's death, 93; Henry's opinion of, 98–9, 100; defends Henry's editorial policy, 101; answers De Quincey's articles in *Tait's*, 105–7; comments on other articles, 107–8; seconds Henry's determination to answer De Quincey in the

COLERIDGE, SARA (*contd.*)

Table Talk, 109–11; regrets various biographical treatments of Coleridge, 111–12; encourages Henry in issuing Coleridge's works, 112–14; falls ill at Ilchester, 115–16; writes *Phantasmion*, 116–20; moves to Regent's Park, 120–1; birth and death of Fanny, 121; draws closer to Hartley, 121; relationship with Derwent, 121–3; troubled by Coleridge's letters to Derwent, 123 and n.; friendship with the Wordsworths, 123–5; relationships with the Southeys, 125–6; continues education of her children, 126–8; resemblances to Coleridge, 130–2; differences from Coleridge, 132; her intellectual heritage, 132; visits Belgium, 133; Henry's last illness, 133, 135–8; devotion between Henry and Sara, 133–4; visit to Oxford, 135; death of Henry, 139; writes to her son, 139; attends funeral, 139–40; struggles for self-control, 140–2; rebuilds Coleridge's vault, 142–3 and n.; edits *Biographia Literaria*, 145–56; defends Coleridge against plagiarism, 145–9, 158–9; discusses Coleridge's religious opinions, 149–51; dedicates *Biographia Literaria* to Wordsworth, 153–4; edits *Notes and Lectures upon Shakespeare*, 156–9; edits *Essays on His Own Times*, 159–62; prepares synopsis of *Treatise on Method*, 162; resents publication of Coleridge's *Theory of Life* by Seth B. Watson, 162–5; re-edits other works, 165–6; learning of, 198–9; recovers after Henry's death, 217–18; portrait painted by Richmond, 218; friendship for de Vere, 219–22; mourns death of Southey, 222–3; financial difficulties of, 223–6; continues publishing with Pickering, 225–6; pride of, in her children, 226–9; last years with her mother, 229–31; loses her mother, 231–2; death of Dora Quillinan, 233–4; receives manuscript sonnet of Coleridge, 234–5; Mrs. Wordsworth sends watch given to Sarah Hutchinson by Coleridge, 235; comes to understand

256

PRINTED IN
GREAT BRITAIN
AT THE
UNIVERSITY PRESS
OXFORD
BY
JOHN JOHNSON
PRINTER
TO THE
UNIVERSITY